Questioning Leadership – it's about time! Leadership is one of the most overused terms in contemporary society. Unfortunately, the concept of leadership has become ambiguous, misleading, a 'catch cry,' and in the end, a meaningless cliché, which makes its systematic analysis, discourse, and study perilous at best. This book is a welcome attempt to balance the glorified rhetoric of leadership with the structural and contextual constraints that make leadership difficult, situational, and paradoxical. *Questioning Leadership* is a timely challenge to the current canons of leader-centrism; it restores equilibrium and reflectiveness to a diverse term that has become a hackneyed slogan. This corrective collection is required reading for all who love to learn and dare to lead.

Wayne K. Hoy, *Professor Emeritus, The Ohio State University, USA*

Just as the reforming school principal has become a key part of the mythology of devolved systems of schooling, so have relatively unexamined notions of school leadership come to dominate academic accounts of contemporary school management. This important book helps us to move beyond such lazy thinking. Following on from her earlier work, *Managing without Leadership*, Lakomski and her colleagues subject over-individualized understandings of leadership to sustained theoretical scrutiny. Although the editors insist they are asking questions rather than providing answers, their impressive array of contributors and commentators offers us a rich choice of alternative ways of understanding school leadership.

Geoff Whitty, *Director Emeritus, UCL Institute of Education,*
UK, and Global Innovation Chair for Equity in Higher Education,
University of Newcastle, Australia

Questioning Leadership edited by Gabriele Lakomski, Scott Eacott and Colin Evers arrives on the scene at a critical time. Educational leadership is in need of critical examination right now, before we jump off a cliff after the next big thing, the next leadership fad or fetish.

Well-conceived and adroitly executed, the book speaks to an important issue of our time: leadership, generally, and educational leadership more specifically. Lest the book be pigeon-holed and, therefore, dismissed, be it known that this book speaks to leadership writ large; any and all can come away from reading it more considerate, more enlightened, more thoughtful. The format of the book is unique and uniquely suited to its intended aim – to look at leadership from top to bottom, head to tail, and inside out, and from multiple vantage points.

Lakomski, Eacott, and Evers have assembled some of the best scholars in the field today, and they provide the reader with some of their best ideas. The tone of the book is such that all can engage with its content, concepts and concerns, and we, our schools and our students will be all the better for it.

Duncan Waite, *Professor, Community and Educational Leadership,*
Texas State University, USA, and Director of The International
Center for Educational Leadership and Social Change

Questioning Leadership

Questioning Leadership offers a diverse mix of cutting-edge research in the field of educational leadership, with contributions from expert and emerging leadership scholars. It contextualises school leadership within broader social and historical contexts and traces its influence on school performance through time, from its relatively modest role within a systems theory paradigm to its growing influence from the 1980s onwards, as exercising leadership came to be perceived as being largely responsible for improving educational outcomes.

This book invites the reader to challenge the current orthodoxy of leader-centrism and instead reflect more broadly on the various structural and institutional interrelationships that determine how a school functions successfully. It poses challenging questions, such as:

- Is leadership really necessary for high-quality school performance?
- Can schools function effectively without leadership?
- Is it possible to describe the work that principals do without using the word 'leadership'?
- How do we challenge the assumption that leadership simply exists and that it is seen as the appropriate default explanation for school performance?

This book does not assume that leadership is the key to organisational performance, although it acknowledges the work that principals do. It goes against current orthodoxy and offers varied perspectives on how leadership might be repositioned vis-à-vis organisational and institutional structures. It also suggests some new directions for leading and learning and throws open a discussion on leadership that for too long has been captured by the assumption that the leader is the cause of organisational performance and learning outcomes in schools.

At a time when leadership's dominance seems unshakeable, this is a bold book that should appeal to postgraduate students of educational leadership and management, those undertaking training in educational administration and current school leaders interested in exploring the value of leadership for educational organisations.

Gabriele Lakomski is Professor Emeritus at the Melbourne Graduate School of Education at the University of Melbourne, Australia.

Scott Eacott is Senior Lecturer at the School of Education at the University of New South Wales, Australia, and Adjunct Professor of Educational Leadership at the University of Saskatchewan, Canada.

Colin W. Evers is Professor of Educational Leadership at the University of New South Wales, Australia.

Foundations and Futures of Education

Peter Aggleton, UNSW, Australia
Sally Power, Cardiff University, UK
Michael Reiss, UCL Institute of Education, UK

Foundations and Futures of Education focuses on key emerging issues in education as well as continuing debates within the field. The series is inter-disciplinary, and includes historical, philosophical, sociological, psychological and comparative perspectives on three major themes: the purposes and nature of education; increasing interdisciplinarity within the subject; and the theory-practice divide.

Questioning Leadership

New directions for educational
organisations

**Edited by Gabriele Lakomski,
Scott Eacott and Colin W. Evers**

LONDON AND NEW YORK

First published 2017
by Routledge
2 Park Square, Milton Park, Abingdon, Oxon OX14 4RN

and by Routledge
711 Third Avenue, New York, NY 10017

*Routledge is an imprint of the Taylor & Francis Group,
an informa business*

British Library Cataloguing in Publication Data
A catalogue record for this book is available from the British Library

Library of Congress Cataloging in Publication Data
A catalog record for this book has been requested

ISBN: 978-1-138-18316-2 (hbk)
ISBN: 978-1-315-64600-8 (ebk)

Typeset in Galliard
by Deanta Global Publishing Services, Chennai, India

Contents

viii   *Contents*

Preface

The purpose of this book is to raise some important questions about leadership in education and to suggest some directions for future travel. It promotes no party line and privileges no model. Indeed, it does not engage in a discussion of individual approaches to school leadership. Rather, it questions the whole enterprise. This was a deliberate choice.

The idea for this book arose from a number of working meetings convened by the editors, which were dedicated to exploring the prominence of 'leadership' in education discourse and to asking whether it is possible to describe and explain the work of school principals and teachers in terms that do not make reference to this term as an *a priori* explanation. The reason we think it important to raise the leadership question in this way can best be appreciated by considering the historical context.

Leadership has not always been considered the prime candidate for explaining the organisational performance of schools. Indeed, from the 1950s to the 1980s, systems theory served as the major explanatory paradigm for educational administration. This is best exemplified by Wayne Hoy and Cecil Miskel's book *Educational Administration: Theory, Research and Practice*, which constituted the core textbook for the field. Its emphasis, true to systems theory, lies in the assumption that organisational phenomena can be explained by reference to the interrelationships that determine how organisations – including schools – function. While leadership was important, it was seen to be constrained and determined by other organisational features. A leader's agency was thus located within the context of the larger quest for a science of organisations, making law-like generalisations possible. This in turn led to the search to identify what all leaders supposedly had in common.

Since the 1980s, a change of emphasis has taken place that focuses more directly on leadership and the leader as the dominant cause of desirable organisational outcomes. The evidence for this change can be seen in the emergence of new academic education journals with *leadership* in their titles. Furthermore, established top-tier educational administration journals such as the erstwhile British journal *Educational Management and Administration* saw fit to amend their titles to include *leadership*. In universities, this change was also evident in job descriptions and promotion criteria, which started to include *leadership* as a required category. Subsequently, research in educational administration shifted to an emphasis on leadership, and leadership training and standards have become prominent in practically all organisations. What has receded into the background are the structural features that affect organisational functioning, making way instead for agent-oriented perspectives, as can be found in many current theoretical accounts.

This book seeks to restore the balance in explanation by exploring the importance of the organisational and, more broadly, the institutional factors that provide both the context for leadership and exercise their own constraints on organisational performance. As such, *Questioning Leadership* places itself in the critical tradition initiated by Lakomski's (2005) earlier book *Managing without Leadership – Towards a Theory of Organizational Functioning*. This examined the very foundations of leadership, advocating for less leader-centric ways of understanding and managing organisations. Since 2005, there has not been another book of its kind.

This edited book takes up the challenge of conceptualising leadership in a new way without necessarily suggesting that we can manage without the *L* word. The perspectives offered by emerging and established scholars are diverse. They illuminate the leadership issue from a rich variety of theoretical standpoints. They challenge the traditional assumptions of leadership as being the default option for the explanation of organisational functioning by emphasising the structural, institutional and generally relational features that constrain organisations and thus challenge the current orthodoxy of leader-centrism.

The perspectives offered include modern French social theory – from Bourdieu to Foucault, Derrida and Lyotard – but extend to encompass the political philosophy of Hannah Arendt. The book's approach incorporates the notions of wisdom, ethics and social justice, as well as the idea of distributed leadership. Eclectic in terms of theoretical perspectives, the common thread at the core of *Questioning Leadership* is that its contributors question leadership! At a time when leadership's dominance seems unshakeable and when its wide acceptance is taken for granted, this book is not just bold; it is controversial. We hope, however, that it will further the growth of knowledge in education, a goal that can best be achieved, as Karl Popper famously suggested, through 'conjectures' and 'refutations'. As editors, we feel this book is overdue in terms of pointing leadership research in more realistic and productive directions that will have real purchase on the functioning of schools and their leaders, wherever they might be.

We have divided the text into three major parts, each part containing four chapters plus an additional chapter that offers a critical commentary. The order in which the parts appear represents a progression from foundational, epistemological and ontological issues in leadership theory in Part 1 to what might be described as the major alternative perspectives in leadership in Part 2, that of Postmodern theory in its various expressions. Part 3 identifies specific issues in leadership theory and practice that are in need of further critical examination, with one exception. A book that advocates questioning leadership, in our view, should also include work that supports leadership as successful practice. This we have done. We end the book by marking out some new directions that leading and learning might take in the future.

We were fortunate to have been able to attract senior international scholars to comment on each part, to provide their assessment of the success (or otherwise) of the type of questioning represented in the chapters they reviewed and to comment on possible theoretical advances emanating from them. As is the case with all books of this kind, the final arbiter, however, is the reader, and the ultimate mark of success is if the book creates new momentum for critical debates in schools and universities – in fact everywhere where leadership is an issue. That is what we hope for!

Gabriele Lakomski, Scott Eacott and Colin W. Evers
Melbourne and Sydney, May 2016

Acknowledgements

The old adage that 'too many cooks spoil the broth' may well apply in the kitchen, but it does not apply to the creation of this book. On the contrary, the richness, diversity, and even 'spiciness' of this book is the result of many contributors who were willing to share their ideas freely and to work towards the common goal of questioning leadership. So first and foremost, we want to record our gratitude to the contributors of this volume. The opportunity afforded to academics to engage with exciting ideas and a diversity of opinion is a real privilege. Reading drafts, reviews and revised papers – and the multitude of exchanges throughout – has highlighted the depth and breadth of scholarship in educational administration and leadership that is represented here. The dialogue and debates that this volume has sparked between us – and hopefully beyond – is something we all wish to continue.

Secondly, the ideas presented throughout this volume have had varied trajectories. Initial stimulus for this collection came from a workshop organized by Scott Eacott and hosted at the Australian Catholic University (North Sydney). Specific thanks go to Dean Tania Aspland for finding the funds to support this initiative. Earlier versions of some of the papers were presented at the Australian Association for Research in Education conference as a symposium of the Educational Leadership Special Interest Group. The questions and discussions with participants at these events helped shape and refine the ideas and push them in new directions.

Thirdly, quality scholarship is forged through rigorous and robust peer review. To that end, we would like to acknowledge the many reviewers who gave their time generously to read (and in some cases, re-read) and comment on chapters in the interests of producing the highest quality arguments. The quality of this collection is a testament to your efforts. Thank you.

Fourthly, we also thank our respective institutions, the University of Melbourne and the University of New South Wales (UNSW) Australia for the ongoing support of rigorous and robust scholarship at a time when edited collections do not count in certain metrics. We greatly appreciate the support of scholarship in all forms that our respective institutions continue to uphold.

Fifthly, we want to express our appreciation and thanks to Peter Aggleton, joint editor of the *Foundations and Futures of Education* series of books, not only for supporting the publication of this book in the series but also, more importantly, for reading drafts of the manuscript and giving constructive advice about our ideas and the ways we expressed them. The end result is all the more polished for his input.

Finally, as all creative endeavours require periods of withdrawal, we owe a debt of gratitude to our families and friends and wish to acknowledge their support and understanding here.

Gabriele Lakomski, Scott Eacott and Colin W. Evers
Melbourne and Sydney, May 2016

Part I

Foundational issues in leadership theory

1 Challenging leadership
The issues

Gabriele Lakomski and Colin W. Evers

Introduction

In the field of educational administration, we live in an age of leadership, both in the material sense of leaders as persons and in a formal sense that concerns the concept, or rather concepts, of leadership. It has not always been so. Although leaders and leadership have been studied since antiquity – Plato's *Republic* and Aristotle's *The Politics* offer fine examples – in the field of educational administration, which began a quest in the 1950s to be more rigorous and scientific, the dominant paradigm has been that of systems theory. This view brought with it an account of how organisations functioned, and when they failed to function adequately, it proffered both diagnostics and remedial action. When a system is characterised by a specification of inputs, the processing of those inputs and a set of desired outputs, the resulting diagnosis that the theory most likely suggests is a failure of adequate integration between the system's components. Perhaps there may be inadequate feedback, causing the system to drift outside its operating parameters, and to fail to return to equilibrium. Perhaps there is a problem with inputs. The point is that a systems-theoretic portrayal of an organisation is not isomorphic to that quintessential representation of an organisation's pattern of leadership – the organisational chart.

Two developments during the 1970s and 1980s prompted more serious questioning of the adequacy of systems-scientific accounts of organisations. One consisted of a series of theoretical attacks on systems science. The first, by Greenfield (1975), argued that the explanatory resources of logical empiricist science were not adequate for social science. He claimed that an understanding of an organisation needs to utilise categories such as intentions, desires and interpretations – the stuff of human subjectivity. The quest for law-like empirical generalisations that might function successfully to explain and predict organisational life was a forlorn one. Other theoretical criticisms of systems theory and its assumed epistemology of logical empiricism soon followed. Hodgkinson (1978) argued that administration involved a consideration of values and that, since science dealt with facts, educational administration was better seen as a humanism rather than a science. Foster (1980), using the resources of critical theory, argued that science was just one type of knowledge. Educational administration needed to deal with hermeneutical knowledge and emancipatory knowledge, a broadening that was not congenial to systems theory in that it was seen to involve the manipulation and control of people. Postmodern approaches that challenged the entire enterprise of scientific evidence and truth were even less congenial in their criticisms. (See Maxcy, 1994.)

The second development, we suggest, was the rise of school-based management in many jurisdictions, especially from about 1980 onwards. This new administrative arrangement required a shift from the more centralised administration of government schools to a decentralised system with greater autonomy for school decision-making at the price of greater accountability. Systems theory struggles with this type of issue, since a central feature of systems is the notion of return to equilibrium when the system is disturbed. It is a model that is weak on theorising systemic change. Caldwell and Spinks (1992, pp. 49–50) understood this perfectly well, claiming that 'a powerful capacity for transformational leadership is required for the successful transition to a system of self-managing schools'. Indeed, transformational leadership became the standard model for schools whereby the leadership had to implement school-based management.

Whatever the merits of these two developments in explaining the decline of systems theory and the rise of leadership theory as the explanatory model of first resort when it comes to organisational functioning in education, there is little doubt that it happened. In this chapter, we recount the evidence for this and then offer a number of arguments to the effect that leader-centric accounts over-reach themselves in some important areas. We first claim that leader-centric accounts of organisational performance appear to be much wedded to the doctrine of methodological individualism, the central feature of which is the idea that explaining what happens in an organisation reduces without remainder to an explanation in terms of what individuals do. We think that this over-states human agency at the expense of structural factors. It is significant that a school principal's agency can be constrained by a school's location in a social matrix of demographic, cultural, economic, ethnic and linguistic constraints. Second, we think that it is not logically possible to explain an agent's actions without recourse to certain structural concepts. We also illustrate this with reference to an example from social network theory. Third, we argue that the concept of the solitary cognitive agent is misleading as it ignores evidence for the extended mind, a condition whereby individual cognition is scaffolded either by outsourcing to artefacts – written notes, calculators, computers, iPads – or is distributed among individuals either statically as variously shared memories or dynamically as time-extended problem solving. We also challenge the notion of the autonomous self by noting findings on the causal antecedents of such autonomy. Finally, we observe that many problems that educational leaders face have their own structure, one dictated by the constraints that go into defining the problem. We conclude that a more balanced approach to understanding schools and other organisations is required, one that gives weight to both individual agency and the structures that constrain the trajectories that such agency can pursue.

Leadership and its discontents

The evidence for a golden age of school leadership (see Drysdale and Gurr, this volume) is plentiful. A Google search of centres for educational leadership produces hundreds of results, most of post-1980 vintage. Named Masters-level qualifications in the field reflect the shift from Masters degrees in educational administration to those in educational leadership. Academic titles also reflect this shift from administration to leadership. The field's main academic journals again reflect the change. For example, *Educational Management and Administration* transitioned to *Educational Management Administration and Leadership* in 2004. A number of new journals commenced after 1990: in 1998, the *International Journal of Leadership in Education*; in 1995, *Leading and Managing*; and in 1991, *Journal of School Leadership*. In 1997, the established journal *School Organisation*, so named in 1981, changed its name to *School Leadership & Management*. (See Evers and Lakomski, 2013, for more detail.) Two other sources of evidence for change are the larger number of handbooks on educational leadership and the number of conferences addressing this theme.

The effect of a strong focus on leadership has consequences for understanding how schools might be improved. For example, among the top 10 jurisdictions surveyed in the Organisation for Economic Co-operation and Development's (OECD) Programme for International Student Assessment (PISA) exercise across mathematics, science and reading could be found Shanghai, Singapore, Hong Kong, Macau and Taiwan, with some combination of Shanghai, Singapore and Hong Kong being in the top three of each area tested. But each of these jurisdictions enjoys the influence of a significant Confucian heritage culture, one that greatly values scholarship and learning. This culture also supports a large shadow education system, one in which many parents pay for private tutoring, either one-to-one or in private classrooms. As Bray (2009, p. 18) notes for China, 'The 2004 Urban Household Education and Employment survey covered 4773 households. It indicated that tutoring was received by 73.8% of primary, 65.6% of lower secondary, and 53.5% of upper secondary students'. In the case of Hong Kong, 'a 2004–2005 survey of 13,600 households suggested that pupils receiving tutoring were 36.0% at the primary level, 28.0% in lower secondary, 33.6% in middle secondary, and 48.1% in upper secondary'.

While methodological individualism counsels the better training of teachers and school leaders, even to the point of borrowing another jurisdiction's pedagogy and training regimes, it is simply not feasible to borrow a jurisdiction's culture. This is a structural matter providing the kind of context in which schooling occurs.

Another possible structural constraint on educational performance is income distribution. Wilkinson and Pickett (2010, pp. 103–117), in analysing the results of PISA 2003, drew attention to the positive correlation between income equality and these PISA results in the various participating jurisdictions. Although leader-centric accounts of school performance might specify the structural constraints under which leaders act, the point remains that leader-centrism is only one part of the available explanatory resources, with other parts placing limits on the attribution of leadership effects. And it should be borne in mind that structural constraints can vary significantly, even among schools within the same jurisdiction.

At a deeper level, there are logical limits to methodological individualism. This depends on how an individual's actions are described. If we just use the resources of behaviourism, then we are basically describing bodily movements as, for example, when describing the movement of a person's arm through a 180-degree rotation from down to up. The kind of inferences this account sustains are extraordinarily thin and are certainly unable to support any inferences rich enough to figure in discussions of leadership. The result would be a failure to distinguish, say, giving a salute, bidding at an auction, swatting away an insect, attracting the attention of a friend or an involuntary Tourette's tic. To do social science, we need the theoretical resources to make distinctions like this, resources that trade in talk of reasons, intentions and understandings. As Lukes (1968, pp. 124–127) observes, the trouble is that these resources invoke structure, a collective intentionality about what counts as reasons, the attribution of intentions or the imputing of understanding. And as Searle (1995, pp. 59–78) remarks, collective intentionality is not a property of individuals. It is an emergent property.

One place where the emergence of properties concerning leadership has been given close study is in social epistemology, where computer simulations of the behaviour of artificial social networks have been undertaken. Here's how the research operates. Consider a network of individuals variously connected for influence and communication. Each individual is given an internal representation of two different theories between which they are deliberating. Posit one individual as a leader, in the sense that they are able to exercise influence over the choices the others make. The simulations (for example, by Hutchins, 1996, pp. 229–262; and Zollman, 2007, pp. 574–587) produce an interesting global result. Inasmuch as the leader exercises strong leadership, that is, s/he is able to strongly influence the views of others in the network, decision-making proceeds quite rapidly. The bad news is that the network also suffers from confirmation bias, which inhibits its learning capacity. That is, once the network reaches a consensus viewpoint, it's very hard to change it with additional evidence. This is known as the 'royal family' effect (Zollman, 2007). On the other hand, with weak leadership, the situation is reversed. The network takes longer to make decisions but suffers much less from confirmation bias.

This general result requires a qualification and some elaboration. First, although we can specify mathematically the learning and decision-making features of each individual in the network, the learning and decision-making properties of the network as a whole are emergent properties. Second, these emergent properties cannot be derived from a precise specification of the same properties for the artificial individuals in the network, that is, because the structure of the network matters, namely the pattern of connectivity. So here is the qualification: even though we keep the same two properties for each individual constant, the emergent properties of the network will be different for different network structures. And holding the leader's level of influence constant, the emergent properties of the network will also be different for different patterns of connectivity. Roughly speaking, a greater amount of connectivity increases the 'royal family' effect; a lesser, the opposite effect. Although these results are based on simulations of toy universes, they can still be highly instructive. (See Evers, 2012, for a detailed discussion.)

Lukes' argument worked because you cannot do social science out of the resources of behaviourism. But once you start enriching explanatory resources for these purposes, you encounter social facts – those that make use of regulatory and constitutively defined patterns (Haig and Evers, 2016). Searle (1995), with his new institutional theory, has done much to theorise the role of language as intrinsic to social functioning.

At some point there needs to be contact between the discourses that contribute to the creation of social reality and the cognitive processes that underwrite those discourses. Organisational theorists have long been interested in the study of human cognition, with the work of Simon (1945) on bounded rationality being a major early initiative. The main reason for this interest is that for Simon, what was viewed as central for understanding and improving organisations was how decision-making occurred. Griffiths (1959) introduced much the same emphasis for educational administration, an emphasis that continues to flourish today. (Chitpin and Evers, 2015.)

The most promising approach to cognition, in our view, is to be found in cognitive neuroscience – theories of how the brain represents and processes information. The best of this work usually takes the form of empirically informed mathematical models.[1] You would think that a focus on cognition as a tool for understanding aspects of leadership would have a focus on individuals. However, this turns out to be only partly true. Theories of educational administration and leadership imply a view of cognition that is enshrined in their epistemologies, and these in turn significantly shape the content and structure of administration and leadership theories. This emphasis on the role of cognition is the first of two main functions of our work (Evers and Lakomski, 1991, 1996, 2000, 2015.) Our epistemology is a form of naturalism, in that it coheres with natural science; and coherentism, in that our best theories enjoy, in addition to empirical adequacy, a number of super-empirical virtues, such as consistency, comprehensiveness, simplicity and coherence. The second function is to see leadership theories as context dependent but developed by leaders in epistemically progressive ways that employ knowledge-building processes that mirror the coherent adjustment of their theories in light of feedback from problem-solving practices. (Evers, 2015.)

In what follows, we make three key points. First, when it comes to understanding knowledge of practice, it is better to see cognition as a form of pattern processing rather than simply sentence crunching. Second, the mind is extended beyond the skull. And third, agency articulates with wider causal contexts. The latter two points imply a view of cognition that extends beyond the individual.

Naturalistic coherentism at work

Cognition in the skull

The adoption of naturalism, and our own version of it, *naturalistic coherentism*, exert a powerful influence in many directions and challenge traditional assumptions of cognition that underlie a range of theories of leadership (see Evers and Lakomski, 2015). Specifically, the modest requirement that what we claim to know we must have been able to acquire or learn given our biological capacities, turned out to be too severe a stipulation for traditional empiricist theories of leadership and their built-in concept of cognition, such as Simon's *bounded rationality*. It was based on a highly implausible theory of the mind that did not provide a realistic account of either learning or knowledge representation. The clearest and most elegant expression of this account of cognition was the *physical symbol system hypothesis* (PSSH) propagated by Newell and Simon (1976), which, they believed, appropriately emulated human rationality. Following the Western philosophical tradition, especially Descartes' view of the *res cogitans* or 'thinking thing' exemplified in the skilful manipulation of abstract symbols, cognition was a matter of formal operations on symbols, human rationality was equated with such skilful manipulation and cognition and rationality were located in the skull. On this view of *disembodied cognition*, 'cognitive processing is not only central, but largely modularized and specialized, and computationally context-independent, essentially independent of motor planning and execution' (Teske, 2013, p. 761).

The view of cognition as disembodied, however, does not cohere well with the scientific evidence of biological brain architecture and function and does not explain the causal processes involved in human thinking and acting. The central difficulty is dealing with knowledge of practice, both how it is developed and how it is exercised. Thus important skills such as sound judgement, influencing and motivating people or being a change agent are difficult to account for. The acquisition of such skills from practice seems to be accountable more realistically by positing that cognising agents learn to recognise characteristic patterns among the complex of elements in dynamic organisational life. The problem of accounting for practical knowledge is particularly acute in theories such as transformational leadership, which place a heavy premium on the leader's cognitive role in leading: a belief that the leader knows best. In view of weaknesses in our social science, it would seem more prudent to adopt a fallibilist approach to leader knowledge, one that requires leaders to engage in much professional self-learning or knowledge-building in their organisational contexts.

Cognition beyond the skull

Much has been accomplished since about 1985 – the year the two-volume work *Parallel Distributed Processing* (Rumelhart and McClelland, 1986) was published – when it comes to the use of artificial neural networks to model aspects of cognition. (Rumelhart, 1993; Evers and Lakomski, 1996, Ch. 9, and

2000, Part 1; Evers, 2000). We also know that despite their amazing capacities, biological brains are computationally limited and need to offload both memory and computation. In order to accomplish complex tasks and to solve problems, we need to draw on external, non-neural, resources, such as the electronic devices developed in recent years, which amplify or extend our brains, and therefore our cognitive grasp, in ways we cannot yet and may never be able to fathom fully. It is this feature that Clark (2008) describes as 'supersizing the mind', enshrined in the concept of the *Extended Mind* (Clark and Chalmers, 1998/2008). Cognition, in this view, 'leaks' into the world, is therefore no longer bounded by skin and skull and can thus more appropriately be understood as constituting *a system* comprising dynamic, reciprocal interactions between people, artefacts and other environmental resources (e.g. Hollan, Hutchins and Kirsh, 2000; Hutchins, 1996; Clark, 1997; Lakomski, 2005, pp. 69–74). What counts as the *relevant unit of analysis* has radically changed from cognition as skull-bound to cognition as externally and socially distributed and situated, and above all, as *embodied* (Anderson, 2003, 2008; Clark, 2003, 2007, 2008, 2010; Teske, 2013; Wilson and Golonka, 2013).

The importance of this change can hardly be overestimated. It poses a number of challenges to understanding where to draw the boundaries of a cognitive system (the problem of *cognitive bloat* (Clark, 2001, p. 156) and how to determine where 'my' mental machinery ends and the world's begins. Furthermore, the extended cognitive unit of analysis invites reconsideration of the traditional notion of human agency ('free will') and specifically about the issue of *control* humans have over their behaviours and decisions. But before we consider these issues, more needs to be said about embodied cognition to understand clearly what is at stake.

The descriptor 'embodied' means specifically that 'thinking is inherently tied to – grounded in – *perceiving and acting*' (Anderson, 2008, p. 423; emphases added). This is an important point, because the link to perceiving and acting connects the body directly to the world in which and upon which the human agent acts. This link seems obvious, but it is in marked contrast to the more disembodied version of cognition that once prevailed. The so-called higher cognitive skills of reasoning, planning and decision-making were not seen to be closely connected to the perceptual and motor systems, on the assumption of a modular brain architecture that sanctioned restricted neural pathways between brain regions. But anatomical modularity has recently been challenged, and neuroscientific evidence suggests that the functional architecture of the brain is better characterised by *dynamic affiliation* (Anderson, 2014, p. 436). It thus exhibits all the hallmarks of a softly assembled dynamical system (Evers and Lakomski, 2015). It is this kind of evidence that supports the claim of intimately connected emotional and cognitive pathways (Pessoa, 2014; for application to educational decision-making, see Lakomski and Evers, 2010, 2012).

At the extreme end of what constitutes a continuum of theories of embodiment (Wilson, 2002) is the claim that 'Our bodies and their perceptually guided motions through the world do much of the work required to achieve our goals, *replacing* the need for complex internal mental representations' (Wilson and Golonka, 2013, p. 1). The critical word here is 'replacing', as it seems to indicate parity between goings-on in the mind/brain and body-bound, environmentally situated processes. Not surprisingly, the *parity principle*, with particular refer- ence to Clark and Chalmers' (1998/2008) *Extended Mind* hypothesis, remains controversial.

On this view, all components, whether internal or externally located, play an active, causal role and determine behaviour (additional criteria that non- biological components must meet to count in an individual's cognitive system are set out in Clark, 2010, p. 46). If the external components were to drop out, 'the system's behavioural competence will drop, just as it would if we removed part of its brain' (Clark and Chalmers, 2008, p. 222). This is a strong claim that has given rise to much critical debate (e.g. Rupert, 2004; Giere, 2007; Gallagher, 2013; Special Issue on Socializing the Extended Mind, *Cognitive Systems Research*, 2013[25–26]). Clark (2007, 2010) has vigorously defended 'pro- foundly embodied agency' and cites evidence from research in human–machine and brain–machine interfaces that help create bodily augmentation and mental augmentation. Regarding the latter, 'body babbling', an infant's exploration of 'which neural commands bring about which bodily effects, which then must be practised until skilled enough to issue those commands without conscious effort' (Clark, 2007, p. 270), is a very good example of this feature. (Further evidence comes from robotics and animal cognition; see Wilson and Golonka, 2013; Shapiro, 2011).

The basic idea here is that humans have plastic neural resources that are sub- ject to continuous monitoring and re-calibration (e.g. Clark, 2003, Ch. 3). This feature of our humanity would be easier to see if we were not stuck on the 'deeply mistaken view of the thinking agent as some distinct inner locus of final choice and control' (Clark, 2010, p. 56). But this is precisely the view implied in leader- centric views of organisational/school functioning, which we will consider next.

Who is in charge? Virtual agency and the neural self

Our brief sketch of the significance of profoundly embodied agency shows that, if true, agency is spread over neural and non-neural components the interactions of which are dynamic and not easily delimited. Furthermore, it follows that the notion of self is extended in a similar manner as it goes beyond the boundaries of consciousness (Clark, 2008, p. 232), a prerequisite for traditional notions of self. This is a challenging notion, as our common-sense understanding of self is that we are in charge, that we freely and intentionally choose our actions and that subsequently we take, or are made to take, responsibility for our actions. In leader-centric views, this assumption is particularly salient (although it applies to everyone else as well), as the principal is legally, and arguably morally, responsible for everything that goes on in a school.

Fundamental to the common-sense idea of self and agency is the assumption that we (consciously) control our behaviour and decisions. Although deeply entrenched, this assumption has been challenged by a wealth of cognitive and social psychological evidence that has shown human behaviour and decisions to be heavily influenced by external, situational contingencies of which agents remain unaware (e.g. Nisbett and Wilson, 1977; Wegner, 2002; Lakomski, 1997, pp. 163–167). This result has invited the conclusion that control, whether conscious or not, is an illusion, and that agency is only *virtual* (e.g. Wegner, 2002). Indeed, Wegner (2003), a prominent proponent of this view, claims that the deeply held idea of humans causing their own actions is 'the mind's best trick'. His *theory of apparent mental causation* (Wegner, 2002) argues that humans experience conscious will 'as a function of the priority, consistency, and exclusivity of the thought about the action. The thought must occur before the action, be consistent with the action, and not be accompanied by other causes.' (Wegner and Wheatley, 1999, p. 480; Wegner, 2005). When these conditions are met, we infer that our thoughts have caused our actions, and Wegner notes that such inference is no more than a construct. And so it is. We know that humans do not have privileged access to the contents of their own minds (Churchland, 1988; Evers and Lakomski, 1991, Ch. 2) and that they make plausibility judgements about the connection between thought and action. Determining causal relations, however, is a matter for scientific investigation rather than introspection, as Wegner (2003) acknowledges.

If we were to accept that human agency is merely virtual, even in ordinary circumstances, then this would have severe consequences regarding the acceptance of responsibility for one's actions. On the face of it, this might let the school principal off the hook in that s/he could plead 'diminished responsibility' for some action on the assumption that the notion of agency-as-control has been discredited. On closer inspection, though, what Suhler and Churchland (2009) dubbed the 'frail control' hypothesis lacks relevant (neuro) scientific evidence, and we explore two critical issues here. The notion of control in the 'frail control' hypothesis is too narrow in that it ties consciousness to control, and secondly, automatic nonconscious processes are falsely considered of little importance. As a consequence of these assumptions, there is no such thing as non-conscious control. Both assumptions, however, are flawed, and non-conscious control is in fact pervasive in everyday life.

We know that brains are fast and furious pattern recognition and completion engines, and it is this ability that provides an explanation of the nature and importance of non-conscious processes and their importance for control. Every skill we exhibit is the expression of 'hidden', non-conscious, neural processes that make possible what we do so well, from driving a car or putting and sinking a golf ball to 'reading' the emotions of a colleague correctly. We do this repeatedly, automatically and mostly well, and thus we demonstrate successful control, engineered by means of neurological activity that aligns the required motor coordination and perception networks to execute the task. As Suhler and Churchland (2009, p. 345) remark, 'habit and routine serve to spare the brain the energetic costs of close attention and to give the benefits of smooth operation… making nonconscious control of this sort a great energy- and face-saving device'.

This conclusion should not come as a surprise, as control is highly likely to have evolved as an adaptive response to environmental possibilities and constraints (Dennett, 2003).

An important (and unsurprising) precondition for non-conscious control to happen at all is that the brain regions and pathways implicated must be intact and function normally. We know from work such as Damasio's (e.g. 1996; 2010) that non-conscious control is severely limited, or even destroyed, in case of certain brain lesions. In addition, as Suhler and Churchland (2009) explain, functionality depends on a range of neurotransmitters that need to be in the 'normal range', a range that recognises a fair degree of individual variability in levels of neurotransmitters present at any given time, so that if one falls below normal range, the person may still be 'in control'. Suhler and Churchland (2009, p. 344) thus argue that 'the physiological requirement for being in control is defined in terms of a hyper-region in an n-dimensional 'control space'. An important consequence of defining control in this way is that there will be many different combinations of neurochemical levels that fall within the 'in control' hyper-region'.

Just as the argument for profoundly embodied agency has undermined the classical notion of the stand-alone thinker by showing just how integrated and interdependent human cognition is with its (non-neural) environment, the novel account of control as neural activity shows that control, and thus agency in an important sense, is real. The idea of virtual agency depended on the identification of control with consciousness and the unimportance of non-conscious processes. But, importantly, consciousness is not a necessary precondition; nonconscious control is pervasive but also more complex. Above all, the fine-grained neural account of control allows for individual variability. It is very early days, as research into non-conscious control has barely begun, but we already see that there may be far-reaching consequences for the determination of responsibility, both morally and legally. Many questions still remain unanswered, but it is clear that the traditional notion of agency and control, so important for leader-centric views of school functioning, is in dire need of revision.

Problems and their structure

Earlier, we spoke of the embodied nature of cognition situated in a causal context of spatially extended cognitive activity. In this last section, we describe a particular dynamical configuration of situated cognitive activity that is focused on epistemic procedures for promoting the solution of problems. The central idea originates in the work of the philosopher of science Karl Popper, who proposed a model for the growth of scientific knowledge (see Popper, 1979). This model begins with the formulation of a problem to be solved, P_1. The next step is to propose a tentative theory, TT_1, to be implemented in order to solve the problem. The process of implementation involves testing the theory in practice, during which limitations to the theory may be discovered. This process is called error elimination, EE_1. Often, problems discovered in implementing a tentative theory arise, P_2. The schema proposed by Popper therefore takes the following form:

$$P_1 => TT_1 => EE_1 => P_2.$$

Call this schema a *Popper Cycle*. Popper suggests that the growth of scientific knowledge is a trajectory defined by a succession of Popper Cycles.

Work done by Chitpin and Evers (2005, 2012) shows that this model can be applied to the study of the growth of professional knowledge among teachers and school leaders (see also Chitpin, 2015; Evers, 2015). The model has utility because even small organisations are complex, and it is often difficult to predict or anticipate the flux of organisational life. Problem-solving is rarely accomplished in one Popper Cycle but more realistically plays out in a trajectory, a succession of such cycles. Sometimes a succession of failures can be a necessary condition for enabling the implementation of a more difficult tentative theory. Uncertainty as to what will work favours the heuristic of trying the easiest to implement tentative theory.

A school faced with the possibility of closure because of falling enrolments will probably start with a programme of promoting the school in the catchment area, even though converting it from a single-sex school to a co-ed school, while complicated to implement, will most certainly work. Also, problems are defined by a constraint set plus the demand that something be done. Getting to a solution may require prior Popper Cycles in order to build up the constraint set to the required level. An analogy would be completing a jigsaw puzzle. You cannot correctly locate the pieces towards the centre in the absence of a substantial build-up of the puzzle because there are insufficient contextual constraints to specify a correct placement.[2]

In this example, the unit of cognition, the extended mind, is the entire material context of activity in which the problem is solved. Since the context is an organisation, the problems, the tentative theories, the acts of implementation and testing for errors and the formulation or discovery of further problems are all distributed across other people, artefacts and resources and courses of action constrained by constitutive and regulative rules. To construe this in a leader-centric way is not only to mis-describe the nature of agency. It is also to misunderstand the conditions that make for the kind of epistemically progressing cognitive activity that leads to the solution of problems.

Conclusion

This chapter should not be construed as a sustained attack on the notion of leadership. Rather, we have tried to offer arguments for seeing leadership as situated in larger structures, processes and contexts, which we think must be taken into account in order to analyse problems and issues realistically and to get a better idea of what those who do perform as leaders (in the distributed arrangements that we suggest obtain) can and cannot do. The current dominance of leader-centrism is itself an artefact of wider social forces. To push back against this dominance with reasoned argument is also an epistemically progressive act in response to these wider social forces.

Notes

1   A good example of this is the work coming out of Paul Thagard's Computational Epistemology Laboratory: http://cogsci.uwaterloo.ca/Index.html.
2   A detailed account of this example can be found in Evers and Katyal, 2008.

References

Anderson, M. L., 2003. Embodied cognition: A field guide. *Artificial Intelligence*, 1491, pp. 91–103.

Anderson, M. L., 2008. On the grounds of x-grounded cognition. In P. Calvo and T. Gomila, eds., *Handbook of cognitive science: An embodied approach*. Oxford: Elsevier, pp. 423–435.

Anderson, M. L., 2014. Complex function in the dynamic brain. Comment on 'Understanding brain networks and brain organization' by Luiz Pessoa, *Physics of Life Reviews*, 11, pp. 436–437.

Bray, M., 2009. *Confronting the shadow education system*. Paris, France: UNESCO Publishing.

Caldwell, B. J. and Spinks, J., 1992. *Leading the self-managing school*. London, UK: Routledge/Falmer.

Chitpin, S., 2015. Capturing principals' decision-making processes in an online professional learning community. In S. Chitpin and C. W. Evers, eds., *Decision-making in educational leadership: Principles, policies and practices*. New York: Routledge.

Chitpin, S. and Evers, C. W., eds., 2015. *Decision-making in educational leadership: Principles, policies and practices*. New York: Routledge.

Churchland, P. M., 1988. *Matter and consciousness*. Cambridge, MA: MIT Press.

Clark, A., 2001. *Mindware*. Oxford: Oxford University Press.

Clark, A., 2003. *Natural-born cyborgs: Minds, technologies and the future of human intelligence*. New York: Oxford University Press.

Clark, A., 2007. Re-inventing ourselves: The plasticity of embodiment, sensing, and the mind. *Journal of Medicine and Philosophy*, 32, pp. 263–282.

Clark, A., 2008. *Supersizing the mind*. New York: Oxford University Press.

Clark, A., 2010. Memento's revenge: The extended mind, extended. In R. Menary, ed., *The extended mind* (pp. 43–66). Cambridge, MA: MIT Press.

Clark, A. and Chalmers, D., 1998. The extended mind. *Analysis*, 58, pp. 10–23. Reprinted in A. Clark, *Supersizing the Mind*, pp. 220–233.

Damasio, A. R., 1996. *Descartes' error*. London: Macmillan.

Damasio, A. R., 2010. *Self comes to mind*. New York: Pantheon Books.

Dennett, D., 2003. *Freedom evolves*. New York: Viking Penguin.

Evers, C. W., 2000. Connectionist modeling and education. *Australian Journal of Education*, 44, pp. 209–225.

Evers, C. W., 2012. Organizational contexts for lifelong learning: Individual and collective learning configurations. In D. N. Aspin, J. D. Chapman, K. R. Evans and R. Bagnall, eds., *Second international handbook of lifelong learning* (pp. 61–76). Dordrecht: Springer.

Evers, C.W., 2015. Decision-making as problem solving trajectories. In S. Chitpin and C.W. Evers, eds., *Decision-making in educational leadership: Principles, policies and practices*. New York: Routledge.

Evers, C. W. and Lakomski, G., 1991. *Knowing educational administration*. Oxford: Elsevier.

Evers, C. W. and Lakomski, G., 1996. *Exploring educational administration*. Oxford: Elsevier.

Evers, C. W. and Lakomski, G., 2000. *Doing educational administration*. Oxford: Elsevier.

Evers, C. W. and Katyal, K., 2008. Educational leadership in Hong Kong schools: Critical reflections on changing themes. *Journal of Educational Administration and History*, 40, pp. 251–264.

Evers, C. W. and Lakomski, G., 2013. Methodological individualism, educational administration, and leadership. *Journal of Educational Administration and History*, 45(2), pp. 159–172.

Evers, C. W. and Lakomski, G., 2015. Naturalism and educational administra-tion: New directions. In S. Eacott and C. W. Evers, eds., 2015, *Educational Philosophy and Theory* (Special Issue on 'New Frontiers in Educational Leadership, Management and Administration Theory'), 47(4), pp. 402–419.

Foster, W., 1980. Administration and the crisis in legitimacy: A review of Habermasian thought. *Harvard Educational Review*, 50(4), pp. 496–505.

Gallagher, S., 2013. The socially extended mind. *Cognitive Systems Research*, 25–26, pp. 4–12.

Giere, R. N., 2007. Distributed cognition without distributed knowing. *Social Epistemology*, 21(3), pp. 313–320.

Greenfield, T. B., 1975. Theory about organization: A new perspective for schools. In M. Hughes, ed., *Administering education: International challenge*. London, UK: Althone Press.

Griffiths, D. E., 1959. *Administrative theory*. New York: Appleton-Century Crofts.

Haig, B. D. and Evers, C. W., 2016. *Realist inquiry in social science*. London, UK: SAGE.

Hodgkinson, C., 1978. *Towards a philosophy of administration*. Oxford, UK: Blackwell.

Hollan, J., Hutchins E. and Kirsh D., 2000. Distributed cognition: Toward a new foundation for human–computer interaction research. *ACM Transactions on Computer–Human Interaction*, 72, pp. 174–196.

Hutchins, E., 1996. *Cognition in the wild*. Cambridge, MA: MIT Press.

Lakomski, G., 1997. Tacit knowledge in teacher education. In D. N. Aspin, ed., *Volume 2: Logical empiricism in educational discourse advanced volume* (pp. 146–159). Durban, SA: Butterworth.

Lakomski, G., 2005. *Managing without leadership*. Oxford: Elsevier.

Lakomski, G. and Evers, C. W., 2010. Passionate rationalism: The role of emotion in decision making. *Journal of Educational Administration*, 48(4), pp. 438–450.

Lakomski, G. and Evers, C. W., 2012. Emotion and rationality in educational problem solving: From individuals to groups. *Korean Journal of Educational Administration*, 30(1), pp. 653–677.

Lukes, S., 1968. Methodological individualism reconsidered. *The British Journal of Sociology*, 19 (2), pp. 119–129.

Maxcy, S. J., ed., 1994. *Postmodern school leadership: Meeting the crisis in educational administration*. Westport, CT: Praeger.

Newell, A. and Simon, H. A., 1976/1990. Computer science as empirical enquiry: Symbols and search. *Communications of the association for computing machinery*. New York: Association for Computing Machinery. Cited as reprinted in Boden,

M. A. (ed.). (1990). *The philosophy of artificial intelligence*. Oxford: Oxford University Press.

Nisbett, R. E. and Wilson, T. D., 1977. Telling more than we can know: Verbal reports on mental processes. *Psychological Review*, 83(3), pp. 231–259.

Pessoa, L., 2014. *The cognitive-emotional brain*. Cambridge, MA: MIT Press.

Popper, K. R., 1979. *Objective knowledge: An evolutionary approach*. Oxford: Oxford University Press.

Rumelhart, D. E., 1993. The architecture of mind: A connectionist approach. In M. I. Posner, ed., *Foundations of cognitive science* (pp. 133–159). Cambridge, MA: MIT Press.

Rumelhart, D. E. and McClelland, J. L., eds., 1986. *Parallel distributed processing*. Volumes 1 and 2. Cambridge, MA: MIT Press.

Rupert, R., 2004. Challenges to the thesis of extended cognition. *Journal of Philosophy*, 101, pp. 389–428.

Searle, J. R., 1995. *The construction of social reality*. New York: The Free Press.

Shapiro, L., 2011. *Embodied cognition*. New York: Routledge.

Simon, H. A., 1945/1976. *Administrative behavior*. New York: The Free Press Macmillan.

Suhler, C. L. and Churchland, P. S., 2009. Control: Conscious and otherwise. *Trends in Cognitive Sciences*, 13(8), pp. 341–347.

Teske, J., 2013. Religion and embodied cognition. *Zygon*, 48(3), pp. 759–787.

Wegner, D. M., 2002. *The illusion of conscious will*. Cambridge, MA: MIT Press.

Wegner, D. M., 2005. Who is the controller of controlled processes? In R. R. Hassin, J. S. Uleman and J. A. Bargheds, eds., *The new unconscious* (pp. 19–37). Oxford: Oxford University Press.

Wegner, D. M. and Wheatley, T., 1999. Apparent mental causation: Sources of the experience of will. *American Psychologist*, 54, pp. 480–491.

Wegner, D. W., 2003. The mind's best trick: How we experience conscious will. *Trends in Cognitive Sciences*, 7(2), pp. 65–69.

Wilkinson, R. and Pickett, K., 2010. *The spirit level: Why equality is better for everyone*. London, UK: Penguin Books.

Wilson, M., 2002. Six views of embodied cognition. *Psychonomic Bulletin and Review*, 94, pp. 625–636.

Wilson, A. D. and Golonka, S., 2013. Embodied cognition is not what you think it is. *Frontiers in Psychology*, 4, pp. 1–13.

Zollman, K. J. S., 2007. The communication structure of epistemic communities. *Philosophy of Science*, 74, pp. 574–587.

2 Beyond leadership

Towards a 'relational' way of thinking

Scott Eacott

Introduction

Since the turn of the century, if not earlier, leadership has been the dominant focus of research attention in educational administration (Bush, 2004; Oplatka, 2010). I argue that claims as to the explanatory importance and robustness of leadership as a construct go too far, as too many theoretical and methodological matters remain unresolved if this concept is simply accepted at face value. Epistemological dialogue and debate was vast during the Theory Movement, the Greenfield revolution and numerous other interventions such as Bates' Critical Theory of educational administration and Evers and Lakomski's naturalistic coherentism. Recently, however, the absence of methodological debate in educational administration has allowed for an under-developed act of human cognition to assume not only ascendency but dominance. This is not to say that leadership has advanced without critique in the broader organisational sciences (e.g. Alvesson and Sveningsson, 2003; Calder, 1977; Miner, 1975; Pfeffer, 1977) and in educational administration (e.g. Eacott, 2013, 2015; Gronn, 2003; Lakomski, 2005), but this critique has been infrequent and not sustained at scale. These alternative stances remain peripheral to the field of educational administration, which, at its core, changes little despite their presence.

In this chapter, I seek to honour the rich epistemological literatures of educational administration, and the many scholars working in the space, with the sort of rigorous analysis that is encouraged in the scholarly exercise embodied by thinkers such as Halpin, Griffiths, Greenfield, Bates, Willower, Hodgkinson and Culbertson; and contemporaries such as Evers, Lakomski, English, Gunter and Samier. In particular, I argue that leadership is an epistemological in addition to, if not more so, an empirical problem, being mindful that, as Bourdieu contends, every act of research is simultaneously empirical (confronting the world of observable phenomena) and theoretical (Bourdieu and Wacquant, 1992). Importantly, though, this chapter does not argue that we should (or should even attempt to) 'apply' or 'map' the works of a great thinker or an alternate meta-narrative onto events commonly described as leadership. As Adkins (2011) argues, such application or mapping is neither desirable nor helpful as it leaves the received terms of those events entirely intact. Instead, I mobilise the *relational* approach that I am advancing both here and elsewhere (e.g. Eacott, 2015) to understand these events in a new light, unsettling many of the normative assumptions regarding leadership and its explanatory value. And in the face of the recasting of our ways of thinking about organising outlined here, it may well be that the work of educational administration theorists will increasingly involve such recasting procedures, making the everyday experiences of organisational life strange.

Leadership is...

Over 50 years ago, Bennis (1959) stated that the concept of leadership continues to elude us, or it turns up in different forms to taunt us with its slipperiness and complexity. After a comprehensive review of literature, Stogdill (1974) claims there are almost as many definitions of leadership as there are definers. In one much-used definition, Yukl (1981) outlines leadership as influence, linking that with performance and collective tasks. If this is so, then leadership is redundant. What does it offer that influence does not? Similarly, Caldwell (2007) argues that leadership is change. Once again, leadership is rendered useless by its very own definition. It is a mere proxy for another term. Alvesson and Sveningsson (2003) argue that the variation in definitions of leadership indicate the non-correspondence between it and something specific out there in organisations and other social settings. The origins of leadership as an empirical phenomenon are the result of subjects being subordinate to the expressions of the observer's assumptions and methodologies. It is the pre-existing – that is, unconscious – orientation of the observer that is the most common experience of leadership. This experience embodies a circular logic built upon an ontological complicity with the dominant ideology of the contemporary social condition. In other words, a leadership worldview is confirmed in experiencing and thinking through events using a leadership worldview. Failure to live up to the expectation of this worldview is perceived as a deficit in individual actors or organisations rather than a questioning of the value of leadership.

Every body of leadership literature includes a degree of advocacy – as it cannot escape its normative generation. Even calls to radicalise leadership (e.g. Bogotch et al., 2008) are frequently replacing one meta-narrative with another. Despite this voluminous literature and regular usage in the ordinary language of the everyday, leadership does not offer itself to the senses. It passes largely unnoticed. This makes leadership somewhat unexperienced. When leadership is described or articulated, it is almost always through past events (the mapping of historical accounts with the lexicon of leadership, such as with contests and the glorification of victors and influential figures) and/or a projection into the forthcoming (a romanticised 'by design' agenda built on sequential steps and perpetual manipulation of materials in pursuit of an idealised future state). This mapping or projection ensures that leadership as a construct is essentially devoid of grounding in time and space. It is beyond context – something I will return to later. For now, suffice it to say that leadership language is reflective of an ideological position on organisational life. Notions of leadership serve as symbols for representing personal causation of social events (Pfeffer, 1977). Therefore, it is the innate human desire to matter, to be significant – that which gives meaning to actions – that is embodied in the language of leadership.

Calder (1977) argues that there is no unique content to the construct of leadership that is not subsumed under other more general models of behaviour. This is arguably why at a certain point in the analysis of the boundaries between leadership, management and administration blur until all that is left are the pre-existing normative assumptions of the researcher. Yet surprisingly, considerable, and far too much, intellectual space in journals, books and theses; and at conferences, seminars and graduate school classes is taken up trying to construct and sustain the distinctions. It is possible to characterise the logic of educational leadership research in a series of steps:

1 A perceived normative organisational need that goes beyond administration and/or management
2 The development of a tentative (leadership) theory for that normative requirement
3 Overlaying organising practice with the normative requirement
4 Transporting the normative beyond the organisation

This logic raises a series of questions concerning the relations between the observer and the observed and our ways of knowing. The first step articulated in the above framing is concerned with the unquestioned belief in leadership. The ontological complicity (Bourdieu and Wacquant, 1992) or intellectual gaze of the educational administration scholar (Eacott, 2015) obscures the relations between the researcher and the researched and the origins of the research object. Failure to attend to this leads to the projection and misrecognition of the objects of human cognition as though they are external and knowable. The unconscious orientation of how the researcher believes organisations *ought* to behave is used as a lens to evaluate how they are currently acting. Any distinctions created between leaders and others (e.g. non-leaders or followers) or between leadership and non-leadership (e.g. administration and management) are the manifestation of the pre-existing normative orientation of the researcher.

The explanatory power of leadership theory is based on its perceived correspondence with organisational behaviour. I want to propose an alternative here that directly engages with the rejection of objective or positivist science and the lack of correspondence. My argument, as will become clear, is based on the belief that leadership is not an external knowable entity but the product of cognition – a social construction. Attempts to get to this point have yet to take effect at scale, or their intents have been misappropriated. For example, Greenfield's body of work has been used to legitimise the choice, and subsequent explosion, of qualitative works in educational administration. Yet the depth of his epistemological critique is diluted, if not confused, when taken to be synonymous with qualitative methods and the legitimation of what are essentially relativist accounts of organisations. The conflation of theory (e.g. post-modern theorising) with method (e.g. qualitative research) is too frequent in the literatures of educational administration. Relational approaches have the potential to attend to the epistemological and content matters raised in the critique of leadership while also offering new ways of thinking through the organising of education.

Thinking relationally

Well-rehearsed arguments of leadership stress that it is relational (Uhl-Bien and Ospina, 2012). While the importance of relationships has been acknowledged since some of the earliest studies in management and administration, namely the Hawthorne studies of Mayo and Roethlisberger (e.g. Mayo, 1933) and the Human Relations movement, in recent decades there has been a somewhat relational turn in leadership studies. This mirrors a similar turn in sociology towards relational theories (Prandini, 2015). As Emirbayer (1997, p. 311) argues, 'social thinkers from a wide variety of disciplinary backgrounds, national traditions, and analytic and empirical points of view are fast converging upon this [a relational] frame of reference'. Relational sociology has strong roots in the US, primarily through what Mische (2011) labels the 'New York School of Relational Sociology' (notably Harrison White at Harvard University; and Charles Tilly at Harvard, then Columbia), but also European scholars such as Donati (1983, 1991, 2011, 2015), Depelteau and Powell (2013; Powell and Depelteau, 2013), Fuhse (2015) and Crossley (2011), with an intellectual tradition drawing upon Marx, Simmel, Tarde, Elias, Luhmann, Bourdieu and Latour, among others. The catalyst for relational approaches is the critique of the individualist and collectivist epistemologies and methodologies that have come to dominate social thought and analysis.

Labeled as being at the forefront of emerging scholarship on leadership (Hunt and Dodge, 2000) and recognised as an established perspective in contemporary leadership studies (Dinh et al., 2014), relational approaches still involve the use of some ambiguous language. Not surprisingly, there are considerable epistemological implications with any language slippage. Sociologists argue for the distinction between substantialist (a focus on things) and relational accounts, whereas in the leadership literatures, both entity-based (substantialist) and relational epistemologies are grouped under the label of *relational* if they focus on relations or relationships (e.g. Uhl-Bien, 2006). To further highlight some of the tensions of language across intellectual fields, Emirbayer's (1997) classic article *Manifesto for a Relational Sociology* uses the term *transactional* somewhat synonymously with *relational* as a label, yet in leadership literatures it has a very different history in opposition to transformational leadership. What remains, however, is a shift from leader- or person-centric accounts to a recognition of practice as being co-constructed by actors (although Uhl-Bien, 2006, mobilises a leader–follower binary), something that, to be understood, requires attention to relations.

It is worth noting that Leithwood and Duke (1999) articulate a form of relational leadership in their contribution to the *Handbook of Research on Educational Administration*. This is built upon four discrete constructs (leadership and followers, environment, organisation and relationships) and the relationships between them. This is what White and colleagues (2007) refer to as relations through a 'measurement construct', wherein relationships are constructed as a way to measure (directionality or strength) or map organisations (activity networks). Recent trends in network analysis/theory do similarly. The reduction of a complex social reality to a series of 1s (ties) and 0s (non-ties) imposes an external reading upon action but also disassembles the very action it claims to measure. In contrast, I take up the Bourdieusian-inspired (e.g. Bourdieu and Wacquant, 1992) focus on the abstract systems of difference or distant (e.g. distinctions) in social spaces and Donati's (2015) argument that society does not have relations but *is* relations. Therefore, relations are the very stuff of what we call 'the social' and the basic unit of analysis for the social sciences.

It is the shifting of the research object that is the primary point of departure for the argument that I am building. In bringing a *relational* approach to educational administration scholarship, there are the intellectual resources to interrogate the ongoing construction of the research object and its relations with others (including the researcher). Thinking relationally goes beyond a focus on traits, behaviours, roles and/or organisational outcomes. Located at the intersection of the humanities, social sciences and the professions, a *relational* approach to educational administration thought and analysis privileges the situated nature of actions. As Crossley (2015) argues, attributes are rethought as positions in a social space rather than as determinants of actions and outcomes. This overcomes the essentialising arguments that often come to dominate educational administration studies by inscribing actors in time and space through rigorous and robust description. Rather than seeking a linear–rational cause and effect and/or generalisability, I argue for detailed accounts of the relations that constitute organising activity. This requires careful attention to grounding description in the particular temporal and socio-spatial conditions. If context matters, something that is almost universally accepted in the leadership literatures, then this is *a* (not *the*) means of acknowledging that actors embody as much as they are embedded in a given temporal–spatial condition. In other words, rather than taking place in a context, relations constitute contexts. This is counter to approaches built upon systems thinking, which construct multiple discrete entities with varying degrees of implied causality determining outcomes. Educational administration scholarship cannot meaningfully engage with relations through theoretical resources that explain practice as determined by social structures, or even that actors interact with social structures. The artificial partitioning of the social world, a scientific reduction required to conceive of the 'individual' or the 'organisation', is an example of an entity-based or substantialist epistemology.

In *Educational Leadership Relationally* (Eacott, 2015), I articulate a particular form of *relational* approach. Built upon a very Bourdieusian craft of scholarship, but without any great loyalty or reverence, I name five *relational* extensions:

- The centrality of 'organising' in the social world creates an ontological complicity in researchers (and others) that makes it difficult to epistemologically break from ordinary language.

- Rigorous social scientific enquiry calls into question the very foundations of popular labels such as *leadership, management* and *administration*;
- The contemporary condition is constantly shaping and shaped by the image of organizing.
- Foregrounding social relations enables the overcoming of the contemporary, and arguably enduring, tensions of individualism/collectivism and structure/ agency.
- In so doing, a productive – rather than merely critical – space emerges in which to theorise educational administration and leadership.

Depelteau (2015) contends that relational approaches are only useful if they can propose new solutions to fundamental issues when compared with existing theorisations. The type of analysis made possible by the *relational* approach offers a means of composing theoretically inscribed descriptions of situated action. It directly engages with the relations between the researcher and the researched, the uncritical adoption of everyday language in scholarship, the role of spatio-temporal conditions in shaping understanding and the limitations of binary thinking, and it seeks to productively theorise – not just critique. As an approach, it does not definitively resolve the epistemological issues of educational administration, but it does engage with them. In so doing, it offers the potential to bring about new ways of understanding rather than simply mapping the intellectual terrain with novel ideas and vocabularies.

The *relational* approach does more than problematise leadership. It illuminates a pre-existing normative assumption at work in the defense and critique of leadership. Specifically, my intervention is to disrupt the dominant epistemologies and methodologies of educational administration. The scholarship of leadership can only proceed on the assumption of the stability and equivalence of the research object across time and space. This is pivotal if leadership is to serve as a reference point for dialogue and debate. My argument is that these claims – stability and equivalence – are indefensible. This is not to say that the study of organising and administration is a flawed pursuit. Rather, the focus on leadership is more the result of a failure of the dominant intellectual resources to handle alternate epistemologies and methodologies for understanding organisations.

Rigour and robustness

Educational administration, and particularly leadership, has contributed to its own legitimacy crisis by failing to deliver on its own promise. In seeking to provide the definitive 'what works' in organisations and increasingly accurate measures of success, educational administration has been stuck within its own normative bounds and has sought to replicate hegemonic notions of scientific methods. I argue that educational leadership research is constrained by three matters: i) the legitimacy of knowledge claims, ii) the nature of scholarly debate, and iii) the matter of relevance. Failure to engage with these matters will continue to draw into question the rigour and robustness of educational leadership research.

A weak quality profile has been an enduring issue for educational administration and is well rehearsed in the literature (Gorard, 2005; Griffiths, 1959, 1965, 1985; Immegart, 1975). Attempts to get beyond this perception have focused on the adoption of particular scientific methods (usually equated, falsely, with logical empiricism). This creates a problem for leadership research. There is no external knowable object to which the label of leadership refers. It does not correspond with material in the empirical world. Leadership is a product of cognition. This construction is overlaid on the empirical. As an act of cognition, there is nothing that is beyond classification and categorisation. To attend to these matters, greater attention should be given to making visible the epistemological preliminaries of work. Following Bourdieu and colleagues (1991), this argument is distinctive in educational administration for its central concern with the logic of discovery as opposed to the logic of validation – so far as the distinction can be sustained. In the case of leadership, this means attention to the constructedness of knowledge and scholarship. Researchers are not external observers of the social world. What distinguishes the knowledge claims of the scholar from the everyday are the scientific methods – making the basis of these explicit goes a long way towards increasing the legitimacy of knowledge claims and lays the foundation for the organisation and functioning of scholarly communities. This has been argued systematically in educational administration by Evers and Lakomski (1991, 1996, 2000) for 25 years.

Educational administration journals and conferences are somewhat devoid of debate. This is not to say that there is a singular overarching narrative; rather it is the absence of engagement with the other that is dominant. For the most part, those with whom we disagree are treated with benign neglect (Donmoyer, 2001; Thrupp and Willmott, 2003). As a result, not only is there a lot of talking past one another but also many parallel monologues. The logic of scholarly life, argument and refutation, is lost in discourse communities that do not meaningfully engage with alternate ways of understanding. Perhaps the most important outcome of this situation is that the available options for understanding educational administration are not particularly satisfactory. There is need for an alternative contribution, one that pays attention not only to the outputs and outcomes of knowledge production but to the actual process of knowledge production. Thinking *relationally* requires attention to the construction and ongoing maintenance of the research object. Doing so locates the work and understanding in wider dialogue and debates. Through attention to matters of ontology and epistemology in addition to content matters, *relational* thinking provides the intellectual resources to think anew.

Holding strong ties to the notion of an applied field, much of the scholarship of educational administration is focused on the improvement of practice. Many classifications and categories are uncritically adopted in research for the purpose of solving empirical problems. Leadership literatures, therefore, have an underlying generative principle of intervention, a desire to generate understandings that can be implemented in schools and preparation programmes at scale. Consistent with contemporary public policy moves, which see leadership as a key leverage point for education reform, particular forms of cause and effect and generalisability dominate educational leadership literatures. For the most part, there is a belief in the stability and equivalence of leadership as a construct across time and space. Additionally, leadership is conceived of as having an effect on organisational performance. In both cases, leadership is constructed as a discrete entity that interacts with others (e.g. context) and has utility. Although the finer details of how it is enacted across time and space may be different, the very idea of leadership remains.

The holy grail of leadership studies is therefore to find the definitive list of behaviours, traits, practices and so on that have maximum, if not complete, utility. To do so requires making some compromises. This utility is only possible through a de-contextualised, or context-free, version of leadership. Leadership is therefore beyond conventional time and space. Simultaneously, there is the rejection of the idea of a leader-less organisation courtesy of an in-built organisational effect from leadership in its conceptualisation. These assumptions, among others, are rarely, if ever, acknowledged in the educational leadership literatures. The mobilisation of more sophisticated methods of analysis (e.g. increasingly powerful statistical tools) or appeals to approximate the standards of internal and external validity of intensive large-scale quantitative research (see Leithwood, 2005) cannot overcome flaws in the original construction of the research object. Irrespective of claims to rigorous and robust research designs, the construction of leadership remains an organisational variable. The key point is that what is overlooked in the majority of contemporary scholarship is the very thing that many argue is most important in understanding organisational action – relations.

Buber (1970) stresses the importance of the 'space between'. He argues that meaning emerges not from discrete entities, or even their relationships, but the spaces between. Although at face value this implies a degree of separation, the argument is actually concerned with the inseparability of action/actors. The attention to space between is even found in what are usually conceived of as the hard sciences. As Bradbury and Lichtenstein (2000) note, in their quest to identify the basic building blocks of the natural world, quantum physicists found atomic particles to be more relational than discrete objects, with space itself being full of potential rather than vacuous. Coming into question here is the explanatory power of leadership research. If leadership is mobilised in such a way that it is an organisational variable interacting with other variables internal and external to the organisation – as is the case in systems thinking – then the spaces between are reduced, at best, to measurement constructs. Irrespective of the sophistication of measures, the meaning of action is lost in the measuring process.

An important contribution here is the work of Geertz (1973), in particular where he draws on Ryle's (1971) discussion of the wink. Ryle discusses two boys rapidly contracting the eyelids of their right eyes. This action could range from an involuntary twitch through to a conspiratorial signal to a friend (and much in between), and the situation becomes more complex as we add a third child into the mix. The two movements are identical in the instrumental measurement of action. It is the relations between actors and their location in temporal and socio-spatial conditions that enables meaning. To a certain extent, this was picked up in a debate between Gronn (1982, 1984, 1987) and Thomas (1986; Thomas et al., 1981), carried out primarily in the pages of *Educational Administration Quarterly*. Gronn (1982, p. 18) challenged the notion of observational studies, arguing that they 'seriously misconstrue the phenomenon they purport to explain: they fail to explicate what it means to 'do' something'. For the most part, educational leadership research does not entertain the question of whether leadership was present or not. Instead, what we have is the identification of it as effective or less effective based on a pre-existing normative orientation.

The explanatory value attributed to leadership is problematic. How we come to know organisations and their relations to other groupings does not necessarily warrant the leap to leadership. The overarching interest appears to be in the organisation of action, or more specifically, organising. This is not to discredit the effect of hierarchies, history, gender, race and so on. Rather, it is to open up the prospect that such things matter. Rigour and robustness can be achieved through grounding the scholarly narrative in the contemporary temporal and socio-spatial conditions. This includes what is actually meant by leadership, why it matters in this place at this time and in what ways. The research object and the researcher are embedded in and embody the contemporary social conditions. Scholarship is the extension of these relations. To illuminate what this means requires description.

Description

The act of description is methodological work. The threshold for scientific description is having the best resources for the task. As an example, Savage (2009) notes that it is the Hubble telescope rather than the personal digital camera pointing to the skies that defines the high ground, or cutting edge, of scientific practice. Inscription devices serve as a key distinction between the physical and social sciences. While increasingly detailed visuals that enable measurement might be useful in the analysis of celestial entities, the mechanical reproduction of social relations through numbers, variables and visual diagrams is not necessarily useful for illuminating the ongoing work of organising.

There are mixed views in educational administration regarding the scholarly value of description. It is frequently mobilised in a derogatory manner, with work being dismissed as merely descriptive and the lowest form of scholarship. Central to such thinking is the artificial partitioning of arguments and the lack of problematising of the research object. The failure to locate work in the broader dialogue and debates of the field means that the specific empirical problem is privileged over the larger theoretical problem. The result is that the description is of little, if any, value beyond itself. In contrast, locating work in broader debates facilitates a contribution to contemporary thought and analysis in the discipline (see Locke and Golden-Biddle, 1997) and even makes it possible to generalise on the basis of a single case study (Evers and Wu, 2006).

What is important here is the embedding and embodying of arguments in broader thought and analysis while also illuminating the particular socio-spatial and temporal conditions of action. Thinking *relationally*, the social world is not divisible into a series of separate – even if inter-related – layers, as is depicted in concentric circles building from the individual/local to the global, but rather flat. This blurs the constructed binaries of the universal and the particular, individual and collective and structure and agency, and it provides the basis for the role of description. It becomes no longer appropriate to assume that the particular is separate to, or merely interacts with, the universal. Spatio-temporal conditions become of central importance in constructing meaning for organising action.

Description provides an avenue to explain, potentially in new ways, what is taking place in the organising of the social world and specifically, for the purpose of this chapter, educational institutions. It is very much a cumulative project, a generative programme contributing to increasing elaborated descriptions of relating actions to other actions. In doing so, a *relational* approach to educational administration and leadership is not defined by the problems it solves but the questions it asks.

Conclusion

Arguments for *leadership* as the label and practice of choice against *administration* and *management* mirror historical tensions between objectivists and subjectivists in educational administrative theory. The leadership programme is positioned as bringing the human element to the structural arrangements of organising. The overarching bureaucratic structures described by Weber (1968) were no longer seen as capable of delivering the types of organisational outcomes expected of contemporary institutions. Herein lies one of the major paradoxes of leadership inquiry. On the one hand, the literatures argue for the uniqueness of every context, yet at the same time, leadership is conceived of as having utility. The result is that leadership becomes beyond context. The establishment of separate knowable objects (entities) that impact *on* leadership is central to the systems thinking evident in much of the educational administration literatures.

Leadership does not offer itself to be felt or sensed and passes largely unnoticed. It is, for the most part, unexperienced. As a product of cognition, leadership is the articulation of a pre-existing normative orientation. It is based on how one believes an organisation, and the individual actors associated with it, *ought* to behave. The *is* is then evaluated against the *ought*, and this constitutes the basis of a substantive proportion of contemporary thought and analysis in educational administration. This leads to significant confusion concerning the meaning of leadership and its relations to management and administration, and it has implications for educational administration as a branch of administrative and organisational sciences. In this chapter, I have mobilised a *relational* approach to expose and explain some important misconceptions about how the social construction of leadership relates to the possibility to make true statements about the world. Significantly, in asking questions of leadership, I have provided an alternate programme that gets beyond the circular logic of leadership and illuminates the situated nature of action. The particular form of *relational* approach that I am advancing seeks not to reduce all social relations to issues of power, as many Marxist inspired accounts do; or to strategies enacted to optimise individual or collective interest. Instead, I call for elaborated descriptions of the unfolding of organising action that are mindful of the abstract systems of difference and distance in the social space. Such descriptions do not necessarily assume the presence or even the desirability of leadership for the achievement of action.

This chapter is not the definitive word on the *relational* approach. But it offers a generative programme that will constantly call into question its own knowledge claims as well as the status quo. Its genesis, and the origins of my critique of leadership, are grounded in a belief that there is a need to promote a narrative of rigorous and robust scholarship in educational administration while at the same time remaining critical of any narrative promoting versions of rigour and robustness. That is, the *relational* approach, or any for that matter, to scholarship must remain critical of its own agenda as much as it is of others. Pursuing this agenda, I encourage others to think with, through and, where necessary, against what I have argued in the interest of the scholarly enterprise. As English (2006) argues, the advancement of any discipline requires deep and sustained criticism of it, philosophically, logically and empirically.

References

Adkins, L., 2011. Practice as temporalisation: Bourdieu and economic crisis. In S. Susen and B. S. Turner, eds., *The legacy of Pierre Bourdieu: Critical essays* (pp. 347–365). London: Anthem Press.

Alvesson, M. and Sveningsson, S., 2003. The great disappearing act: difficulties in doing 'leadership'. *The Leadership Quarterly*, 14(3), pp. 359–381.

Bennis, W. G., 1959. Leadership theory and administrative behaviour: The problem of authority. *Administrative Science Quarterly*, 4(3), pp. 259–301.

Bogotch, I. E., Beachum, F., Blount, J., Brooks, J. S., English, F. W. and Jansen, J., eds., 2008. *Radicalizing educational leadership.* Rotterdam, the Netherlands: Sense Publishers.

Bourdieu, P. and Wacquant, L., 1992. *An invitation to reflexive sociology.* Cambridge: Blackwell Publishers.

Bourdieu, P., Chamboredon, J.-C. and Passeron, J.-C., 1991. *The craft of sociology: Epistemological preliminaries.* R. Nice, Trans. New York: Walter de Gruyter.

Buber, M., 1970. *I and thou.* W. Kaufmann, Trans. New York: Scribner's Sons.

Bush, T., 2004. Editorial: What's in a name? Leadership in the ascendancy. *Educational Management Administration and Leadership*, 32(1), pp. 5–9.

Calder, B. J., 1977. An attribution theory of leadership. In B. M. Staw and G. R. Salancik, eds., *New directions in organisational behaviour* (pp. 179–204). Chicago, IL: St. Clair.

Caldwell, B. J., 2007. Educational leadership and school renewal: Introduction by the guest editor. *Australian Journal of Education*, 51(3), pp. 225–227.

Crossley, N., 2011. *Towards a relational sociology.* New York: Routledge.

Depelteau, F., 2015. Relational sociology, pragmatism, transactions and social fields. *International Review of Sociology: Revue Internationale de Sociologie*, 25(1), pp. 45–64.

Depelteau, F. and Powell, C., eds., 2013. *Applying relational sociology: relations, networks and society*. New York: Palgrave McMillan.

Dinh, J. E., Lord, R. G., Garder, W. L., Meuser, J. D., Liden, R. C. and Hu, J., 2014. Leadership theory and research in the new millennium: Current theoretical trends and changing perspectives. *The Leadership Quarterly*, 25(1), pp. 36–62.

Donati, P., 1983. *Introduzione alla sociologia relazionale [Introduction to relational sociology]*. Milan: Franco Angeli.

Donati, P., 1991. *Teoria relazionale della societa [Relational theory of society]*. Milan: Franco Angeli.

Donati, P., 2011. *Relational sociology: A new paradigm for the social sciences*. London: Routledge.

Donati, P., 2015. Manifesto for a critical realist relational sociology. *International Review of Sociology: Revue Internationale de Sociologie*, 25(1), pp. 86–101.

Donmoyer, R., 2001. Evers and Lakomski's search for leadership's holy grail (and the intriguing ideas they encountered along the way). *Journal of Educational Administration*, 39(6), pp. 554–572.

Eacott, S., 2013. 'Leadership' and the social: Time, space and the epistemic. *International Journal of Educational Management*, 27(1), pp. 91–101.

Eacott, S., 2015. *Educational leadership relationally: A theory and methodology for educational leadership, management and administration*. Rotterdam, the Netherlands: Sense Publishers.

Emirbayer, M., 1997. Manifesto for a relational sociology. *American Journal of Sociology*, 103(2), pp. 281–317.

English, F. W., 2006. The unintended consequences of a standardized knowledge base in advancing educational leadership preparation. *Educational Administration Quarterly*, 42(3), pp. 461–472.

Evers, C. W. and Lakomski, G., 1991. *Knowing educational administration: Contemporary methodological controversies in educational research*. Oxford: Pergamon Press.

Evers, C. W. and Lakomski, G., 1996. *Exploring educational administration*. Oxford: Elsevier.

Evers, C. W. and Lakomski, G., 2000. *Doing educational administration*. Oxford: Elsevier.

Evers, C. W. and Wu, E. H., 2006. On generalising from single case studies: Epistemological reflections. *Journal of Philosophy of Education*, 40(4), pp. 511–520.

Fuhse, J., 2015. Theorizing social networks: The relational sociology of and around Harrison White. *International Review of Sociology: Revue Internationale de Sociologie*, 25(1), pp. 15–44.

Geertz, C., 1973. *The interpretation of culture*. London: Hutchinson.

Gorard, S., 2005. Current contexts for research in educational leadership and management. *Educational Management Administration and Leadership*, 33(2), pp. 155–164.

Griffiths, D. E., 1959. *Research in educational administration: An appraisal and a plan*. New York: Teachers College.

Griffiths, D. E., 1965. Research and theory in educational administration. In W. W. Charters, ed., *Perspectives on educational administration and the behavioural sciences* (pp. 25–48). Eugene, Oregon: Center for the Advanced Study of Educational Administration.

Griffiths, D. E., 1985. *Administrative theory in transition*. Melbourne: Deakin University.

Gronn, P., 1982. Neo-Taylorism in educational administration? *Educational Administration Quarterly,* 18(4), pp. 17–35.

Gronn, P., 1984. On studying administrators at work. *Educational Administration Quarterly,* 20(1), pp. 115–129.

Gronn, P., 1987. Obituary for structured observation. *Educational Administration Quarterly,* 23(2), pp. 78–81.

Gronn, P., 2003. Leadership: Who needs it? *School Leadership and Management,* 23(3), pp. 267–290.

Hunt, J. and Dodge, G. E., 2000. Leadership deja vu all over again. *The Leadership Quarterly,* 11(4), pp. 435–458.

Immegart, G. L., 1975. *The study of educational administration 1954–1974: Myths, paradoxes, facts and prospects.* Columbus, Ohio: Ohio State University.

Lakomski, G., 2005. *Managing without leadership: Towards a theory of organizational functioning.* Oxford: Elsevier.

Leithwood, K., 2005. Understanding successful principal leadership: Progress on a broken front. *Journal of Educational Administration,* 43(6), pp. 619–629.

Leithwood, K. and Duke, D., 1999. A century's quest to understand school leadership. In J. Murphy and K. S. Louis, eds., *Handbook of research on educational administration* (2nd ed., pp. 45–72). San Francisco: Jossey-Bass.

Locke, K. and Golden-Biddle, K., 1997. Constructing opportunities for contribution: Structuring intertextual coherence and 'problematizing' in organisational studies *The Academy of Management Journal,* 40(5), pp. 1023–1062.

Mayo, E., 1933. *The human problems of an industrial civilization.* New York: Macmillan.

Miner, J. B., 1975. The uncertain future of the leadership concept: An overview. In J. G. Hunt and L. L. Larson, eds., *Leadership frontiers* (pp. 197–208). Kent, OH: Kent State University Press.

Mische, A., 2011. Relational sociology, culture and agency. In J. Scott and P. Carrington, eds., *The SAGE handbook of social network analysis* (pp. 80–97). London: SAGE.

Oplatka, I., 2010. *The legacy of educational administration: A historical analysis of an academic field.* Berlin: Peter Lang.

Pfeffer, J., 1977. The ambiguity of leadership. *The Academy of Management Review,* 2(1), pp. 104–112.

Powell, C. and Depelteau, F., eds., 2013. *Conceptualizing relational sociology: Ontological and theoretical issues.* New York: Palgrave McMillan.

Prandini, R., 2015. Relational sociology: A well-defined sociological paradigm or a challenging 'relational turn' in sociology? *International Review of Sociology: Revue Internationale de Sociologie,* 25(1), pp. 1–14.

Ryle, G., 1971. *Collected papers.* London: Hutchinson.

Savage, M., 2009. Contemporary sociology and the challenge of descriptive assemblage. *European Journal of Social Theory,* 12(1), pp. 155–174.

Stogdill, R. M., 1974. *Handbook of leadership: A survey of theory and research.* New York: Free Press.

Thomas, A. R., 1986. Seeing isn't believing? Neither is hearing! In defense of observational studies. *Educational Administration Quarterly,* 22(1), pp. 29–48.

Thomas, A. R., Willis, Q. and Phillipps, D., 1981. Observational studies of Australian school administrators: Methodological issues. *Australian Journal of Education,* 25(1), pp. 55–72.

Thrupp, M. and Willmott, R., 2003. *Educational management in managerialist times: Beyond the textual apologists.* Buckingham, UK: Open University Press.

Uhl-Bien, M., 2006. Relational leadership theory: Exploring the social processes of leadership and organizing. *The Leadership Quarterly,* 17(6), pp. 654–676.

Uhl-Bien, M. and Ospina, S., eds., 2012. *Advancing relational leadership research: A dialogue among perspectives.* Charlotte, NC: Information Age Publishing.

Weber, M., 1968. *Economy and society: An outline of interprise sociology.* Berkeley, CA: University of California Press.

White, H., Fuhse, J., Thiemann, M. and Buchholz, L., 2007. Networks and meanings: Styles and switchings. *Soziale Systeme,* 13, pp. 543–555.

Yukl, G., 1981. *Leadership in organisations.* Englewood Cliffs, NJ: Prentice-Hall.

3 Everything we know about educational leadership is wrong

Rethinking scholarship and practice for a fractured field[1]

Jeffrey S. Brooks

Introduction

Educational leadership, as a field of both practice and inquiry, has undergone remarkable growth over the past 100 years. From relatively modest beginnings related to a religious and moral emphasis in schooling, thought and practice, it progressed through the eras of scientific management, a focus on humanistic values, the theory movement, the postmodern and critical theory turn of the 1980s, the social justice movement and neo-accountability (Brooks and Miles, 2008; Callahan, 1962; Cuban, 1988; Glass, 1986; Tyack and Hansot, 1982). To be sure, I am painting with a broad brush here – there are multiple perspectives on whether or not these eras offer a fair characterisation of the field of educational leadership; ideas born in each of them have later resurfaced (or disappeared), and antecedent ideas and practices from each of these times continue to influence the field to varying degrees. This chapter is less an exercise in looking backward and more an attempt to describe a perspective and to critique the present from that perspective. I begin the inquiry with a provocative question and, over the course of the chapter, explore possible answers and the many questions that such a question raises.

This chapter represents an initial attempt to document and explore a central question – *is everything we know about educational leadership wrong?* I do not view this as a holistic or even systematic critique but rather as a set of interrelated issues, some of which are fairly benign and widely discussed. However, other issues I will raise have perhaps fundamentally undermined the very way we think about, study and practise educational leadership, from the field's inception to the present day (e.g. Callahan's 1962 critique). Accordingly, the purpose of this chapter is to share and critique the way that certain ideas, questions and problems shape the field of educational leadership, in terms of both its scholarship and its practice in schools. I conceptualise this as a continuation of critical conversations started by scholars such as Fenwick English, Joseph Murphy, Peter Gronn, Jill Blackmore, Thomas and William Greenfield, Gabriele Lakomski, Bill Mulford, Jackie Blount, Catherine Marshall, Harry Wolcott and others too numerous to list who have questioned the theoretical and empirical foundations of the fields of educational and school leadership.[2]

The field(s) of educational leadership

Over the past 100 years, both the research and practice of educational leadership has changed. In some ways, that change has been drastic; in other ways, it has simply represented the next steps in a slow conceptual and empirical evolution (Beck and Murphy, 1993; Campbell et al., 1987; English, 1994, 2002a, 2003). Moreover, as English (2002b) points out, the field is perhaps more rightly char- acterised as a loosely coupled set of fields than a coherent corpus of inquiry, each of which variously includes and excludes certain ideas and traditions. For example, there are many scholars who look at educational leadership research through a social justice lens while ignoring studies that approach things from a functionalist or value-neutral perspective (Larson and Murtadha, 2002). There is a similar schism in the field between those who accept or reject quantitative or qualitative research (Brooks and Normore, 2015), those whose work connects to policy studies and those whose work does not (Diem and Young, 2015), those who relate their work to other educational research such as content areas like science or mathematics (Theoharis and Brooks, 2012; Saka et al., 2009) and so on. To be sure, no scholar can take every dynamic into account when they design and execute their studies. Yet, it would be one thing to reject another perspective based on strong argumen- tation or the results of new work, but I suggest that there is an ongoing discon- nect between lines of inquiry that leave the field fractured and discrete rather than integrated and pluralistic (English, 2002b, 2003). That is to say that there is no one set of ideas, concepts or research methods that scholars and practitioners use to understand and explore their work – there are only disjointed lines of inquiry that seek to understand certain issues, albeit it from wildly different perspectives.

While that claim is quite strong, educational leadership is not the only research field to confront fragmentation. For example, the field of medicine has had its own histories of organising principles up-ended and reordered – thanks not only to scientific discovery but also to the importation of other research disciplines. For instance, an example from sociology relates to work on alienation, which existed as several lines of disconnected inquiry until it was categorised into sev- eral empirical domains by Melvin Seeman (1959, 1967, 1975, 1983). This then helped scholars whose work was theretofore disconnected to situate their work in the context of various related lines of inquiry.

Given this contested and messy backdrop, it seems useful to identify some recent areas of interest to educational leadership scholars and practitioners:

1   The use and misuse of accountability and various forms of research and data (Johnson, 2002)
2   The relationship between leadership and learning (Brooks and Theoharis, 2012; Mulford et al., 2004)
3   The preparation of school leadership and the research that examines and informs said preparation (Darling-Hammond et al., 2010)
4   The conceptualisation of administration, management and leadership as dis- tinct parts of a whole that is distributed in a fluid manner between leaders and followers (Brooks et al., 2007; Gronn, 2003; Spillane, 2006)

5   The role of internationalisation and globalisation in the preparation and practice of educational leadership (Brooks and Normore, 2010)
6   The nature of trust and educational leadership (Tschannen-Moran, 2004, 2001)

To be sure, those interested in educational leadership also continue to understand the way that some classic tensions are manifest in educational organisations and policies: freedom versus control; equity versus equality; direction versus support; coercion versus cooperation; centralisation versus decentralisation; the influence of business literature and practices on the practice of administration and management in education (Callahan, 1962); and effectiveness versus individualisation versus standardisation (Beck and Murphy, 1993). I do not intend to present an historical perspective on the field of educational leadership; rather I note that it is important to situate any contemporary critique of the field within this perspective. The remainder of this chapter relates and explains a series of points that I feel scholars and practitioners should question as they conduct their work.

Issue #1: Educational leadership theories often do not include or connect in any way to student learning processes and outcomes and often have only a tenuous connection to teaching. In writing and research on educational leadership, we tend to be heavy on 'leadership and management' and light on 'education'. This means that very little of our research or training in the field actually connects to current thinking in critical areas such as learning, teaching or instruction (Brooks and Normore, 2015). Educational and school leadership scholars commonly cite very little research from teacher education in their studies, and often publish works that are completely uninformed by areas such as curriculum, educational psychology, educational philosophy and sociology of education, even when they are ostensibly researching those areas. In many cases, educational leadership scholars are not up to date on research in these related areas and are likewise in the dark about best practices and inquiry in various content areas such as science education, mathematics, reading, art, disability studies and so on. This disconnect means that educational leadership is seldom about education and more commonly focuses on managerialism and administration (Foster, 1986). To be sure, there are many contextual variables that influence this dynamic. For example, in the USA, this isolation is at least partially structural, thanks to legal mandates requiring educational leaders to focus on managerial aspects far more intensively than on curricular matters and student learning. From zero-tolerance discipline policies, special education reports, labour relations and the like, school principals and superintendents are mired in a managerial imperative that is strongly resistant to attempts to transform the entire enterprise into student-centred leadership (Cuban, 1988).

One would think that in a field called educational leadership, students and student learning should be central to educational leadership theory, not marginalised or treated as a contextual or latent factor. The basic relationship that defines the field of educational leadership is that between the principal and teachers – or the workers and the managers, much like the beginning of the field in the late nineteenth century (Nasaw, 1979). In both eras, students and their learning are merely a product, or worse, a by-product, of this relationship. What this means in the end is that we can say very little about the relationship between leadership and learning. We know very little about how students lead students, how parents act as leaders of students, how school principals lead teachers and so on. In far too many studies in the field, student learning is treated as part of the background rather than being the central focus of the study. To be sure, certain scholars have explored this phenomenon directly, notably Ken Leithwood, Bill Mulford (e.g. Mulford et al., 2004) and others have also examined the relationship indirectly, but as a field, the paltry amount of work devoted to understanding student learning and leadership behaviour is shocking.

That said, the relationship between leadership and learning must finally challenge and transcend the idea that standardised test outcomes are a viable proxy for student learning. There are so many learning theories ripe for exploration yet they are rarely considered. Among these are various cognitive learning theories, such as social cognitive theory, cognitive information processing theory, content-area learning, motivation and so on. There are few (if any) educational leadership studies of learning-related issues such as memory, transfer, self-regulation, modelling, metacognition, forgetting, cognitive growth, attribution or self-concept (Schunk, 2008).[3] Yet while there are exciting advances in each of these areas, educational leadership scholars and practitioners are often dreaming up words and terms that sound like they are educational when they are not.

Much of educational leadership research sounds like it is about education when it is in fact more squarely focused on efficiency (Callahan, 1962; Cuban, 1988). Terms like 'organisational learning' or 'professional learning communities' are often little more than ways of describing better ways for an organisation to function – they may connect, in the most abstract way, to the ways in which adults in the organisation learn, but they certainly do not connect explicitly to student learning. I acknowledge that methodologically, this may be, at present, a nearly impossible task. That is not to say that organisational studies are not needed and there has not been some fine work done on these specific phenomena. What I am calling into question is whether or not such 'false' education constructs actually contribute to a greater understanding of the way learning, cognition, instruction and the like are practiced. As an example, I will use one of the more popular leadership theories as an illustration: distributed leadership.

Distributed leadership is a theory often explained as leadership practice enacted between leaders and followers that evolves over time during particular situations (Brooks et al., 2007; Spillane, 2006). The theory has been helpful to leadership scholars attempting to understand leadership as a fluid phenomenon, wherein people are at times leaders and at times followers. The theory points out that this dynamic evolves over time, and that an organisation develops idiosyncratic working norms around the way leadership is distributed (see Figure 3.1). As an organisational theory, distributed leadership has helped scholars and practitioners gain new insights about the way that people interact in specific situations and the ways that those situations become institutionalised depending on the situation.

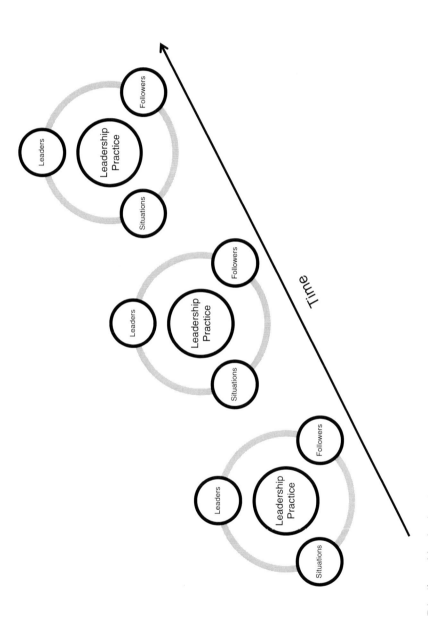

Figure 3.1 Distributed leadership (adapted from Brooks and Kensler, 2011).

However, while distributed leadership has been applied to the study of schools, it is not an educational leadership theory; it is an organisational theory. The theory does not include learning, instruction or any other construct that is distinct to education or even to schooling. It is not informed by educational research, and it is questionable whether or not it informs us of anything that is particularly insightful or useful with regard to education. It is at worst a useless theory and at best an incomplete one in terms of telling us something about education. Do not get me wrong – distributed leadership tells us something about organisations, and schools can be thought of that way – but it tells us nothing about student learning.

Figure 3.2 is an attempt to reimagine distributed learning as an educational leadership theory. Note that a specific content area is at the heart of this model, with the student leadership, teacher leadership and administrative leadership all influencing learning in this area. The model also suggests that these activities are fluid, and that instead of leadership being always fluid and distributed, it is conceived of as activity that is at times differentiated (connecting to differentiated learning pedagogies), at times distributed and at other times dynamic (connecting to research that suggests school is only part of the learning experience and that learning comes from formal and informal sources). Though this is a crude model, it serves to illustrate the point that Figure 3.1 is without an intentional and specific connection to education, while Figure 3.2 is explicitly informed by educational research.

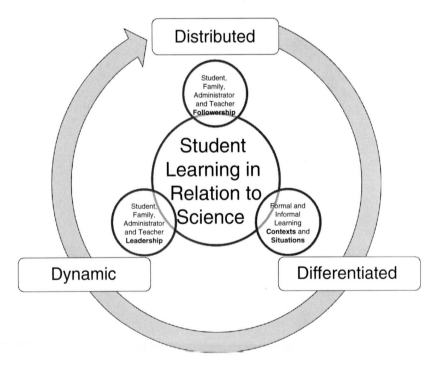

Figure 3.2 Distributed leadership as an educational theory.

Issue #2: There is no 'one size fits all' approach to educational leadership. For many years, scholars and professional development gurus have generated lists of 'suggested', 'successful' or 'best' practices or behaviours in the field of educational leadership, even though they have failed consistently to produce success. Many of these ideas come uncritically from the world of business, and it is important to interrogate them as both conceptual constructs and empirical practices. Because of the context-specific nature of the work and the ever-changing carousel of personnel, policies, projects, structures and strategies, generalising about processes and outcomes is a dubious and likely unattainable goal. Yet this has not slowed down the number of scholars who generate lists of critical factors, sets of 'new' standards and professional development schemes that will 'change everything'. Surely, such efforts should be seen as a platform rather than a frame for knowledge in the field or a recipe for success. The complex nature of schooling, leadership and learning suggests that there can be no single approach to the work, and that any list of factors will have a unique configuration in situ. Leaders are not the same, nor are followers, organisations or situations, and all change over time – the same goes for schools, students, families, knowledge, administrators, teachers and a whole host of other variables that shape the formal and informal aspects of education.

There are two other aspects of one-size-fits-all, a 'one best system' (Tyack, 1974) thinking that undermines educational leadership. First, it is time for leaders and followers alike to eschew the 'My way or the highway' threats that are commonly delivered to people in organisations with a different perspective on the way leadership should be practised in schools. Yet this is often lazy, unethical and self-centred (rather than learner centred) misleadership or an abuse of power. Such proclamations rarely reflect thoughtful, student-centred leadership focused on the best interests of the students. However, this abusive understanding of leadership has often been repackaged as school reform or 'school turnaround' mantras like 'no excuses'. Second, there is often a great confusion between equity versus equality in leadership practice and scholarship. Equity means distributing resources based on people's individual needs and talents, whereas equality means giving each person the same opportunity to access resources (Brooks, 2012). This distinction is critical, and each leader must continually make decisions based on either equity or equality – they are two different ways of thinking about leadership and are not interchangeable. In some instances, leaders will want to make sure that they are making decisions based on equity that ameliorate systemic inequities or that support students with special talents or needs. Developing an understanding that both are important in the overall scope of the organisation, and that this basic decision shapes the educational experiences of people throughout the organisation, has a tremendous bearing on student and educator experiences.

Issue #3: Pollyanna language and entrepreneurialism have undermined research and practice in educational leadership. The knowledge industry has shaped the way we think about education and leadership for profit – not for improved education (Wirt and Kirst, 1972). It is critical that educational leaders interrogate neo-liberalism and that they question whether the educational resources they bring into the school are the best possible educational resources for their students and educators. Are the resources, be they books, digital resources, assessments, consultants or the like, based on solid *educational* research? Who is making the resources and to what end? Does the cost merit the educational benefit? What is excluded and included in the resource? What is the likelihood that the resource will make a meaningful and positive change in the daily life of students and educators? It is particularly important to beware of high dollar, one-shot consultants; train-the-trainer models; and initiatives that are headed by a few champions. Because of the transient nature of schools and their disconnect from the daily work of the school, it is important to try and ascertain whether the resource is sprung from the mind of one of the many snake-oil salespeople in the field or from strong and research-based work.

In addition to keeping up with the latest research on issues related to education, leaders must also be cognisant of entrepreneurialism in educational leadership, which often amounts to little more than putting old wine in new bottles. There are many recycled ideas in the field, both in terms of scholarship and practice. Different school reform ideas like mastery learning, total quality management, data-driven decision-making and many others have appeared and receded over the past 75 years in education, yet leaders seldom have an appreciation for a history of the field, which would help them make informed decisions about ostensibly 'new' efforts.

It is also important to note the language leaders use to describe their work (Anderson, 1991). The language of leadership is often a barrier rather than a bridge. Terms like *visions, missions, values, aims, goals, principles, school improvement* and the like are the language administrators adopt to talk about organisational and systemic change, but it is not the language of teachers, students or communities. They also smell dangerously like fashionable jargon and are in many cases completely untested processes that routinely produce inconsistent outcomes (Mintzberg, 1993). This disconnect is handled well by some leaders, who make sure that the ideas take life in the everyday work of the school; and poorly by others, whose use of these words and concepts alienate their staff and students, who then transform these into terms of mocking and derision – aimed precisely at the leader. Corollary to the way some leaders speak is a solitary focus on the positive while studiously ignoring the negative. This is unethical, miseducational and deprofessionalising. Consequently, teachers and students learn to ignore problems of practice and life.

Issue #4: Too much of what happens in schools is designed for the edification of adults rather than the education of students. School leaders must reflect on who benefits from the processes and outcomes in their school. Are the processes and outcomes in the school student-centred or educator-centred? Are decisions made for convenience or with the students' best interests in mind? Are decisions informed by local and global research? Where are students' voices in leadership at school and where are students not heard? In many instances, leaders allow decisions to be based on the wants of the staff rather than the needs of the students. This is in part due to the way that leadership is often explained in terms of leading staff rather than leading students. It is in part due to the fact that staff members are better and more effective at advocating for their interests then students. It is important in schools for leaders to advocate for those least equipped to advocate for themselves – in nearly every case this means the students, but in too many cases this simply does not happen (Doyle and Feldman, 2006; Lee, 1999; Mitra, 2008; Mitra and Gross, 2009).

Issue #5: We must not champion conformity over creativity. One of the things that makes schools special organisations is that they are full of smart, and sometimes brilliant, people – students, staff and administrators should be part of decision-making in schools but are at times excluded from various conversations. Part of a leader's core responsibility is to establish structures and processes that facilitate a culture of conflict rather than a culture of complicity in schools. If we can agree that schools should be democratic institutions (of course this is disputed, but I am evoking an oft-proclaimed maxim), then we must accept that they thrive on conflict, not complicity. Respectful and ongoing conflict – the coming together and critique of ideas – is the path to creativity. Schools that facilitate creativity rather than conformity are full of possibility and offer constant renewal, challenge and discovery. As a caveat, we must not value creativity solely for creativity's sake. Many ambitious educational leaders strive to inflict reform on a school, which might be better served by a more conservative approach. Radical reform for the sake of proving one's worth as a creative leader harms the very people that schools are designed to serve – students.

Issue #6: Educational leadership has borrowed too heavily and too uncritically from business literature and not enough from the social sciences or other educational research, and key concepts remain undertheorised. Educational leadership practitioners and scholars can learn from every field, business included, but they must be critical and adapt, experiment and explore rather than copy. There are fundamental differences between the purposes and practice of institutions designed to make money and those designed to facilitate learning (Gelberg, 1997). Yet still, leaders have a tendency to uncritically adopt strategies from sectors that have no knowledge of the work of schools and at times no real track record of success in their own sector. One excellent example of education adopting failed business strategies is strategic planning. Mintzberg's (1993) analysis of the failure of this business fad to substantively improve processes or outcomes in companies suggests that educational leadership should approach the strategy with great caution, yet even 30 years after strategic planning rose and fell in the business world, school administrators continue to ignore the lessons that the business world learned long ago. Critically, business differs from education because in schools, the outcome is a process rather than a product. To be sure, the untapped potential of learning more deeply from (and teaching in) other fields (particularly service and human relational fields like nursing) and from social sciences and other fields of educational research remains unrealised, but all must be approached with a healthy scepticism and critical eye.

Issue #7: Thinking about our schools as closed systems in competition rather than as open systems in cooperation is stealing resources from children and renewal from our educators. It is important for leaders to recognise that every school, every classroom, every teacher is an ongoing creative experiment in process and outcome. As such, competition, while highly prized in capitalism, is anathema to education. There is a strong body of research that suggests that the pressure and anxiety created by high-stakes competition does not help people learn (Kohn, 1999). Cooperation and coordination must replace competition and commodification if education systems are to realise their full potential. Educators have an ethical and moral responsibility to their students and communities to do their best, to seek critique and to learn from self and others. Moreover, they have a moral responsibility to the profession and to their communities to share their best work so that all may benefit. We have created far too many systems where bonuses, teacher and student recruitment and ranking by test scores prevent rather than facilitate the kind of broad ethic of care that should distinguish teaching from other professions. Additionally, this extends into the community. Education is not only school; learning, teaching and leadership are dynamic and they happen outside of the classroom. An acknowledgement of this means that creating a false market with fabricated measures of success creates a consumer mentality with respect to education rather than the ethic of care that should be at the heart of the educational endeavour.

Issue #8: Difference-blind conceptualisations of leadership are a form of misleadership. Too many theories of leadership, instructional practices and educational programmes are conceived as though many social dynamics do not exist. Students are mass produced widgets – unraced, unsexed, completely inhuman. Yet every social science indicates that discrimination and oppression, as well as unearned privilege are real; dynamics such as racism, sexism, classism, ableism, ageism and many more are manifest in both society and school, and they inequitably influence processes as well as outcomes. Leadership cannot be practised as though these dynamics do not exist, and in fact it should be practised with leaders and scholars taking intentional opposition to the negative dynamics that undermine their work. To practice leadership and scholarship from a 'difference-blind' perspective ignores every social science and over 100 years of solid empirical research (Brooks, 2012; Bogotch et al., 2008). We need to be vigilant against micro-aggressions and macro-aggressions in school and society, and leaders' heightened agency means they are uniquely positioned to have a positive influence on them. We must endeavour to unlearn our miseducation and to use this agency as leaders to counter inequity, not be complicit as it happens in our organisations and communities (Brooks and Brooks, 2013).

Issue #9: Organisations are not ahistorical, but much leadership is practised as though they were. Each organisation and individual has a unique history in relation to educational and leadership practice. Importantly, this suggests that there is not a single history but multiple histories in every school. Leadership practice that ignores the lessons of these intertwined histories is destined to fall short of potential. Listening to and understanding history will give the leaders and the organisation the benefit of experience when moving forward with a decision or project (Tyack and Hansot, 1982). That said, there are three types of organisations with respect to history.

Schools are one of three types of educational organisations, those whose leaders, members and constituents are *history-informed*, *history-ignorant* or *history-inert*. History-informed schools are aware of the individual and institutional histories of the organisation. They have clear processes in place that allow people to share their perspectives on how current and proposed changes are similar or different to what has been done before. These histories are discussed and critically interrogated, meaning that it is important to be informed by the past but also to talk through why or why not something that happened once may happen again. History-ignorant schools have no idea what has come before. They are often stuck in reform churn (Brooks, 2006) and repeat ineffective practices over and over. History-inert school personnel are paralysed by the past – and do not change for fear of repeating past mistakes. Clearly, leaders should be striving to create and sustain history-informed schools, where the plurality of experiences people bring to their work can inform current and future practice without holding it back.

Issue #10: Educational leadership research methods have failed to take into account the special dynamics of influence, power, control and so on. Scholars should be informed by classic social science research methods and methodologies but should not be a slave to them. In the fields of educational leadership, our current approaches routinely fail to account for many known individual and organisational leadership dynamics (Brooks and Normore, 2015). As an example, one glaring omission in many studies of educational leadership is a lack of attention to the relational, power and gatekeeper dynamics that influence the study. Nearly all qualitative interview-based studies in educational leadership are some form of elite interview, yet most studies fail to account for the special position and perspectives of the people they interview (Harvey, 2010). The field needs new research designs, data collection techniques, data analysis procedures, ways to establish rigour and forms of communicating findings (Brooks and Normore, 2015). In today's data-rich schools, mixed methods hold a great deal of promise, as do various forms of increasingly sophisticated quantitative and qualitative methods. The field could also explore new forms of narrative inquiry, indigenous leadership perspectives or even methods like existential sociology. We must also look for ways to incorporate global educational leadership phenomena into our work and consider new ways to investigate issues of race, sexuality, ableism and many, many more aspects of educational leadership (Apple et al., 2005; Brooks and Normore, 2010).

Conclusion

At the onset of this chapter, I asked the provocative question, 'is everything we know about educational leadership wrong?' The easy answer is 'no', with the qualification that it seems likely that much of the field is misconceptualised and that the current methodologies we employ are ill-suited to answer educational leadership research questions. There is a desperate need for research that deeply explores the relationships between leadership and learning. Further, there is a corollary need for work that investigates what leadership looks like in relation to specific content areas and in relation to new ways of conceptualising learning. There is a need for practice and policy that is research-generative not research-reductive, meaning that we go beyond lists of standards or purportedly effective practices and really seek to embrace the complexity of leadership practice and scholarship. As in any field, we need a great many scholars to eschew conformity and authentically to explore, discover, question, test, learn and share new ideas and approaches to leadership practice. We must find meaningful ways of disseminating and utilising high-level findings quickly but without sacrificing quality. We must design and conduct research that comes *to* and *from* schools and society, and in sum, we need more people questioning everything – looking at their work and other's work with a curious heart and a critical perspective. Only then can we begin to understand the ways that we are right or wrong.

Notes

1 I would like to thank Catherine A. Lugg for her comments on earlier drafts of this chapter.
2 Specific references of many of the central works by these writers appear in other chapters of this book.
3 There are two notable exceptions to this absence: Evers, C.W. and Lakomski, G. (1996). *Exploring educational administration.* Oxford: Pergamon and Spillane, J. P. (2006). *Distributed leadership.* San Francisco, CA: John Wiley.

References

Anderson, G. L., 1991. Cognitive politics of principals and teachers: Ideological control in an elementary school. In J. Blasé, ed., *The politics of life in schools: Power, conflict, and cooperation* (pp. 120–130). Newbury Park: SAGE.

Apple, M., Kenway, J. and Singh, M., eds., 2005. *Globalizing education: Policies, pedagogies, and politics.* New York: Peter Lang.

Beck, L. G. and Murphy, J., 1993. *Understanding the principalship: Metaphorical themes 1920s–1990s.* New York: Teachers College Press.

Bogotch, I., Beachum, F. Blount, J., Brooks, J. S. and English, F. W., 2008. *Radicalizing educational leadership: Toward a theory of social justice.* Netherlands: Sense.

Brooks, J. S., 2012. *Black school, white school: Racism and educational (mis)leadership.* New York: Teachers College Press.

Brooks, J. S. and Miles, M. T., 2008. From scientific management to social justice ... and back again? Pedagogical shifts in educational leadership. In A. H. Normore, ed., *Leadership for social justice: Promoting equity and excellence through inquiry and reflective practice* (pp. 99–114). Charlotte, NC: Information Age Publishing.

Brooks, J. S. and Normore, A. H., 2010. Educational leadership and globalization: Toward a global perspective. *Educational Policy,* 24(1), pp. 52–82.

Brooks, J. S. and Kensler, L. A. W., 2011. Distributed leadership and democratic community. In F. W. English, ed., *The SAGE handbook of educational leadership: Advances in theory, research, and practice* (2nd ed., pp. 55–66). Thousand Oaks, CA: SAGE Publishing.

Brooks, M. C. and Brooks, J. S., 2013. What can school leaders do about violence in schools? *Journal of Curriculum and Pedagogy*, 10(2), pp. 115–118.

Brooks, J. S. and Normore, A. N., 2015. Qualitative research and educational leadership: Essential dynamics to consider when designing and conducting studies. *International Journal of Educational Management*, (29)7, pp. 1–9.

Brooks, J. S., Normore, A. H., Jean-Marie, G. and Hodgins, D., 2007. Distributed leadership for social justice: Influence and equity in an urban high school. *Journal of School Leadership*, 17(4), pp. 378–408.

Callahan, R.E., 1962. *Education and the cult of efficiency*. Chicago: University of Chicago Press.

Campbell, R. F., Fleming, T., Newell, L. J. and Bennion, J. W., 1987. *A history of thought and practice in educational administration*. New York: Teachers College Press.

Cuban, L., 1988. *The managerial imperative*. Albany, NY: SUNY Press.

Darling-Hammond, L., Meyerson, D., LaPointe, M. and Orr, M. T., 2010. *Preparing principals for a changing world: Lessons from effective school leadership programmes*. San Francisco, CA: Jossey-Bass.

Diem, S. and Young, M. D., 2015. Considering critical turns in research on educational leadership and policy. *International Journal of Educational Management*, 29(7), pp. 838–850.

Doyle, M. C. and Feldman, J., 2006. Student voice and student choice in Boston pilot high schools. *Educational Policy*, 20(2), pp. 367–398.

English, F. W., 2002a. *The fateful turn: Understanding the discursive practice of educational administration*. Huntsville, TX: NCPEA.

English, F. W., 2002b. The point of scientificity, the fall of the epistemological dominos, and the end of the field of educational administration. *Studies in Philosophy and Education*, 21(2), 109–136.

English, F. W., 2003. *The postmodern challenge to the theory and practice of educational administration*. Springfield, IL: Charles C. Thomas.

Foster, W., 1986. *Paradigms and promises: New approaches to educational administration*. Buffalo, NY: Prometheus Books.

Gelberg, D., 1997. *The 'business' of reforming American schools*. Albany: State University of New York Press.

Glass, T. E., 1986. Factualism to theory, art to science: School administration texts 1955–1985. In T. E. Glass, ed., *An analysis of texts on school administration 1820–1985: The reciprocal relationship between the literature and the profession* (pp. 93–114). Danville, IL: Interstate.

Gronn, P., 2003. *The new work of educational leaders*. London: Paul Chapman Publishing.

Harvey, W. S., 2010, Methodological approaches for interviewing elites. *Geography Compass*, 4(3), pp. 193–205.

Johnson, R. S., 2002. *Using data to close the achievement gap: How to measure equity in our schools*. Thousand Oaks, CA: Corwin Press.

Kohn, A., 1999. *Punished by rewards: The trouble with gold stars, incentive plans, A's, praise, and other bribes*. Boston: Houghton Mifflin.

Larson, C. and Murtadha, K., 2002. Leadership for social justice. In J. Murphy, ed., *The educational leadership challenge: Redefining leadership for the 21st century* (pp. 134–161). Chicago: University of Chicago Press.

Lee, P. W., 1999. In their own voices: An ethnographic study of low-achieving students within the context of school reform. *Urban Education*, 34(2), pp. 214–244.

Mintzberg, H., 1993. *The rise and fall of strategic planning: Reconceiving roles for planning, plans, planners.* New York: Simon and Schuster.

Mitra, D. L., 2008. *Student voice in school reform: Building youth–adult partnerships that strengthen schools and empower youth.* Albany, NY: State University of New York Press.

Mitra, D. and Gross, J., 2009. Increasing student voice in high school reform: Building partnerships, improving outcomes. *Educational Management Administration and Leadership,* 37(4), pp. 522–543.

Mulford, W., Silins, H. and Leithwood, K., 2004. *Educational leadership for organisational learning and improved student outcomes.* Dordrecht, The Netherlands: Kluwer Academic Publishers.

Nasaw, D., 1979. *Schooled to order.* New York: Oxford University Press.

Saka, Y., Southerland, S. A. and Brooks, J. S., 2009. Becoming a member of a school community while working toward science education reform: Teacher induction from a cultural historical activity theory (CHAT) perspective. *Science Education,* 93(3), pp. 1–30.

Schunk, D. H., 2008. *Learning theories: An educational perspective.* New York: Pearson Prentice Hall.

Seeman, M., 1959. On the meaning of alienation. *American Sociological Review,* 24(6), pp. 783–791.

Seeman, M., 1967. On the personal consequences of alienation in work. *American Sociological Review,* 32(2), pp. 273–285.

Seeman, M., 1975. Alienation studies. *Annual Review of Sociology,* 1, pp. 91–123.

Seeman, M., 1983. Alienation motifs in contemporary theorizing: The hidden continuity of the classic themes. *Social Psychology Quarterly,* 46(3), pp. 171–184.

Spillane, J. P., 2006. *Distributed leadership.* San Francisco: John Wiley and Sons, Inc.

Theoharis, G. and Brooks, J. S., eds., 2012. *What every principal needs to know to create equitable and excellent schools.* New York: Teachers College Press.

Tschannen-Moran, M., 2001. Collaboration and the need for trust. *Journal of Educational Administration,* 39(4), pp. 308–331.

Tschannen-Moran, M., 2004. *Trust matters: Leadership for successful schools.* San Francisco: Jossey-Bass.

Tyack, D. B., 1974. *The one best system: A history of American urban education.* Cambridge, MA: Harvard University Press.

Tyack, D. B. and Hansot, E., 1982. *Managers of virtue: Public school leadership in America, 1920–1980.* New York: Basic Books.

Wirt, F.M. and Kirst, M.W., 1972. *Political and social foundations of education.* Berkeley, CA: McCutchan Publishing Corporation.

4 Disambiguating leadership

The continuing quest for the philosopher's stone

Fenwick W. English and Lisa Catherine Ehrich

Introduction

In recent years, the concept of *leadership* in education has become the fabled *philosopher's stone* of mediaeval times. The *stone* represented the search for the chemical formula that could turn lead into gold. While the alchemists of the day suspected that lead and gold were quite close, they were never able to pull it off.

This chapter aims to disambiguate or make unambiguous the shift in thinking regarding educational direction from administration to leadership and discusses why, in reviewing the history of educational administration as viewed through its textbooks, Glass declared (2004, p. 121), 'Perhaps the future of general texts is a focus on leadership. Leadership texts supported by casebooks may become dominant adoptions in the standards-driven era of twenty-first century reform'.

We review possible explanations for this shift and posit a perspective regarding the nature and potency of leadership that has heretofore not been considered, in our on-going research on leadership as connoisseurship (Ehrich and English, 2013a; English and Ehrich, 2016). In doing so, we will visit the intersection of the intellectual/conceptual history of educational administration and consider that record with the politics of ideas as they compete for influence and dominance in our field. In this analysis, we attempt to engage in Bourdieu's *reflexive thinking*, (Bourdieu, 1999, p. 608) that is, to question how we have been thinking about leadership and how we have been thinking about disambiguating leadership.

To clarify further the perspective of this chapter, our view of leadership remains individualistic. This perspective sits solidly within an over 1,200 year understanding of the concept. We note that before the year 725, the verb *laedan* meant 'to cause to go with one, *lead* cognate with Old Frisian *leda* to lead' (Barnhart, 1995, p. 425). The etymological history of *lead* signifies a turning to and in this case a turning to a person as a guide. We think here of the great community organiser Saul Alinsky (1969, p. 66) who commented on people occupying formal roles in organisations who called themselves leaders, and the 'Native' or 'Indigenous leaders' who gained respect and support from their followers because of who they were and what they did. To help construct a workable and successful community organisation, one had to learn how to recognise the 'Native' or 'Indigenous leader'.

Our notion of a leader is (1) a person who emerges in a religious, labour or political movement to guide or direct (Ehrich and English, 2012); (2) a person who is an acknowledged expert, scientist or artist in a specific field (Gardner, 1995), or (3) a person in a formal organisation who is appointed to occupy a role where he or she is expected to provide inspiration and/or direction and to organise and/or facilitate a group's energy in reaching a desired goal or outcome, which could be a service or a product (Peters, 2010). These definitions are not endorsements of what has been called 'the hero leader' (see Gronn, 2004, p. 34). We have no need for heroes, but when it comes to the magnitude of reforming of educational institutions, we agree with Gandhi, who observed:

> *We must worship heroism, not heroes. The hero may later on disgrace himself* [sic] *and in any case must cease to exist, but heroism is everlasting.*
>   (as cited in Iyer, 1973/2000, p. 138)

While we are not opposed to what Nielsen (2004) has called the 'leaderless organisation', in which rank-based leadership is replaced by peer-based leadership, we think it will be a long time before formal, central bureaucratic organisations, which began in the eleventh century in France (Samier, 2013a, p. 909) and are now a 'world historical phenomenon with complex causal relations spread across empires, colonial systems, and nations' (Samier, 2013a, p. 909), disappear from the cultural landscape. We do not pose an alternative concept of a leader as utopian, but rather as practical and doable within such structures even as we do not embrace those structures as optimal. This is similar to some scholars who propose distributed leadership (see Gronn, 2004, pp. 27–50; Woods, 2015, pp. 85–90) as a different division of labour in formal organisations but not a total abolition of bureaucratic structure. Further, by continuing to embrace individualism in leadership, we are similarly not embracing a 'command and control' concept of leadership within them.

The contested space of a social/intellectual field

We locate our discussion within Bourdieu and Wacquant's (1992) concept of a *field*. A field is not a static entity but rather a social space of fluidity and contestation. It is comprised of players, that is, agencies and groups competing with one another for influence and dominance. Nothing is stable in this space, and influence is pursued with many forms of capital, the most obvious of which is money. Because there is no person or agency that can bestow ultimate legitimacy, it must be fought for and acquired (Bourdieu and Passeron, 1970/2000, p. 18). The struggle is ceaseless. One form of capital involved is cultural, and that is comprised of linguistic and symbolic forms of which degrees, diplomas and other forms of distinction become highly prized and sought after (Bourdieu, 2009). In the university, one form of distinction is represented in the scholarship, research or unusual insight that comes to be accepted as 'the way things are or should be', that is, the creation of a mindset to which others refer and defer and that they accept. We see the rise of leadership in the literature of educational administration as an example of this struggle over mindset or what Thomas Kuhn (1996) called a *paradigm*. From a Bourdieusian perspective, the rise of leadership as the centre of intellectual gravity represents the outcome of a struggle for political power in an academic sphere. From humble beginnings around 1900, the number of books on educational leadership has grown, reaching a 100 percent growth in the 1920s and 250 percent in the 1950s (Google books Ngram Viewer, 2015). As it pertains to the topic today, it is estimated that 'approximately every six hours, somewhere, someone publishes a paper on leadership in English' (Grint, 1995, p. 124). We now explore some of the reasons for this growth.

The big tent metaphor: The intersection of politics and power in Bourdieusian social space

In the second edition of the *Handbook of Research on Educational Administration*, edited by Joseph Murphy and Karen Seashore Louis (1999), Robert Donmoyer surveyed the seismic shifts in the changing intellectual landscape of educational administration. Many of these shifts, akin to the movement of intellectual tectonic plates, occurred outside the educational administration field but heavily impacted on the thinking of academics in the field. Among these were critiques of the idea of a scientific base for knowledge from Apple (1979) and Giroux (1981) as well as Pinar (1975) and Eisner (1975, 1979, 1988). These scholars stressed the politics of intellectual change and disputed the notion that the idea of a science was without the taint of politics. Also outside the field were frontal attacks on methodology in intellectual inquiry that had favoured almost exclusively quantitative approaches, especially from influential methodologists like Lee Cronbach (1975), a scholar in educational psychology who first abandoned the search for 'laws that were universal and context free' (Donmoyer, 1999, p. 27) to a point where he similarly rejected searching for cause–effect interactions because such relationships cannot inform practice and are pointless – in his words, like 'waiting for Godot' (Donmoyer, 1999, p. 27). According to Donmoyer (1999), Cronbach was the most influential scholar in educational psychology and quantitative research methodology, and he arrived at the conclusion that 'social action was constructed and not caused' (Donmoyer, 1999, p. 27). Cronbach's apotheosis was similar to the critiques of educational administration by T. B. Greenfield (1978) and Richard Bates (1980). These intellectual shifts produced great doubts about the efficacy of educational administration as a sustainable metadiscourse even in the minds of those who had been strong advocates. For example, Jack Culbertson (1983, p. 15), the influential educational administration scholar and executive director of the University Council of Educational Administration (UCEA, a consortium of higher education institutions in the USA committed to advancing the preparation and practice of educational leaders), wrote, 'I am coming not to know what educational administration is and to doubt that it ought to continue an existence as an independent field of inquiry'.

There were also full-scale attacks on educational administration from within the discipline, not only in terms of a methodological assault on heretofore regnant quantitative methods, but also from feminists who pointed out the patriarchal, misogynist and hierarchically gendered aspects of the field, which had moved from one that at first would not admit women at all to one where quotas were established because it was feared that the field might become over-feminised (Blount, 1998, p. 141). There were critiques of the racist heritage of educational administration (Delgado, 1998), cries for social justice (Shoho et al., 2005; Marshall and Oliva, 2006) and finally postmodern critiques (Maxcy, 1994; English, 2003).

The outcome of this intellectual shift produced a situation whereby what was once considered a fairly established intellectual field (Griffiths, 1959) was eventually replaced by another, which was 'nonlinear, essentially plotless, somewhat disjointed, and riddled with ruptures, contradictions, and inconsistencies' (Donmoyer, 1999, p. 30). The result was the creation of a 'big tent' that would hold all of these anomalies together without insisting that there must be agreement or unification of interests, individuals or conceptions of knowledge or methodology. The 'big tent' nowadays is essentially a Bourdieusian holding pen in which competition and struggle are the rule of the day. Since all of these movements undermined the idea of a stable knowledge base that once supported educational administration as a science, that term became passé, much too limited in its view and burdened with heavy negative intellectual baggage. In its place came *leadership*, a more ambiguous and amorphous term but one much more suitable to the change in the intellectual landscape than *educational administration*. In Bourdieusian contested social space, leadership fulfils a viable political function, and its continued rise in professional discourse has signalled that there are more voices (actors, agencies and groups) involved in that expanded discourse than in the case of the older terminology. Of particular note was that educational administration was largely the hegemonic discourse dominated by white heterosexual males interested in perpetuating a patriarchal, hierarchical system that reflected their own cultural perspectives, which were misogynist, racist and classist (Katz, 1971; Bowles and Gintis, 1976; Blount, 1998; Young and Marshall, 2013).

Educational administration and the loss of paradigmatic dominance

Of some importance in this contestation over terminology, some academics in the field have lamented the loss of the defined borders and content of the older notion of *educational administration*. When serving on the executive board of UCEA in the USA, a senior professor lamented to one of the co-authors of this chapter after looking over the annual conference programme, 'When are we going to get back to what educational administration is about? What's all this social justice stuff have to do with educational administration?' It is instructive to note that both national professorial associations in the USA have discussed at times changing the 'administration' in their names to 'leadership', as the British

Educational Leadership Management and Administration Society (BELMAS) did in the UK.

Recent scholarship has focused on educational leadership as anti-racist, feminist, spiritual, distributed, culturally proficient and democratic, among other concepts (see Griffiths and Portelli, 2015). Each of these terms is purported to resolve a most significant issue in matters facing schools (Horsford, 2010), and each is a kind of philosopher's stone for turning lead into gold. While we do not decry any of these manifestations of leadership nor of the serious problems they are purported to resolve, by using Bourdieusian reflexivity (1999, p. 608) and exposing their presuppositions, we note that virtually all of them stand on the assumed existence of a line of demarcation between the conceptual categorical binary of leader and non-leader. Such binaries have been shown to be easily deconstructed by exposing the fact that the oppositional term in a binary remains suspended with the other, though silent. For example, the classic binary 'subjective/objective' requires that for one term to make sense the other must be present as well (though unspoken). Otherwise the binary does not work. In this case where is the line of demarcation, that is, the categorical exclusivity which is necessary to substantiate claims of one or the other as true? (see Rapaport, 1989, p.62).

Pattison (1997, p.32) commented on this state of affairs:

> The only thing that can be safely concluded here is that effective leadership... is an elusive, perhaps longed-for chimera, a kind of holy grail for managers. This is not to say that leadership does not exist, nor that it is inessential. It is just to acknowledge that it is difficult to grasp and analyse in any concrete way. Leadership is thus another part of the myth and faith world that surrounds contemporary management.

The loss of the paradigmatic dominance of educational administration and the many new and emergent concepts of *leadership* have permitted more voices and perspectives to enter into the field than before. The field, such as it was, has been permanently changed, and it does not seem to us that it will ever be possible to get the new genie back in the old bottle. Rather than see this as a weakness, Lakatos (1999, p. 69) advances the position that the situation is healthy and normal:

> The history of science has been and should be a history of competing research programmes (or, if you wish, 'paradigms') but it has not been and must not become a succession of periods of normal science, the sooner competition starts, the better for progress. Theoretical pluralism is better than theoretical monism.

The questioning of leadership as the solution to improving school performance appears to be a healthy re-examination of the implicit assumption that somehow a change in the leader can perform a similar sort of alchemy with poor or failing schools. This belief has become a kind of social fact irrespective of the evidence. In 2010 in the USA, the Barack Obama administration implemented a *Blueprint for Reform* and provided funds to the states for their implementation of its agenda. The blueprint stipulated four possible models for improving and/ or reforming failing schools. They were *the transformation model, the turnaround model, the restart model* and *the school closure model.* Every model required the firing of the principal or the replacement of the principal by converting to a charter school or an education management organisation. When asked where the research was to support the federal requirement for the termination of the principal as the school leader, the US Department of Education could cite none (Papa and English, 2011, pp. 40–41).

An alternative perspective of *doing* leading

We posit that so-called scientific studies of leadership can only be partially understood from an empirical perspective and from the traditional logical–rationalistic methods affiliated with scientific discourse (Heilbrunn, 1996). We have observed that logico-empirical approaches to leadership have proven to be disappointing (Jacob et al., 2015), have approached outcome measures without appreciation for the complexities involved (Grissom et al., 2015) and have failed to discern anything novel or new for a long time (English and Ehrich, 2015). Further, we support Lakatos's (1999) argument that the line of demarcation between science and non-science is unsustainable in the short term and perhaps even over some period of time. Furthermore, a field founded on such a line of demarcation is easily deconstructed and becomes essentially a non-entity (English, 2002).

Instead, we would suggest that leading and leadership are much better understood from the perspective of aesthetics for the following reasons: (1) the emotional and intuitive aspects of leadership are important areas for inclusion if the whole human being is to be considered in the leadership equation; (2) aesthetics and aesthetic theory are critical in 'designing analytical models, taxonomies, and maps of the field' (Samier, 2013b, p. 945) and furthermore, aesthetics 'also has theoretical importance to identifying and analysing expressive qualities' (Samier, 2013b, p. 945); and (3) it 'also allows for a clearer integration of disciplines integrating the humanities and social sciences' (Samier, 2013b, p. 946).

Aesthetics emerged as a separate branch of philosophy in the eighteenth century in England and Europe. It represented a second way of assembling knowledge, not from logic (the dominant mode of scientific discourse) but from 'sensory experience coupled with feeling' (Feagin, 1999, p. 12). One of the hallmarks of aesthetics is the difficulty with definitions or rules, an issue also in defining leadership. Aesthetic judgment is not amenable to rules because

> we could not use rules to produce in ourselves felt responses to objects; we could not, in cases of disagreement, reasonably ask another person to relinquish his or her judgment on the grounds that it conflicted with the rules;

and whatever our own responses departed from the rules, we would quite rightly repudiate the rules rather than our response.

(Gardner, 1996, p. 230)

Furthermore, 'To judge according to rules is to miss the uniqueness of objects, and so to fail to judge aesthetically' (Gardner, 1996, p. 230).

At work in aesthetic judgment is a subjective element that situates any definition as being in the mind of the observer, influenced by his or her tastes and within the culture of that individual. There is no way that the divergence, an essential feature of aesthetic taste and judgment, can be brought into a single focal point. 'Aesthetic qualities are deeply elusive: the "positioning" of the observer needed to discern aesthetic qualities involves a plethora of temperamental and culturally parochial factors, all strongly indicative of subjectivity' (Gardner, 1996, p. 231).

As an aesthetic concept, there is wide divergence and no rules to fall back on to negotiate one definitive version of leadership. It clearly is a matter of taste, judgement and subjective interpretation. With so many versions, it is no wonder that rational/logical empirical approaches which depend upon accurate definitions in order to determine methods of measurement often flounder in the garden of ambiguity.

The potential of doing leading as an aesthetic construct

Sebastian Gardner (1996, p. 229) wrote, 'A world without aesthetic qualities would be an inferior, if not uninhabitable, world, and a person without any capacity for aesthetic response, if imaginable, would not qualify as a fully developed human being'. Assuming for the moment that many adults within and outside organisations today (including schools) would be more or less fully developed, they would certainly recognise the aesthetics involved in leadership.

Imagine the Elizabethan audience who experienced leaders in Shakespeare's immortal plays. This is a representation of the aesthetics and the full range of senses of experiencing leadership. Harold Bloom (1998, p. 4) wrote of the scholarship of the Bard and his continued universality (a thing that the quantifiers of human actions on the scientific side hold out as their philosopher's stone):

> The idea of Western character, of the self as a moral agent, has many sources: Homer and Plato, Aristotle and Sophocles, the Bible and St. Augustine, Dante and Kant, and all you might care to add. Personality, in our sense, is a Shakespearean invention, and is not only Shakespeare's greatest originality but also the authentic cause of his perpetual pervasiveness. Insofar as we ourselves value, and deplore, our own personalities, we are the heirs of Falstaff and of Hamlet, and of all the other persons who throng Shakespeare's theater of what might be called the colors of the spirit.

We know of no research conducted on leadership in general or on educational research specifically that would even venture into this arena. It would be struck down as too subjective and unverifiable by scientific procedures. Where is the evidence? The evidence in an aesthetic experience is the linkage between the representation of art, in whatever form that may take, and how that representation connects to us as observers and participants in a common experience.

Aesthetic assessment is certainly a more encompassing procedure than the research procedures typically employed to study leadership in many university programmes today. How did audiences assess the leadership of Hamlet, Falstaff, Cleopatra, Julius Caesar, King Lear, Macbeth and so many others? There were no sociological texts in which to locate their decisions or actions. But what audiences saw was the whole human being. Some may have loved Hamlet or empathised with him. Others may have despised him. But what is going in is an appraisal of the leader as developed, a whole human being with motives, feelings and dreams.

We mention here the recent travails of Gary Loveman, the CEO of *Caesars Entertainment*, a billion-dollar organisation with branches worldwide. Loveman, a former Harvard Business School professor, had to downsize the number of employees from 87,000 to 68,000 after a very bad decision regarding a buyout, which left *Caesars* with a debt load of $22 billion dollars. In stepping down as CEO, Loveman indicated that 'revenue and earnings aren't the best way to assess Caesars performance' (O'Keeffe, 2015, p. B1). A former *Caesars* executive reflected on Loveman's tenure as the leader and remarked, 'If Gary had led more with his heart than his intellect, people wouldn't be asking what happened to the heart and soul of Caesars Entertainment' (O'Keeffe, 2015, B1).

'Leading with the heart' is not likely to appear on any list of executive skills we know of for business or education. One would not find it in many of the existing textbooks (if any) in educational administration either. Yet, leading with the heart is a metaphor of the demeanour of a leader. We aver it is a sensory experience that is almost purely aesthetic. Aesthetic knowledge often results in metaphorical data as opposed to quantitative expressions. One can see an example of an aesthetic analysis in Morgan's (1986) *Images of Organization*, Lumby and English's (2010) *Leadership as Lunacy* and Ehrich and English's (2013b) paper 'Leadership as dance: A consideration of the applicability of the 'mother' of all arts as the basis for establishing connoisseurship'.

Eisner (1991, p. 227) spoke of the power of metaphor when he said 'metaphorical precision is the central vehicle for revealing the qualitative aspects of life'. Hence, it is the ability of a leader to put the ineffable aspects of life into words in the stories he/she tells to prospective audiences and to embody those aspects that is seen as a measure of his/her or authenticity (Gardner, 1995, p. 9). The embodiment of stories a leader tells is regarded as a key to his/her credibility. This domain is an anchor of the basis of trust and is an aesthetic judgment.

Leadership as a form of connoisseurship

Our own recent research attempts to reconcile the aesthetic and rational aspects of leadership in the notion of connoisseurship called by Schwandt (1994) 'the art of apperception. It is grounded in the "consummatory function" of aesthetic knowing [that is] the developed ability to experience the subtleties of form' (Eisner, 1985, p. 28).

In our quest to re-imagine the field of leadership and to consider its aesthetic dimensions, we commenced our explorations with the metaphor of leadership as dance (Ehrich and English, 2013b), wherein we argued that leadership is a type of bodily performance that draws upon a leader's emotions, intuition, ethics and senses. This work led us further into the realm of *connoisseurship*, a term often used in the arts (Eisner, 1991) to describe an expert or a person who is highly knowledgeable and in a strong position to render judgements. We undertook interviews commencing firstly with ten artists (i.e. a writer, director, sculptor, choreographers, composers and visual artists) in order to understand how they create art and deal with constraints and how they developed a 'discerning eye' in their respective fields. This was followed by a round of interviews with ten school leaders in which we were interested to explore both the similarities and differences that emerged amongst the participants' accounts.

There were many similarities regarding the way in which artists and leaders spoke about their work. The joy of doing one's work and the necessity of working within constraints were embraced by artists more so than leaders. Moreover, developing a 'discerning eye' was an evolutionary developmental process that required sheer hard work and personal efforts to improve. An important difference was that the educational leaders were part of a formal organisation in which their roles had been designated, whereas the artists, for the most part, had more space in which to create and experiment. Like grassroots leaders, some of the artists in our sample were not bound or tightly defined by clear roles or rules. Yet like the leaders, those with more freedom to create what and how they desired still worked within constraints, even if those constraints were only the medium or the structures inherent in the discipline itself. Another finding we would highlight here is the way in which the leaders, like the artists, found the space to enact forms of artistry in their day-to-day performance. Since school leaders work within bureaucratic systems, they had to find ways to work within existing spaces, often defying bureaucratic rules and regulations in forms of what can only be called 'creative insubordination'.

Based on our work to date, we have determined that connoisseurs of leadership performance are those people who use their discerning eye to make finely grained judgements often based on intuition and tacit knowledge. They are aesthetically aware and not afraid to draw upon their emotions, senses, intuitions, passions and perceptions as well as using more conventional approaches when confronted with decisions (English and Ehrich, 2016). Finally, our work in this arena convinced us that the descriptive term connoisseurship is not a binary (i.e. connoisseur vs. non-connoisseur) but rather a continuum of human development and that most humans are on this continuum.

We believe that our journey of understanding connoisseurship has taken us into new intellectual and conceptual territory that restores to leadership its much needed human-centred side. Further, it combines perception, discernment and action. We believe that this perspective offers a deeper and broader understanding of *doing leadership.*

In conclusion

In this chapter, we have proffered that leadership is a metaphorical construct centred on a form of knowledge that is based in aesthetics. This is the reason it has so many definitions and has proven to be illusive in the strict logical empirical tradition of the modernistic sciences. Solving the leadership issue is like asking 'what is art?' A response to that question is highly interpretative and subjective. Empirical investigations of leadership have proven to be disappointing for this reason. They have largely failed to validate even its importance let alone its existence, especially in organisational studies and in various forms of organisational theory, which continue to dominate the context of educational administration.

In presenting our case for leadership as a different concept, we began with the assertion, now factually established, that it is possible to turn lead into gold, only not by chemical means. All that is required is a particle accelerator and lots of energy, and by slamming 'beams of carbon and neon nuclei nearly to light speed' into lead, one can in fact produce gold; it is just prohibitively expensive to do so and not worth the effort (Matson, 2014). We proffer that a similar shift, which would be worth the effort, can identify leadership as connoisseurship and confirm its presence, but not in the manner in which it has been historically conceptualised; and that when it is confined to formal bureaucratic structures, its actual nature is camouflaged and marginalised. We concur with Lakomski (2005, p. 146) that organisations can run without leaders and survive and prosper with versions of group collectivities, at least for a time. If, as she avers, 'knowledge management' represents the key to 'decentered forms of organization with flatter hierarchies as optimal design for turbulent environments', then in our opinion, such knowledge must include whole human beings who both think and feel. We are creatures of logic and emotion. We believe our preliminary research on leadership aesthetics as connoisseurship offers a promising and different perspective on the more central and illusive nature of understanding leadership. Such a perspective might be the real goal that has so far eluded our best efforts, leading to many broken dreams and promises.

References

Alinsky, S., 1969. *Reveille for radicals.* New York: Vintage Books.
Apple, M., 1979. *Ideology and curriculum.* London: Routledge and Kegan Paul.
Barnhart, R. K., ed., 1995. *The Barnhart concise dictionary of etymology.* New York: Harper Collins.
Bates, R., 1980. Educational administration, the sociology of science, and the management of knowledge. *Educational Administration Quarterly,* 16(2), pp. 1–20.
Bloom, H., 1998. *Shakespeare: The invention of the human.* New York: Riverhead Books.

Blount, J. M., 1998. *Destined to rule the schools: Women and the superintendency, 1873–1995.* Albany, NY: SUNY Press.

Bourdieu, P., 1999. Understanding. In P. Bourdieu, *The weight of the world: Social suffering in contemporary society* (pp. 607–629). Stanford, CA: Stanford University Press.

Bourdieu, P., 2009. *Distinction: A social critique of the judgment of taste.* R. Nice, Trans. New York: Routledge.

Bourdieu, P. and Passeron, J.-C., 1970/2000. *Reproduction in education, society and culture* (2nd ed.) R. Nice, Trans. London: SAGE (original work published in French in 1970).

Bourdieu, P. and Wacquant, L. J. D., 1992. *An invitation to reflexive sociology.* Chicago, IL: University of Chicago Press.

Bowles, S. and Gintis, H., 1976. *Schooling in capitalist America.* New York: Basic Books.

Cronbach, L., 1975. Beyond the two disciplines of scientific psychology. *American Psychologist,* 30, pp. 116–127.

Culbertson, J. A., 1983. Theory in educational administration: Echoes from critical thinkers. *Educational Researcher* 12(10), pp. 15–22.

Delgado, B. D., 1998. Using a Chicana feminist epistemology in educational research. *Harvard Educational Review,* 68(4), pp. 555–582.

Donmoyer, R., 1999. The continuing quest for a knowledge base: 1976–1998. In J. Murphy and Karen Seashore Louis, eds., *Handbook of research on educational administration,* (2nd ed., pp. 25–72) San Francisco, CA: Jossey-Bass.

Ehrich, L. C. and English, F. W., 2012. What can grassroots leadership teach us about school leadership? *Halduskultuur-Administrative Culture* 13(2), pp. 85–108.

Ehrich, L. C. and English, F. W., 2013a. Towards connoisseurship in educational leadership: Following the data in a three stage line of inquiry. In S. Eacott and R. Niesche, eds., *Empirical leadership research: Letting the data speak for themselves* (pp. 165–198). Niagara Falls, NY: Untested Ideas Research Center.

Ehrich, L. C. and English, F. W., 2013b. Leadership as dance: A consideration of the applicability of the 'mother' of all arts as the basis for establishing connoisseurship. *International Journal of Leadership in Education.* 16(4), pp. 454–481.

Eisner, E., 1975. The perceptive eye: Toward the reformation of educational evaluation. Address to the American Educational Research Association, Division B. Washington, D.C.

Eisner, E., 1979. *The educational imagination.* New York: Macmillan.

Eisner, E., 1985. Aesthetic modes of knowing. In E. Eisner, ed., *Learning and teaching the ways of knowing: Eighty-fourth yearbook of the National Society for the Study of Education* (Part II, pp. 23–36). Chicago: National Society for the Study of Education.

Eisner, E., 1988. The primacy of experience and the politics of method. *Educational Researcher,* 7(5) pp. 15–20.

Eisner, E., 1991. *The enlightened eye.* Upper Saddle River, NJ: Prentice-Hall.

English, F. W., 2002. The point of scientificity, the fall of the epistemological dominos, and the end of the field of educational administration. *Studies in Philosophy and Education,* 21(2), pp. 109–136.

English, F. W., 2003. *The postmodern challenge to the theory and practice of educational administration.* Springfield, ILL: Charles C. Thomas Publisher, Ltd.

English, F. W. and Ehrich, L. C., 2015. Innovatus interregnum: Waiting for a paradigm shift. *International Journal of Educational Management,* 29(7), pp. 851–862.

English, F. W. and Ehrich, L. C., 2016. *Leading beautifully: Educational leadership as connoisseurship*. London and New York: Routledge.

Feagin, S. L., 1999. Aesthetics. In R. Audi, ed., *The Cambridge dictionary of philosophy* (2nd ed., pp. 11–13). Cambridge: Cambridge University Press.

Gardner, H., 1995. *Leading minds: an anatomy of leadership*. New York: Basic Books.

Gardner, S., 1996. Aesthetics. In N. Bunnin and E. P. Tsui-James, eds., *The Blackwell companion to philosophy* (pp. 229–256). Oxford: Blackwell.

Giroux, H., 1981. *Ideology, culture and the process of schooling*. Philadelphia: Temple University Press.

Glass, T. E., 2004. A retreat from theory in an era of reform: 1985–2000. In T. E. Glass, ed., *The history of educational administration viewed through its textbooks* (pp. 109–126). Lanham, MD: Scarecrow Education.

Google books Ngram Viewer, 2015. Educational leadership. Accessed on August 30, 2015 at https://books.google.com/ngrams/graph?content=educational+leadership&year_start=1800&year_end=2000&corpus=0&smoothing=3&share=&direct_url=t1%3B%2Ceducational%20leadership%3B%2Cc0

Greenfield, T. B., 1978. Reflections on organizational theory and the truths of irreconcilable realities. *Educational Administration Quarterly*, 14(2), pp. 1–23.

Griffiths, D. E., 1959. *Administrative theory*. New York: Appleton-Century-Crofts.

Griffiths, D. and Portelli, J. P., 2015. *Key questions for educational leaders*. Burlington, Ontario, Canada: Word and Deed Publishing Incorporated and Edphil Books.

Grint, K., 1995. *Management: A sociological introduction*. Cambridge, UK: Polity Press.

Grissom, J. A., Kalogrides, D. and Loeb, S., 2015. Using student test scores to measure principal performance. *Educational Evaluation and Policy Analysis*, 37(1), pp. 3–28.

Gronn, P., 2004. *The work of educational leaders*. London: Paul Chapman Publishing.

Heilbrunn, J., 1996. Can leadership be studied? In P. Temes, ed., *Teaching leadership: Essays in theory and practice* (pp. 1–12). New York: Peter Lang.

Horsford, S. D., 2010. *New perspectives in educational leadership*. New York: Peter Lang.

Iyer, R. N., 1973/2000. *The moral and political thought of Mahatma Gandhi*. New York: Oxford University Press.

Jacob, R., Goddard, R., Kim, M., Miller, R. and Goddard, Y., 2015. Exploring the causal impact of the McREL balanced leadership programme on leadership, principal efficacy, instructional climate, educator turnover, and student achievement. *Educational Evaluation and Policy Analysis*, 37(3), pp. 314–332.

Katz, M. B., 1971. *Class, bureaucracy and schools: The illusion of educational change in America*. New York: Praeger Publishers.

Kuhn, T., 1996. *The structure of scientific revolutions*. Chicago: University of Chicago Press.

Lakatos, I., 1999. *The methodology of scientific research programmes*. J. Worrall and G. Currie, eds., Cambridge: Cambridge University Press.

Lakomski, G., 2005. *Managing without leadership: Towards a theory of organizational functioning*. Amsterdam: Elsevier.

Lumby, J. and English, F. W., 2010. *Leadership as lunacy: And other metaphors for educational leadership*. Thousand Oaks, CA: Corwin Press.

Marshall, C. and Oliva, M., 2006. *Leadership for social justice: Making revolutions in education*. Boston, MA: Pearson.

Matson, J., 2014. Fact or fiction? Lead can be turned into gold. *Scientific American*. Accessed on June 16, 2015, at www.scientificamerican.com/article/fact-or-fiction-lead-can-be-turned-into-gold

Maxcy, S., 1994. *Postmodern school leadership: Meeting the crisis in educational administration.* Westport, CT: Praeger.

Morgan, G., 1986. *Images of organization.* Beverly Hills, CA: SAGE.

Murphy, J. and Seashore Louis, K., eds., 1999. *Handbook of research on educational administration* (2nd ed.), San Francisco, CA: Jossey-Bass.

Nielsen, J. S., 2004. *The myth of leadership: Creating leaderless organizations.* Palo Alto, CA: Davies-Black Publishing.

O'Keeffe, K., 2015. Weary but unbowed, Caesars CEO defends his tenure. *The Wall Street Journal.* Updated June 29, 2015.

Papa, R. and English, F. W., 2011. *Turnaround principals for underperforming schools.* Lanham, MD: Rowman and Littlefield Education.

Pattison, S., 1997. *The faith of the managers: When management becomes religion.* London: Cassell.

Peters, A. L., 2010. Rethinking transformational leadership in schools: The influence of people, place, and process on leadership practice. In S.D. Horsford, ed., *New perspectives in educational leadership* (pp. 29–46). New York: Peter Lang.

Pinar, W., 1975. *Curriculum theorizing: The reconceptualists.* Berkeley, CA: McCutchan.

Rapaport, H., 1989. *Heidegger and Derrida: Reflections on time and language.* Lincoln, NE: University of Nebraska Press.

Samier, E. A., 2013a. Bureaucratic theory: Myths, theories, models, critiques. In B. J. Irby, G. Brown, R. Lara-Alecio and S. Jackson, eds., *The handbook of educational theories* (pp. 909–916). Charlotte, NC: Information Age Publishing.

Samier, E. A., 2013b. The aesthetics of leadership and administration. In B. J. Irby, G. Brown, R. Lara-Alecio and S. Jackson, eds., *The handbook of educational theories* (pp. 945–952). Charlotte, NC: Information Age Publishing.

Schwandt, T. A., 1994. Constructivist, interpretivist approaches to human inquiry. In N. K. Denzin and Y. S. Lincoln, eds., *Handbook of qualitative research* (pp. 118–137). Thousand Oaks, CA: SAGE.

Shoho, A., Merchant, B. M. and Lugg, C. A., 2005. Social justice: Seeking a common language. In F. English, ed., *The SAGE handbook of educational leadership: Advances in theory, research, and practice* (pp. 47–67). Thousand Oaks, CA: SAGE.

Woods, P. A., 2015. What is democratic leadership? In D. Griffiths and J. Portelli, eds., *Key questions for educational leaders* (pp. 85–89). Burlington, Ontario, Canada: Word and Deed Publishing Inc.

Young, M. D. and Marshall, C., 2013. Critical feminist theory. In B. Irby, G. Brown, R. Lara-Alecio and S. Jackson, eds., *The handbook of educational theories* (pp. 975–984). Charlotte, NC: Information Age Publishing.

Commentary
The rise and rise of leadership

Tony Bush

The rise of leadership

The terminology used to characterise school organisation has shifted over the past 50 years, as noted in the chapters by Lakomski and Evers and by English and Ehrich. Both chapters appear to point to the growth in importance of leadership at the expense of administration. It should also be noted that, in some contexts, including the UK, management supplanted administration as early as the early 1980s because administration in this context tends to denote routine processes. This is reflected in the gradual expansion of the title of its professional society to the *British Educational Leadership, Management and Administration Society* (BELMAS), as noted by English and Ehrich; and of its academic journal, *Educational Management, Administration and Leadership*.

The English National College for School Leadership (NCSL), founded in 2000, reinforced this shift (Bush, 2011). Plotting such changes in nomenclature is easier than explaining their significance, although the chapters by both Lakomski and Evers and English and Ehrich offer plausible, if not entirely convincing, explanations. Elsewhere (Bush, 2008), I ask if this shift is purely semantic or signals a more fundamental change in the ways in which the field is understood and practised. One fruitful line of enquiry might be changing assumptions about the link between structure and agency, and I will return to this relationship later.

Eacott's chapter argues that claims about leadership's explanatory importance go too far, while English and Ehrich comment that leadership has become the alchemy of the twenty-first century, offering the equivalent of turning lead into gold. The greater the optimism about the power of leadership to bring about school improvement, the greater the likelihood of disappointment. For leadership to succeed in this way, two sets of changes would be required. First, school principals and other leaders would need to change their behaviours to enact leadership rather than administration or management. This may be compromised by weak and contested assumptions about the differences between and among these constructs. Second, leadership would need to be enacted in ways that meet the needs of their schools and students, rather than simply following the often generic precepts found in many texts and official pronouncements.

We should note the caution expressed by Leithwood (1994) that the differences between leadership, management and administration are not easily observable in the practices of school principals. If behavioural changes are not observable, they are unlikely to be significant. Leithwood et al. (1999) also include managerial leadership in their typology, a model that is very similar to contemporary definitions of management (Bush, 2011). The reality may be that leadership is normatively preferred, as in the name chosen for the NCSL, but that practice has changed more slowly, if at all. This may also be reflected in the tightening accountability frameworks in many countries, as noted in Brooks's chapter.

Agency and structure

Traditional approaches to understanding educational organisations, variously described as systems theory (Lakomski and Evers), bureaucratic organisations (English and Ehrich) and scientific management (Brooks), have been dominant since the industrial revolution through the work of Weber (1989), although English and Ehrich, with Samier (2013), argue that the trend began in the eleventh century. Briefly, this formal model is characterised by the following features:

- A hierarchical structure
- Goal-seeking
- Rational decision-making
- Positional authority
- Vertical accountability patterns

(Bush, 2011; Bush and Glover, 2014)

Lakomski and Evers comment on the 'serious questioning' of this model, noting the powerful challenge by Greenfield (1973, 1975) in particular. There is insufficient space here to rehearse all his arguments against this orthodoxy, but Greenfield (1973, p. 553) was especially eloquent and persuasive in asking: 'what is an organisation that it can have such a thing as a goal?' However, more than 40 years later, bureaucratic assumptions about goals remain dominant, re-emerging as 'mission statements' or 'the school's vision' (Hoyle and Wallace, 2005).

In practice, such organisational goals tend to reflect the personal aims and values of senior members of the school, notably those of the principal. This view leads to consideration of the relationship between structure and agency. In the bureaucratic model, the structure is paramount, reflected in organisational charts, as Lakomski and Evers note. These figures are almost always vertical and are remarkably similar across national contexts. One central assumption underpinning such representations is that people are subordinate to the structure and that principal agency is limited. Little change is expected as one post-holder replaces another. Power accrues to principals because of their position, not because of their personal qualities.

Much leadership theory, in contrast, stresses and often celebrates the personal characteristics of the principal. This leads some writers, including English and Ehrich, to assert that 'leadership remains individualistic', although they comment that this is rank based, suggesting that hierarchy remains important. Much of the literature stresses that principals should act in ways that are consistent with their values, professional and personal, and that these should anchor leadership practice. Because leaders differ in numerous ways, including background, experience, gender, ethnicity and religion, they are thought to perceive events differently, leading to potentially different responses to events, problems and situations (Bush, 2011). The difficulty with this analysis is that it underestimates the accountability pressures associated with high-stakes testing, often treated by administrators and politicians as 'a viable proxy for student learning', as Brooks notes. Even in ostensibly decentralised systems, leadership is constrained by systemic mandates and imperatives.

School-based management

Most education systems remain highly centralised, notably in Africa, Asia and Eastern Europe. Such systems have a central education ministry and one or more administrative levels, depending on the size of the population. The People's Republic of China, with 375,000 schools, understandably has a more complex structure than the Republic of Seychelles, which has only 33. Most of the major decisions, including curriculum, staffing and budgets, are made outside the school. In such contexts, the main role of school principals is to implement policy, with limited scope to interpret or contextualise top-down decisions. Bureaucracy, with its vertical hierarchies, is helpful in understanding how schools operate within such centralised systems.

Lakomski and Evers note the rise of school-based management in many jurisdictions from the 1980s onwards, with greater autonomy for school decision-making. While the details vary across systems, decentralisation typically involves devolving powers over staffing, financial and real resources, and student admissions, to the school level. The UK, for example, with its landmark Education Reform Act (1988), enabled schools to develop their own budgets, appoint their own staff and determine their own admissions policies. Funding was largely based on student numbers, enabling schools to budget with a degree of confidence, as most students stay in their school for several years. Legally, powers were devolved to school governing bodies, but in practice, the scope for leadership and management was greatly extended.

As Lakomski and Evers note, traditional theories are weak in explaining how schools operate within this more distributed model. The enhanced scope for principals provides much greater potential for leadership agency and, arguably, diminishes the role of formal structures. It also increases the potential for leaders to differentiate their schools from their competitors in order to enhance their appeal to parents. The neo-liberal assumption is that competition leads to higher standards, although empirical support for this contention is limited (but see the Organisation for Economic Co-operation and Development [OECD], 1994). It is likely that the growing significance of leadership, in contrast to administration and management, is connected to decentralisation and, certainly, the two developments occurred at broadly the same time.

Leadership models

The normative shift towards leadership has led to a plethora of different, and competing, explanations about the nature of leadership, sometimes caricatured as 'adjectival' leadership. Several of these models are mentioned in the four chapters in this section but, perhaps surprisingly, they are not prominent features of the discussion. Brooks argues that leadership is characterised as a 'loosely coupled' set of fields rather than a coherent corpus of enquiry, and this is an implicit recognition of the different models prevailing in educational leadership. I will briefly review some of these models, drawing on Leithwood et al. (1999), Bush (2011 and 2015) and Bush and Glover (2014). Crawford (2012) distinguishes between solo and shared models, and I will structure this section in this way.

Solo leadership models

I noted earlier that English and Ehrich maintain that leadership is individualistic, but there are several different solo models. I review some of these in this sub-section.

Managerial leadership

As noted earlier, Leithwood et al. (1999) include managerial leadership as one of five models in their typology. It assumes that the focus of leaders ought to be on functions, tasks and behaviours and that, if these functions are carried out competently, the work of others in the organisation will be facilitated. Most approaches to managerial leadership also assume that the behaviour of organisational members is largely rational. Influence accrues largely because of the formal authority of leaders, and Leithwood et al. (1999) argue that influence is allocated in proportion to the status of those positions in the organisational hierarchy. They also note that 'positional power, in combination with formal policies and procedures, is the source of influence exercised by managerial leadership' (Leithwood et al., 1999, p. 17).

One difficulty with this leadership model is that it scarcely differs from management, suggesting that the differences between the two constructs may be exaggerated. This form of leadership appears to be well suited to the highly centralised education systems discussed earlier. One of the main problems is the danger of managerialism, where there may be value-free management, focusing on efficiency for its own sake – what Hoyle and Wallace (2005, p. 68) describe as 'management to excess'.

Transformational leadership

Lakomski and Evers argue that transformational leadership 'became the standard model for schools' where leaders had to implement school-based management, citing Caldwell and Spinks (1992) in support of this claim. This model assumes that the central focus of leadership ought to be the commitments and capacities of organisational members. Higher levels of personal commitment to organisational goals and greater capacities for accomplishing those goals are assumed to result in extra effort and greater productivity (Leithwood et al., 1999, p. 9).

Because so many aspects of organisation are school-centred in devolved systems, staff and stakeholders are likely to seek guidance and direction from internal leaders, especially the principal, rather than external bodies. Much of the visionary rhetoric associated with leadership arises from this model, as leaders are expected to inspire followers to perform at higher levels as they commit to what are presented as school goals. Leithwood's (1994, p. 506) research suggests that there is some empirical support for the essentially normative transformational leadership model, but critics (e.g. Allix, 2000) argue that it may lead to manipulation, or be 'despotic', because of its heroic and charismatic features. English and Ehrich stress that they do not endorse 'the hero leader', but this may be seen as a likely outcome of a successful attempt to inspire followers.

The transformational model stresses the importance of values but the debate about its validity relates to the central question of 'whose values?' Critics of this approach argue that the decisive values are often those of government or of the school principal, who may be acting on behalf of government. Educational values, as held and practiced by teachers, may be subjugated to internally or externally imposed values.

Transactional leadership

Transactional leadership is often contrasted with transformational approaches (Bush, 2011; Miller and Miller, 2001). Transactions involve an exchange process between leaders and followers. At the most basic level of transaction, followers offer educational services, including teaching, assessment and student welfare, in exchange for salaries and other rewards. Principals may also seek the cooperation of staff and offer rewards, such as promotion or supportive references, in exchange. The major problem with this model is that it does not engage followers beyond the issue that is the subject of the exchange.

Eacott's discussion of relational leadership notes that it has been used synonymously with transactional approaches. However, he also argues that relational approaches foreground social relations leading to theoretically inscribed descriptions of situated action. This seems to connect with Spillane's (2005) view that distributed leadership focuses on interactions rather than actions. Eacott seeks to 'disrupt' the dominant epistemologies and methodologies of educational administration but, as I suggest below, dominance is also temporal, as previously favoured models decline as new ideas take hold. Eacott's claim that educational administration journals and conferences are somewhat devoid of debate is also contentious, although his subsequent point that leadership classifications may be adopted uncritically is valid. The search for a 'magic bullet' that will secure school improvement is a naïve fallacy.

Moral and authentic leadership

The conceptualisation of leadership discussed earlier stresses the importance of professional and personal values. This is a distinctive feature of moral leadership, which assumes that the critical focus of leadership ought to be on the leaders' values, beliefs and ethics (Leithwood et al., 1999). Several other terms have also been used to describe values-based leadership, including spiritual leadership (Woods, 2007). The latter may be particularly evident in faith schools but could also arise in secular settings.

The concept of authentic leadership has grown in significance but essentially covers similar ground to that of moral leadership. Begley (2007, p. 163) defines it as 'a metaphor for professionally effective, ethically sound and consciously reflective practices'. Moral and authentic leadership are underpinned strongly by leaders' values. The models assume that leaders act with integrity, drawing on firmly held personal and professional values. These serve to inform the school's vision and mission and to underpin decision-making.

Shared leadership models

The models discussed above are essentially about individual (usually principal) leadership. However, despite English and Ehrich's assertion that leadership 'remains individualistic', there have been several approaches that seek to widen the debate to include shared approaches to leadership. Crawford (2012) notes the shift from solo to shared leadership and attributes this, in part, to well-documented failures of high-profile 'superheads' in England, leading to scepticism about individual, or 'heroic', leadership.

Several shared models have been advanced in the literature, including collegiality, once described as 'the official model of good practice' (Wallace, 1989) in England; and teacher leadership (Frost, 2008). Leithwood et al. (1999) include participative leadership as one of the five models in their typology derived from scrutiny of four leading journals. In the twenty-first century, however, the most favoured shared model is that of distributed leadership.

Distributed leadership

Distributed leadership has become the normatively preferred leadership model in the twenty-first century. Gronn (2010, p. 70) states that 'there has been an accelerating amount of scholarly and practitioner attention accorded [to] the phenomenon of distributed leadership'. An important starting point for understanding distributed leadership is to uncouple it from positional authority. As Harris (2004, p. 13) indicates, 'distributed leadership concentrates on engaging expertise wherever it exists within the organization rather than seeking this only through formal position or role'.

Gronn (2010, p. 70) refers to a normative switch 'from heroics to distribution' but also cautions against a view that distributed leadership necessarily means any reduction in the scope of the principal's role. Heads and principals retain much of the formal authority in schools, leading Hartley (2010, p. 82) to conclude that 'distributed leadership resides uneasily within the formal bureaucracy of schools'. Harris (2005, p. 167) argues that 'distributed and hierarchical forms of leadership are not incompatible' but it is evident that distribution can work successfully only if formal leaders allow it to take root.

Leithwood et al.'s (2006) important English study shows that multiple leadership is much more effective than solo approaches. Total leadership accounted for a quite significant 27 per cent variation in student achievement across schools. This is a much higher proportion of explained variation (two to three times higher) than is typically reported in studies of individual headteacher effects. Hallinger and Heck (2010) also found that distributed leadership was significantly related to change in academic capacity and thus to growth in student learning.

As suggested earlier, the existing authority structure in schools and colleges provides a potential barrier to the successful introduction and implementation of distributed leadership. As Lakomski and Evers note, the school principal is legally, and arguably morally, responsible for everything that goes on in the school. Fitzgerald and Gunter (2008) also refer to the residual significance of authority and hierarchy and note the 'dark side' of distributed leadership – managerialism in a new guise. Gronn's (2010, p. 77) 'hybrid' model of leadership may offer the potential to harness the best of both individual and distributed approaches. English and Ehrich argue that distributed leadership represents a different division of labour in formal organisations, but this also links to the distinction made, for example by Bolden et al. (2009), between allocative distribution, which may align with formal structures; and emergent distribution, which may arise from anywhere in the organisation and suggests much looser relationships.

Distributed leadership provides the most significant contemporary example of the nature of theory in educational leadership. To what extent is theory a representation of practice (description), and to what extent does it constitute advocacy, a normative perspective? Lumby (2013, p. 582) comments that discussion of distributed leadership as a heuristic tool gave way to an evangelical approach, for example in NCSL publications. Distributed leadership is popular, in part, because it accords with the notion that values should be shared by teacher professionals and other adults in the schools. Difficulties arise when the assumption of shared values is contradicted by the reality of conflicting values. Distributed leadership is the most recent model to be subject to a strongly normative approach – 'the theory of choice for many' (Lumby, 2013, p. 581).

Contingent leadership

The models of leadership examined here are all partial. They provide valid and helpful insights into one particular aspect of leadership. None of these models, however, provide a complete picture of school leadership. As Lambert (1995, p. 2) notes, there is 'no single best type'. The contingent model provides an alternative approach, recognising the diverse nature of school contexts and the advantages of adapting leadership styles to the particular situation rather than adopting a 'one size fits all' stance. Lakomski and Evers make a similar point, noting that leadership theories should be seen as context dependent. However, Eacott argues that leadership as a construct is 'beyond context' and 'devoid of grounding in time and space'. These apparently irreconcilable positions may be aligned through the recognition that some normative approaches to leadership assume that 'good' leaders can operate equally well regardless of context. This is evidenced in the English government's plans to offer rewards to headteachers who are willing to move to challenging inner-city or coastal contexts, regardless of whether they have had previous experience of working in such settings. English and Ehrich are right to comment that a change of leader is often seen as the 'alchemy' for poor and failing schools 'irrespective of the evidence'. (This text, p. 49)

The prevalence of so many leadership models provides the 'raw material' for a contingent approach and demonstrates the pluralist nature of the field, with more voices and perspectives (English and Ehrich). However, Brooks goes beyond this to claim that the field is 'fractured' rather than pluralist, leading to disjointed lines of inquiry. This is open to debate, but it is possible to argue that evangelical adherence to particular models limits the potential for coherence.

Leadership and learning

There is wide recognition that a focus on managing teaching and learning is essential for school leaders. This is reflected in leadership theory through the well-established instructional leadership model. Hallinger (1992) argues that this had become the 'new orthodoxy' by the mid-1980s. It became discredited and superseded by other models because it focused mainly on the role of principals, neglecting other leaders; and also because the main emphasis was on teaching (instruction) rather than learning (Bush, 2011). However, the recognition that leaders should engage with learning led to instructional leadership being 'reincarnated' as 'leadership for learning' in the twenty-first century (Hallinger and Heck, 2010) but as a shared function.

Robinson's (2007) meta-analysis of published research shows that the nature of the leader's role has a significant impact on learning outcomes. Direct leader involvement in curriculum planning and professional development is associated with moderate or large leadership effects. 'This suggests that the closer leaders are to the core business of teaching and learning, the more likely they are to make a difference to students' (Robinson 2007, p. 21). This finding indicates that instructional leadership effects are much greater than those of other leadership models.

Given Robinson's evidence, it is surprising that Brooks claims that educational leadership theories often do not include or connect in any way to student learning processes and outcomes and often have only a tenuous connection to teaching, citing an old (1986) source in support of this argument. While the term *often* is open to interpretation, this claim seems to be inaccurate, as is his argument that 'we can say very little about the relationship between leadership and learning'. His assertion that only a 'paltry' amount of work has been devoted to understanding student learning and leadership behaviour is polemical and not supported by the evidence. He is on stronger ground in stating that standardised test outcomes are not a viable proxy for student learning.

Conclusion: Leadership as a normative construct

Concepts of administration and of management have been joined or superseded by the language of leadership, but the activities undertaken by principals and senior staff resist such labels. School principals face unprecedented accountability pressures in many countries in what is clearly an increasingly 'results driven' business. As these environmental pressures intensify, leaders and managers require greater understanding, skill and resilience to sustain their institutions. Headteachers, principals and senior staff need an appreciation of the theory, as well as the practice, of educational management.

Theory is one of the four essential building blocks of school leadership. Alongside policy, research and practice, it provides helpful insights into how schools are led and managed. The theory of leadership is important for two main reasons. First, it provides a way of understanding and interpreting the actions of leaders. Second, understanding theory provides a guide to leadership practice for principals and other leaders. It widens horizons and avoids drawing only on the inevitably limited individual or collective experience of any school's leaders.

I noted earlier that leadership theory is subject to fashion and that models increase and decrease in perceived importance over time. The reasons for such changes are not always apparent, but one way of understanding them is through explicit recognition of the normative basis of leadership models, as noted by Eacott and by Brooks. Eacott's comments about the pre-existing normative assumptions of the researcher and the ideological nature of leadership language help us to recognise the fallacy of relying on a single approach as the elixir for school improvement. As with managerial, collegial and transformational approaches at different times in the last century, distributed leadership has become the normatively preferred leadership model in the twenty-first century. Its endorsement by the NCSL confirms this preference in the English context.

The four chapters in this section all question the dominance of leadership as the default option for explaining organisational activity or, in Lakomski and Evers' language, 'the explanatory model of first resort'. Recent research (Leithwood et al., 2006; Robinson, 2007) has raised expectations about the potential for leadership to explain and to bring about school improvement. The chapters question several aspects of the significance attributed to this phenomenon. First, it tends to exaggerate its importance. Leadership is not alchemy (English and Ehrich) or an elixir, and we need to know much more about how and why some leaders appear to be successful while others are not. This may relate to individual variables or to a lack of 'fit' between the leaders and school contexts, as will be discussed here.

The second consideration relates to the current dominance of 'leadership' at the expense of 'administration' and 'management' in the language of organisations. Leithwood (1994) and Bush (2008) both cast doubt on whether such changes are substantive or simply semantic. Questioning the normative preference for leadership, as both Brooks and Eacott do, is helpful. We need to know more about what distinguishes leadership from these alternative descriptors in understanding and practicing headship.

The third issue concerns the almost bewildering number of different leadership models, each promoted by their advocates as the 'best' way to lead schools, often with little evidence to support such claims. The rise and fall of these models, for example, from managerial to instructional to transformational to distributed, over the past four decades suggests frustration as each once-fashionable model fails to achieve what was claimed for it and is then superseded by the latest fad without a solid body of research to explain the limitations of the once-preferred approach. The currently popular distributed leadership is coming under closer scrutiny, leading to notions of hybridity (Gronn, 2010) or allocative distribution (Bolden et al., 2009) as theorists try to find an accommodation between distribution and the enduring power of managerial leadership.

The fourth factor, foregrounded by Eacott and by Lakomski and Evers, is that leadership is often uncoupled from context by those who make extravagant claims for its potency. Policy-makers may then simply assume that moving 'successful' leaders to underperforming schools will turn them around. However, much of the evidence, for example from the English NCSL, is that context is vitally important and that a 'fit' between school and leader is essential.

Contingent leadership acknowledges the diverse nature of school contexts and the advantages of adapting leadership styles to the particular situation rather than adopting a 'one size fits all' stance. The educational context is too complex and unpredictable for a single leadership approach to be adopted for all events and issues. Contingent leadership is pragmatic rather than principled but provides a helpful way to avoid excessive dependency on the latest 'fad' and to enable leaders to assess what works best for the specific context. Claims about the universal utility of leadership theory should be challenged. As Eacott notes, leadership is not 'beyond context'.

The four chapters each contribute to an overdue debate about the value of leadership theory as a vehicle for explaining school practice. By questioning current assumptions about the efficacy of leadership as a broad construct and the claims associated with specific models, the authors provide a helpful caution. Sustainable improvement in school and student learning cannot be achieved by unquestioning adherence to a particular approach but only through mature understanding that educational change requires situational analysis, leading to grounded action and careful evaluation of the effects of such interventions.

References

Allix, N., 2000. Transformational leadership: Democratic or despotic, *Educational Management and Administration*, 28(1), pp. 7–20.

Begley, P. T., 2007. Editorial Introduction: Cross-cultural perspectives on authentic school leadership. *Educational Management, Administration and Leadership*, 35(2), pp. 163–164.

Bolden, R., Petrov, G. and Gosling, J., 2009. Distributed leadership: Rhetoric and reality. *Educational Management, Administration and Leadership*, 37(2), pp. 257–277.

Bush, T., 2008. From management to leadership: Semantic or meaningful change? *Educational Management, Administration and Leadership*, 36(2), pp. 271–288.

Bush, T., 2011. *Theories of educational leadership and management.* Fourth edition. London: SAGE.

Bush, T., 2015. Organisational theory in education: How does it inform school leadership? *Journal of Organizational Theory in Education*, 1(1), pp. 35–47.

Bush, T. and Glover, D., 2014. School leadership models: What do we know? *Journal of School Leadership and Management*, 34(5), pp. 553–571.

Caldwell, B. and Spinks, J., 1992. *Leading the self-managing school.* London: Falmer Press.

Crawford, M., 2012. Solo and distributed leadership: Definitions and dilemmas. *Educational Management, Administration and Leadership*, 40(5), pp. 610–620.

Fitzgerald, T. and Gunter, H., 2008. Contesting the orthodoxy of teacher leadership. *International Journal of Leadership in Education*, 11(4), pp. 331–340.

Frost, D., 2008. Teacher leadership: Values and voice. *School Leadership and Management*, 28(4), pp. 337–352.

Greenfield, T., 1973. Organisations as social inventions: Rethinking assumptions about change. *Journal of Applied Behavioural Science*, 9(5), pp. 551–574.

Greenfield, T., 1975. Theory of organisations: A new perspective and its implications for schools. In M. Hughes, ed., *Administering education: international challenge.* London: Athlone Press.

Gronn, P., 2010. Where to next for educational leadership? In T. Bush, L. Bell and D. Middlewood, eds., *The principles of educational leadership and management.* London: Sage.

Hallinger, P., 1992. The evolving role of American principals: From managerial to instructional to transformational leaders. *Journal of Educational Administration*, 30(3), pp. 35–48.

Hallinger, P. and Heck, R., 2010. Leadership for learning: Does collaborative leadership make a difference in student learning? *Educational Management, Administration and Leadership*, 38(6), pp. 654–678.

Harris, A., 2004. Distributed leadership and school improvement: Leading or misleading? *Educational Management, Administration and Leadership*, 32(1), pp. 11–24.

Harris, A., 2005. Distributed leadership. In B. Davies, ed., *The essentials of school leadership.* London: Paul Chapman.

Hartley, D., 2010. Paradigms: How far does research in distributed leadership 'stretch'? *Educational Management, Administration and Leadership*, 38(3), pp. 271–285.

Hoyle, E. and Wallace, M., 2005. *Educational leadership: Ambiguity, professionals and managerialism.* London: Sage.

Lambert, L., 1995. New directions in the preparation of educational leaders. *Thrust for Educational Leadership*, 24(5), pp. 6–10.

Leithwood, K., 1994. Leadership for school restructuring. *Educational Administration Quarterly*, 30(4), pp. 498–518.

Leithwood, K., Day, C., Sammons, P., Harris, A. and Hopkins, D., 2006. *Seven strong claims about successful school leadership.* London: DfES.

Leithwood, K., Jantzi, D. and Steinbach, R., 1999. *Changing leadership for changing times.* Buckingham: Open University Press.

Lumby, J., 2013. Distributed leadership: The uses and abuses of power. *Educational Management, Administration and Leadership*, 41(5), pp. 581–597.

Miller, T. and Miller, J., 2001. Educational leadership in the new millennium: A vision for 2020. *International Journal of Leadership in Education*, 4(2), pp. 181–189.

Organisation for Economic Cooperation and Development, 1994. *Effectiveness of schooling and educational resource management*. Synthesis of Country Studies, Paris: OECD.

Robinson, V., 2007. School leadership and student outcomes: Identifying what works and why. Winmalee, NSW: Australian Council of Leaders.

Samier, E., 2013. Bureaucratic theory: Myths, theories, models, critiques. In B. Irby, G. Brown, R. Lara-Alecio and S. Jackson, eds., *The handbook of educational theories*. Charlotte, NC: Information Age Publishing.

Spillane, J., 2005. Distributed leadership. *The Education Forum*, 69, pp. 143–150.

Wallace, M., 1989. Towards a collegiate approach to curriculum management in primary and middle schools. In M. Preedy, ed., *Approaches to curriculum management*. Buckingham: Open University Press.

Weber, M., 1989. Legal authority in a bureaucracy. In T. Bush, ed., *Managing education: Theory and practice*. Buckingham: Open University Press.

Woods, G., 2007. The 'bigger feeling': the importance of spiritual experience in educational leadership. *Educational Management, Administration and Leadership*, 35(1), pp. 135–155.

Part II

Postmodernist perspectives on leadership

5 Zombie ~~leadership~~, a *différend* and deconstruction

Richard Niesche

Introduction

How do you kill a concept that will not die? Killing a zombie is relatively easy … simply cut off its head. However, a dubious concept such as 'leadership', which has been constructed via numerous intersecting discourses, is not so easy (or even desirable to many scholars in the field of educational leadership, management and administration). In thinking about the problems associated with the term *leadership* – for example, its requisite instrumentalism, exceptional individualism, selling of best practice models, incestuous repetitive adjectival approaches, performative standards–based discourses – these discourses of leadership refuse to die. They are the 'living dead' of educational leadership and continue to spread quicker than the plague of zombies on *The Walking Dead*[1]! The metaphor of the zombie seems appropriate for these relentless, uncritical, unreflective and often mindless movements of scholarship, a leadership industry that cannot – nor, it often seems, desires to – transition away from particularly narrow modes of thinking. The field of cultural studies, for example, has frequently used the metaphor of the zombie to highlight the anxieties and malaise of our current cultural and social troubles (see Dendle, 2007; Stratton, 2011). Of course, this may seem like an overly playful and extravagant analogy to which to compare leadership; however, there is also a serious point to be made concerning the problematic nature of the field.

The field of education has also had a longstanding fascination with the notion of leadership. Lauren Berlant's notion of cruel optimism (Berlant, 2011, p. 1) is useful here for framing and understanding some of this obsession. She argues that 'a relation of cruel optimism exists when something you desire is actually an obstacle to your flourishing'. The desire to describe human activity as a form of leadership that adequately represents the link to organisational outcomes or success is a relation of cruel optimism in the sense that this relentless desire impedes the initial aim of capturing all there is to know about that activity. The complexity of factors at work makes this link between the 'leadership' of an individual and organisational outcomes almost impossible to ascertain (no matter what some scholars may claim). As a result, the field of educational leadership is at an *impasse* that it cannot see through (Berlant, 2011, p. 4). Further to Berlant's earlier claim, she says that cruel optimism is also the condition of maintaining an attachment to a significantly problematic object (Berlant, 2011, p. 24). There is still a need to understand how such a term is problematic in the way it is conceptualised and being put to use. In order to understand this condition, I am putting to work the ideas of both Foucault and Derrida to unsettle this attachment to leadership as a concept.

While there have already been numerous excellent critiques of the kinds of leadership discourses I have referred to here, as well as an acknowledgement of the marginalisation of more critical perspectives, I will not focus on those here. My focus instead is on how we can respond to the difficulties and problems with continuing to use the term *leadership*. In thinking about this issue, I propose to point out what Jean François Lyotard would term a *différend* (Lyotard, 1988) between two possible responses. A first response is the idea that we must do away with or not mention the word *leadership*. While in practice this would be a difficult undertaking, it would still be possible to feel the *trace* (Derrida, 1973) of the word *leadership* at work, and this is what provoked elements of this chapter as I seek to engage with the term *leadership* while at the same time acknowledging its limitations.

This leads me to a second response (and the one I favour in this chapter), which could be the act of deconstructing ~~leadership~~², or engaging with and using the term in order that its problematisation (Foucault, 1996a) and deconstructions (Derrida, 1997) can be seen. I believe there is a *différend* (Lyotard, 1988) between these two responses, statements or phrases. By this, Lyotard refers to the notion that the rules and genres of discourse applicable to each phrase are not commensurable; that is, there is a lack of a rule of judgement between the two, resulting in a *différend*. This incommensurability between statements indicates that there is no form of judgement that can accommodate both sets of concerns. It is this *différend* that is the impetus for this chapter although not necessarily its object. In summary, my argument as a response to this problematisation of leadership as a term and discourse is to argue that one needs to use the language and discourse of leadership in order for a witnessing of its deconstruction to occur. This chapter is then divided into two main sections: first, I explore Michel Foucault's notion of problematisation in relation to leadership discourse; and second, I draw on Jacques Derrida's approach to deconstruction to indicate an awareness of the limitations of what leadership can and does represent. By developing these perspectives (and I am keenly aware of the differences and tensions between the two approaches; however, I am not using them to form a coherent approach to leadership but more to outline two possible interventions into working with the term *leadership* while also acknowledging the problematics of doing so), it may then be possible to seek genuinely different alternatives for understanding and capturing particular behaviours, practices and actions in organisations. That is, it is possible to create a discursive space for different approaches to the range of models currently 'on the market'.

Problematising zombie leadership

When Michel Foucault contemplated the 'death of man' along with the emergence of the human sciences in the nineteenth century, he was referring to the constitution of man as an object of knowledge and the coinciding failure of the discovery of a human nature, human essence or essential human feature (Foucault, 2002a). The following is illustrative of Foucault's point:

> In the course of their history, men have never ceased to construct themselves, that is, to continually displace their subjectivity, to constitute themselves in an infinite, multiple series of different subjectivities that will never have an end and never bring us in the presence of something that would be "man". Men are perpetually engaged in a process that, in constituting objects, at the same displaces man, deforms, transforms, and transfigures him as a subject.
>
> (Foucault, 2002b, p. 276)

The notion of 'the death of man' is one that must cause great pain to many leadership scholars, as much of the effort in this field has been directed towards finding this essence of leadership (Lawler, 2005), this essence of man. The death of the 'leader', or 'leadership' as a concept, is also one that is difficult to accept, but it points more to the idea of the concept, the particular rules of discourse that no longer live and speak for themselves. Leadership has become so meaningless that, as I and others have argued elsewhere (Gronn, 2003; Kelly, 2008; Niesche, 2013), we must consider the death of leadership before we can properly consider alternatives. Foucault famously said that one needs 'to cut off the king's head' in terms of an analysis of power (1980, p. 121). That is, an individual does not hold power. It is not a thing but a relation between individuals or groups of individuals. It is not simply top down (i.e. sovereign power) or held by an individual but exercised at innumerable points through a range of practices and strategies. In order to kill a zombie, one must cut off its head or severely damage the brain (according to whichever popular culture source you refer to!). We need to cut off the head of zombie leadership in order to think differently about leadership. Leadership is not the proviso of an individual and is not solely exercised at the head of an organisation. Foucault's analysis of power is helpful in this regard. That is, it is necessary to problematise the top-down analysis of power as a form of leadership[3] (see Gillies, 2013; Niesche, 2011).

Gabriele Lakomski's provocative work (Lakomski, 2005), while also critical of many of the poststructuralist ideas I draw upon, speaks to these critiques of leadership in proposing that leadership accounts for little in the functioning of organisations, and the constant drive for a causal link between the actions of individuals and outcomes is misguided and flawed. Others have critiqued this leadership drive over the years (Kelly, 2008; Pfeffer, 1977; Kerr and Jermier, 1977) and even more recently there have still been those who would proclaim the end of leadership (Kellerman, 2012). What this points to is dissatisfaction with the conceptualisation, development and use of the term *leadership* to describe the behaviours, actions and practices of individuals.

It is also important to point out that there has been an extensive history of critique or critical approaches to educational leadership. While there has been a relentless drive for positivist accounts of leaders' work, best-practice models, standards frameworks and the like, there has concurrently been a range of more critical perspectives on these instrumentalist approaches. Some of these include gender in the form of feminist critiques (Blackmore, 1999; Halford and Leonard, 2001; Hall, 1996; Lambert, 2007); those exploring equity, diversity and social justice (Anderson, 2009; Blackmore, 2006, 2008; Smyth, 2008, 2011; Wilkinson, 2008); postmodern and poststructuralist critiques (English, 2002; Niesche, 2011, 2013; Maxcy, 1994); critiques of the standards movements (Anderson, 2001; English, 2000, 2003, 2006); critiques of portraits of headship (Thomson, 2009); critiques of heroicism and methodological individualism (Evers and Lakomski, 2013; Gronn, 2003); critiques of the 'what works' phenomenon (Gorard, 2005; Gunter 2001, 2011); and the over-reliance on prescriptive, adjectival models (Eacott, 2011). This list is not meant to be exhaustive by any means but serves to highlight some of the important work that has been done and continues to be done to bring a range of theories and critical tools to the study of leadership in education.

When explaining his overall approach and body of work, Foucault often used the term *problematisation*. For Foucault, problematisation refers to studying the history of problems in specific fields, to question the meanings, conditions and goals of certain ideas and practices. It is a movement of critical analysis that tries to see how different solutions to problems have been constructed and also how these different solutions result from specific forms of problematisation (Foucault, 1996b). For example, in *Madness and Civilization*, Foucault examined how and why madness had been problematised through particular institutional practices at a specific point in time; in *Discipline and Punish*, he analysed the problematisation of carceral institutions in the late eighteenth century; and in the three volumes of *The History of Sexuality*, he problematised the multiplication of discourses surrounding sexuality in various societies. Foucault was also quick to point out that problematisation is not concerned with a pre-existent object but rather the 'set of discursive or non-discursive practices that makes something enter into the play of the true and false, and constitutes it as an object for thought' (Foucault, 1996c, pp. 456–457).

Therefore, moving this notion of problematisation into the realm of educational leadership would entail exploring the practices that construct leadership as a concept to be used in describing the link between the individual and organisational processes and outcomes. Such an approach is not concerned with building models of good practice or good leadership but rather examining how leadership is mobilised in different ways in the formation of particular truths and also questioning the assumptions underlying such discursive practices. For example, Foucault's work can help us to understand how school leaders are inserted into sets of power relations whereby they are both the targets of power and governance and also the vehicles though which power operates (see Gobby, 2013; Niesche and Keddie, 2015; Thompson and Mockler, 2015). These are not just abstract investigations; they analyse leadership from specific practices at the points where people are constituted as subjects and grasp the minutiae of the relationship between power and knowledge formation (Niesche and Gowlett, 2015). This is important work for opening up spaces of contestation and discussion rather than closing down debates through the identification of leadership as specific adjectival models and other forms of representation such as standards.

Deconstructing zombie leadership

To reiterate the point I made at the start of the chapter, if we are unhappy with the term ~~leadership~~, then the choices are to avoid it or to use it while knowingly engaging with its problems in order to witness the occurrence of its deconstruction. Going back to the terms *administration* or *management* as the key terms is also difficult as not only have the distinctions between these three terms proven difficult and problematic, but the re-insertion of this terminology would now leave a *trace* of ~~leadership~~ with their use. The entire history of the study of leadership has been the search for a fixed origin, a centring, of presence. However, thinking with Derrida, one can consider the 'centre' (or human essence of ~~leadership~~ via various adjectival models) as a series of substitutions of centre for centre (see Niesche, 2013). This serves to displace the centring of ~~leadership~~ as *the* term or concept that describes such human activity. Let me explain a little more.

Deconstruction

Jacques Derrida is most commonly associated with the term *deconstruction*, which usually refers to a form of critical or close reading and analysis[4] that offers an interpretation of Western metaphysics, including the Western philosophical tradition, as well as everyday thought and language (Johnson, 1981, p. viii). The term *deconstruction* is often misused and represented to refer to a method or a set of conventions or rules to be applied. Deconstruction occurs or 'takes place' (Derrida, 1991, p. 273) when texts are opened up by careful reading and scrutiny. Deconstruction works in identifying the contradictions of logic within a text, exploring those assumptions that are often taken for granted and meaning in relation to the author and the intended audience.

Derrida's philosophy is difficult to capture as he explored the works of other philosophers such as Plato, Aristotle, Descartes, Kant, Hegel, Rousseau, Marx, Heidegger, Husserl and Nietzsche, amongst others. His very close readings of these philosophers' work make an engagement with his ideas difficult in the absence of a significant familiarity with this larger body of theory. Nevertheless, Derrida was largely concerned with metaphysics, which he sees as being associated with structures of language that determine being as presence. It is through *logocentrism* that this structuring of language works to make sense of the world. For example, Derrida argues that Western metaphysical thought seeks to provide stability to meaning through such language structures as binaries like presence/absence, nature/culture, speech/writing, good/evil, man/woman, leader/follower, true/false, normal/abnormal, being/nothing, mind/body and so on. It is through these systems of signs that words have meaning. That is, they form a stable platform on which to make sense of the world. These dualisms work with a privileging of the first term over the second. It is this structural hierarchy that Derrida seeks to challenge. The second term of the binary is usually considered in relation to the first as a form of negative or lacking. In the example of speech/ writing, *logocentrism* is that which gives preference to speech over writing. To counter this privileged position of speech over writing, Derrida developed a new science of writing: grammatology (Derrida, 1997). Derrida is concerned with inserting instability into this structuring, not a reversing of the binary. He does this by developing new concepts such as *différance* and *trace*.

Différance

One of the concepts Derrida uses to disrupt our use of language and to explore the limits of language's ability to signify concepts is the notion of *différance*. *Différance* is used to both blur the lines of sense by separating different significations as well as at the same time binding some together. In French, the verb 'to differ' (*différer*) has two meanings. The first indicates a distinction, while the second refers to a deferring or putting off till later. Derrida uses the *a* in *différance* to link the common root between the two meanings, as the word sounds similar whether it has an *e* or an *a*. That is, the difference between the two spellings is written but not heard. Derrida uses this to argue how phonetic writing is poorly described by the concept of signs and that one must resort to writing, and not speech, to mark the difference. *Différance* both describes and performs the deferral of language.

Trace

For Derrida, language is a play of forces that, according to Western metaphysics, seeks to structure language around a process of centring, such as through binaries, as I mentioned earlier. It is this centring that needs to be deconstructed:

> The function of this center was not only to orient, balance, and organize the structure – one cannot in fact conceive of an unorganized structure – but above all to make sure that the organizing principle of the structure would limit what we might call the *play* of the structure…the center also closes off the play which it opens up and makes possible. As center, it is the point at which the substitution of contents, elements, or terms is no longer possible.
>
> (Derrida, 1978, pp. 178–179)

Derrida argues that the centre is simply an endless chain of signifiers that do not designate an ultimate truth of representation but a *trace* in the form of absence of presence. The meaning of signs is only understood in terms of their difference from other signs, that is, a displaced presence that functions as a form of anti-structuralism. As Derrida writes:

> The trace is not a presence but is rather the simulacrum of a presence that dis-locates, displaces, and refers beyond itself. The trace has, properly speaking,

no place, for effacement belongs to the very structure of the trace…in this way the metaphysical text is understood; it is still readable, and remains read.

(Derrida, 1973, p. 156)

The idea of *trace* then presents a way of undoing structures as it challenges the temporality of making meaning from structures of language. Derrida is also clear to point out that his 'critique' of metaphysics is not from a position exterior to metaphysics. This is where I think Derrida's work may be helpful for making the case for using the term ~~leadership~~ in order for its deconstructions to occur. As Derrida states,

> There is no sense in doing without the concepts of metaphysics in order to shake metaphysics. We have no language – no syntax and no lexicon – which is foreign to this history; we can pronounce not a single destructive proposition which has not already had to slip into the form, the logic, and the implicit postulations of precisely what it seeks to contest.
>
> (Derrida, 1978, p. 280)

This is why Derrida draws extensively on particular texts for his deconstructions to highlight the inherent problems within these texts to achieve what they claim. For example, in *Of Grammatology*, Derrida deconstructs Rousseau's work in a detailed, long and painstaking reading; in *Dissemination*, Derrida explores Plato; and in numerous other texts, he deconstructs the writings of Hegel, Saussure and Husserl. It is within these texts themselves that Derrida's deconstructions work, and it is within the educational ~~leadership~~ texts that similar deconstructions must also work. In order to witness these deconstructions in action, we must retain the concept of ~~leadership~~ and strive to reveal the tensions from within:

> The movements of deconstruction do not destroy structures from the outside. They are not possible and effective, nor can they take accurate aim, except by inhabiting those structures. Inhabiting them *in a certain way*, because one always inhabits, and all the more when one does not suspect it. Operating necessarily from the inside, borrowing all the strategic and economic resources of subversion from the old structure, borrowing them structurally, that is to say without being able to isolate their elements and atoms, the enterprise of deconstruction always in a certain way falls prey to its own work.
>
> (Derrida, 1997, p. 24)

The issue is not about destroying ~~leadership~~ but rather inhabiting it with a certain deconstructive disposition and working with the texts to analyse the competing forces of signification, to tease out multiple readings and meanings in the text, to expose the contradictions and to raise questions about its assumptions. This is only a brief précis of some of Derrida's concepts that form deconstruction; therefore it is worth making a few further comments about putting these ideas to work in relation to educational ~~leadership~~.

Witnessing deconstruction in educational ~~leadership~~

Thinking with Derrida in educational ~~leadership~~ is no easy task, for scholarship in the field is largely concerned with articulating what ~~leadership~~ is and particularly what 'good' ~~leadership~~ is. However, this search for an objective truth leads to a closing down of what ~~leadership~~ can be. The sign of a model ascribed to a particular practice serves to centre the structure of play in a possible war of signification. If we want to develop a productive space for alternate understandings of ~~leadership~~ to come, then it is necessary not only to resist the seductive paradigms of best practice captured through rigid models and standards discourses but also to show how these models are examples of *différance* at work and cannot represent what they prescribe. ~~Leadership~~ must be shown to be a signifier of signifiers forming a chain of supplements. As Derrida writes:

> The signified concept is never present in itself, in an adequate presence that would refer only to itself. Every concept is necessarily and essentially inscribed in a chain or a system, within which it refers to another and to other concepts, by the systematic play of differences.
>
> (Derrida, 1973, p. 140)

Exploring ~~leadership~~ in this way then allows for an opening up of the concept to designate something other than what its author intends. This is not an 'anything goes' form of relativism but an openness to that which is wholly 'other' to what has previously been constructed. This is to open up the texts' grammatology at work, to offer an approach that can be affirmative (Peters and Biesta, 2009). For example, in the transformational ~~leadership~~ model as articulated by Burns (1978), the leader–follower relationship follows a Western metaphysical binary whereby *leader* is conceptualised as a form of presence as being, while *follower* is conceptualised as a form of lack in relation to leader. It is through the relation with leaders that followers are signified through this particular subordinate relationship. As I have argued elsewhere (Niesche, 2013), this is symptomatic of most ~~leadership~~ models, with the ascribed adjective in front of the word leadership being really just an example of a *trace* of other relations. In saying this, there is no real truth claim to the presentation of a ~~leadership~~ model but simply a repeating chain of supplements that are minor variations on the original binary. For instance, the claims of distributed ~~leadership~~ models are also a form of leader–follower structuring that is really a re-inscribing of similar hierarchies to models such as transformational ~~leadership~~ (for a much more detailed analysis see Niesche, 2013). Transformational models are primarily concerned with a top-down flow of power in which the leader is constructed as the primary instigator of change. This is a particular configuration of the leader–follower dynamic in which the *leader* is the privileged term.

Many proponents of a distributed approach draw their critique and distinction from transformational approaches by the distributing of leadership across a number of people or groups. More recently, Peter Gronn, well known for his contributions to the development of a distributed perspective as a unit of analysis for the division of labour, has drawn attention to the limitations of how such a concept has been taken up (Gronn, 2010). The significance of Gronn's shift in position is that it acknowledges the persistence of a binary between leader and follower, and the prioritising of any one term over the other does not shift the power relation involved. Derrida's work is important here in working to interrupt such binaries in a way that opens space for alternatives and in highlighting how the texts of ~~leadership~~ models are formed via the transformation (or not) of other ~~leadership~~ texts. There is a displacing of the core foundation upon which ~~leadership~~ as a concept has been built. The discourse of ~~leadership~~ through such a model also carries with it the potential for the deconstruction of the very same model.

Furthermore, the notions of *trace* and *différance* imply a temporality that is not a simple linearity. Much research on ~~leadership~~ is undertaken by describing what people do after it has been witnessed (if it even can be) or talked about in an interview or a survey and then projected into the future as an example of what should or should not be done (mostly in the form of what is thought of as best practice). Models of ~~leadership~~ that are developed this way, as well as other texts such as standards, fall prey to linear temporality that have already within them deconstructions that must be accounted for. To not witness these deconstructions allows these standards and models to close down alternate perspectives and avenues for allowing 'otherist' perspectives to flourish. The aim of a ~~leadership~~ model is to project and idealise future behaviour based on assumptions from a deferring (in the temporal sense) of a description of activity, for example, the simple process of designating a sign to an observed or described activity. As a result, there is a double deferral, first in the process of undertaking the research and then second in writing the text at a later stage. According to Derrida, if we cannot take hold of or show the thing in its presence, then we signify or go through the detour of signs (Derrida, 1973). This making up of signs is therefore a deferred presence. As Derrida argues:

> Différance is what makes the movement of signification possible only if each element that is said to be "present," appearing on the stage of presence, is related to something other than itself but retains the mark of a past element and already lets itself be hollowed out by the mark of its relation to a future element. This trace relates no less to what is called the future than what is called the past, and it constitutes what is called the present by this very relation to what it is not, to what it is absolutely not.
>
> (Derrida, 1973, pp. 142–143)

The designation of a model of ~~leadership~~ as a mark of signification of presence seems to be an example of its deconstruction at work. This notion certainly has implications for how research into ~~leadership~~ is undertaken or can even possibly be undertaken. This is not to say that there is no value in undertaking empirical research but serves more to highlight how the truth claims made require some very cautionary work and an awareness of how deconstructions work through a process of double deferral. There is also scope here for new forms of texts and poststructuralist research approaches.[5]

The question of ~~leadership~~ will begin upon its death

The aim of this chapter has been to think critically about how we might respond to the crisis of ~~leadership~~, and specifically ~~leadership~~ in education, to problematise the use of the term. I do not think that avoiding using the term will allow for the necessary problematising and deconstructing that is necessary for new and different alternatives to come about. Derrida tells us that deconstruction must work from the inside and inhabit particular structures and discourses. Thinking again with Lyotard's work on phrasing, he argues that silence is still a phrase (Lyotard, 1988); that is, not using the term ~~leadership~~ is still to make a particular statement. Furthermore, Derrida uses the term *trace* to signify the inhabiting of this space via a chain of significations and not a centring of the construction of ~~leadership~~ in a metaphysical sense. Taking this a step further, developing different models or ideas still leaves a trace of ~~leadership~~; these become substitutions for one another.

As I have argued here, we need to consider the possibility of the death of ~~leadership~~ in its current conceptual sense – in other words, as it stands in its various current forms and models and the structuring according to a particular binary of leader–follower – in order for different ideas about ~~leadership~~ to occur. We may not be able to prescribe or predict what these different ideas are, nor should we, but we can create a space for them to occur and try to capture them at the time and place of that occurrence. We have to cut off the head of zombie ~~leadership~~. Although perhaps on further reflection, through the writing of this chapter, it is not so much the end or death of ~~leadership~~ that matters (although that too I think is necessary), but questioning how it may continue as a useful concept (Lyotard, 1988).

Notes

1   A popular comic that is now a television series. The zombie phenomenon has been around for decades in movies, books and so on but it saw a resurgence in the late 1990s and 2000s. The zombie analogy has also been taken up in academic writing (e.g. see *Zombie Economics* [Quiggan, 2012] and *Zombies in the Academy* [Whelan et al., 2013]) and also in postgraduate programmes (see a course titled 'Zombies in Educational Administration' by Paul Newton at the University of Saskatchewan).
2   Derrida draws on Heidegger's practice of crossing out key terms as a form of *sous rature*, or writing under erasure, to indicate that a word or concept is both inaccurate but also necessary (Derrida, 1997). The word *leadership* is thus crossed out to show its operation and also its deletion. I use this here with the term *leadership* to indicate both its dubious nature but also its necessity as a term for deconstruction. I resume this move in later sections of the chapter.
3   Scott Eacott's recent programme of exploring relational approaches is a useful endeavour in response to these concerns (See Eacott, 2015).

4   To attempt to define deconstruction is inherently problematic, for Derrida has said that deconstruction is not a method nor can be transformed into one and to claim 'what deconstruction is' is to offer a false statement or miss the point (Derrida, 1991).

5   Some recent work in post-qualitative approaches can be of significant value (See Honan, 2014; Lather and St. Pierre, 2013; MacLure, 2013). However, a more detailed discussion of this work is not possible here.

References

Anderson, G., 2001. Disciplining leaders: A critical discourse analysis of the ISLLC National Examination and Performance Standards in educational administration. *International Journal of Leadership in Education*, 4(3), pp. 199–216.

Anderson, G., 2009. *Advocacy leadership: Toward a post-reform agenda in education.* London: Routledge.

Berlant, L., 2011. *Cruel optimism.* Durham: Duke University Press.

Biesta, G., 2009. Witnessing deconstruction in education: Why quasi-transcendentalism matters. *Journal of Philosophy of Education*, 43(3), pp. 391–404.

Blackmore, J., 1999. *Troubling women: Feminism, leadership and educational change.* Buckingham: Open University Press.

Blackmore, J., 2006. Social justice and the study and practice of leadership in education: A feminist history. *Journal of Educational Administration and History*, 38(2), pp. 185–200.

Blackmore, J., 2008. Leading educational re-design to sustain socially just schools under conditions of instability. *Journal of Educational Leadership, Policy and Practice*, 23(2), pp. 18–33.

Dendle, P., 2007. The zombie as barometer of cultural anxiety. In N. Scott, ed., *Monsters and the monstrous: Myths and metaphors of enduring evil* (pp. 45–60). Leiden, Netherlands: Brill Publishing.

Derrida, J., 1973. *Speech and phenomena and other essays on Husserl's theory of signs.* Evanston: IL: Northwestern University Press.

Derrida, J., 1978. *Writing and difference.* Chicago: Chicago University Press.

Derrida, J., 1997. *Of grammatology.* Corrected edition. Baltimore: John Hopkins University Press.

Derrida, J., 1991. Letter to a Japanese friend. In P. Kamuf, ed., *A Derrida reader: Between the blinds* (pp. 270–276). New York: Columbia University Press.

Eacott, S., 2011. New look at leaders or a new look at leadership? *International Journal of Educational Management*, 25(2), pp. 134–143.

Eacott, S., 2015. *Educational leadership relationally: A theory and methodology for educational leadership, management and administration.* Rotterdam: Sense.

English, F. W., 2000. Pssssst! What does one call a set of non-empirical beliefs required to be accepted on faith and enforced by authority? [Answer: a religion, aka the ISLLC standards]. *International Journal of Leadership in Education*, 3(2), pp. 159–167.

English, F. W., 2002. The point of scientificity, the fall of the epistemological dominos, and the end of *the field* of educational administration. *Studies in Philosophy and Education*, 21, pp. 109–136.

English, F. W., 2003. Cookie-cutter leaders for cookie-cutter schools: The teleology of standardization and the de-legitimization of the university in educational leadership preparation. *Leadership and Policy in Schools*, 2(1), pp. 27–46.

English, F. W., 2006. The unintended consequences of a standardized knowledge base in advancing educational leadership preparation. *Educational Administration Quarterly,* 42(3), pp. 461–472.

Evers, C. W. and Lakomski, G., 2013. Methodological individualism, educational administration, and leadership. *Journal of Educational Administration and History,* 45(2), pp. 159–173.

Foucault, M., 1980. Truth and power. In C. Gordon, ed., *Power/knowledge: Selected interviews and other writings 1972–1977.* Sussex: The Harvester Press.

Foucault, M., 1996a. The concern for truth. In S. Lotringer, ed., *Foucault Live: Michel Foucault Collected Interviews, 1961–1984.* New York: Semiotext(e).

Foucault., M., 1996b. Problematics. In S. Lotringer, ed., *Foucault Live: Michel Foucault Collected Interviews, 1961–1984.* New York: Semiotext(e).

Foucault, M., 1996c. Concern for truth. In S. Lotringer, ed., *Foucault Live: Michel Foucault Collected Interviews, 1961–1984.* New York: Semiotext(e).

Foucault, M., 2002a. *The order of things.* London: Routledge.

Foucault, M., 2002b. Interview with Michel Foucault. In James D. Faubion, ed., *Power: Essential works of Foucault: 1954–1984.* Volume 3. London: Penguin Books.

Gillies, D., 2013. *Educational leadership and Michel Foucault.* London: Routledge.

Gobby, B., 2013. Principal self-government and subjectification: The exercise of principal autonomy in the Western Australian Independent Public Schools programme. *Critical Studies in Education,* 54(3), pp. 273–285.

Gorard, S., 2005. Current contexts for research in educational leadership and management. *Educational Management Administration and Leadership,* 33(2), pp. 155–164.

Gronn, P., 2003. Leadership: Who needs it? *School Leadership and Management,* 23(3), pp. 267–290.

Gronn, P., 2010. Leadership: Its genealogy, configuration and trajectory. *Journal of Educational Administration and History,* 42(4), pp. 405–435.

Gunter, H., 2001. *Leaders and leadership in education.* London: Paul Chapman Publishing.

Gunter, H., 2011. *Leadership and the reform of education.* Bristol: Policy Press.

Halford, S. and Leonard, P., 2001. *Gender, power and organisations.* New York: Palgrave.

Hall, V., 1996. *Dancing on the ceiling: A study of women managers in education.* London: Paul Chapman Publishing.

Honan, E., 2014. Disrupting the habit of interviewing. *Reconceptualizing Educational Research Methodology,* 5(1), pp. 1–17.

Johnson B., 1981. Translator's introduction. In J. Derrida, *Dissemination.* Chicago: Chicago University Press.

Kellerman, B., 2012. *The end of leadership.* New York: HarperCollins.

Kelly, S., 2008. Leadership: A categorical mistake? *Human Relations,* 61(6), pp. 763–782.

Kerr, S. and Jermier, J., 1977. Substitutes for leadership: Their meaning and measurement. *Organization and Human Performance,* 22, pp. 374–403.

Lakomski, G., 2005. *Managing without leadership: Towards a theory of organizational functioning.* Oxford: Elsevier.

Lambert, C., 2007. New labour? New leaders? Gendering transformational leadership. *British Journal of Sociology of Education,* 28(2), pp. 149–163.

Lather, P. and St. Pierre, E. A., 2013. Post-qualitative research. *International Journal of Qualitative Studies in Education,* 26(6), pp. 634–645.

Lawler, J., 2005. The essence of leadership? Existentialism and leadership. *Leadership*, 1(2), pp. 215–231.

Lyotard, J. F., 1988. *The différend: Phrases in dispute*. Minneapolis: University of Minnesota Press.

MacLure, M., 2013. Researching without representation? Language and materiality in post-qualitative methodology. *International Journal of Qualitative Studies in Education*, 26(6), pp. 658–667.

Maxcy, S. ed., 1994. *Postmodern school leadership: Meeting the crisis in educational administration*. Westport, CT: Praeger.

Niesche, R., 2011. *Foucault and educational leadership: Disciplining the principal*. London: Routledge.

Niesche, R., 2013. *Deconstructing educational leadership: Derrida and Lyotard*. London: Routledge.

Niesche, R. and Gowlett, C., 2015. Advocating a post-structuralist politics for educational leadership. *Educational Philosophy and Theory*, 47(4), pp. 372–386.

Niesche, R. and Keddie, A., 2015. *Leadership, ethics and schooling for social justice*. London: Routledge.

Peters, M. A. and Biesta, G., 2009. *Derrida, deconstruction and the politics of pedagogy*. New York: Peter Lang.

Pfeffer, J., 1977. The ambiguity of leadership. *The Academy of Management Review*, 2(1), pp. 104–112.

Quiggan, J., 2012. *Zombie economics: How dead ideas still walk among us*. Princeton: Princeton University Press.Smyth, J., 2008. Australia's great disengagement with public education and social justice in educational leadership. *Journal of Educational Administration and History*, 40(3), pp. 221–233.

Smyth, J., 2011. The disaster of the 'self-managing school': Genesis, trajectory, undisclosed agenda, and effects. *Journal of Educational Administration and History*, 43(2), pp. 95–117.

Stratton, J., 2011. Zombie trouble: Zombie texts, bare life and displaced people. *European Journal of Cultural Studies*, 14(3), pp. 265–281.

Thompson, G. and Mockler, N., 2015. Principals of audit: Testing, data and 'implicated advocacy'. *Journal of Educational Administration and History*, ifirst.

Thomson, P., 2009. *School leadership: Heads on the block*. London: Routledge.

Whelan, A., Walker, R. and Moore, C., eds., 2013. *Zombies in the academy: Living death in higher education*. Chicago: Intellect.

Wilkinson, J., 2008. Good intentions are not enough: A critical examination of diversity and educational leadership scholarship. *Journal of Educational Administration and History*, 40(2), pp. 101–112.

6 Problematisations, practices and subjectivation

Educational leadership in neo-liberal times

Brad Gobby

Introduction

The mainstream educational leadership expertise and its literature need disrupting. Despite the more recent entry into the field of critical voices and perspectives (Bates, 2010; Lakomski, 2005), the field tends to be sociologically realist; it assumes that changing social and political realities are self-evident and unproblematic. It is not uncommon for leadership gurus like Fullan (2011), Hargreaves (2011) and Leithwood et al. (2006) to take neo-liberal reform and its effects on education systems in liberal democratic countries as inevitable and largely beyond interrogation. With the exception of feminist, critical and post-structuralist analyses, how political and governmental discourses constitute or shape the notions, practices and expertise of educational leadership has avoided critical inquiry. The mainstream leadership literature has instead attempted to be responsive to these changes by offering models, technical skills, personal attributes and best practice solutions to the supposedly immutable circumstances of political, social and educational reform. This has made the expertise of educational leadership a resource for government authorities who have sought to 'script the performance' of politically responsive educational leadership through government policy and programmes (Fitzgerald and Savage, 2013). The purpose of this chapter is to move beyond accepting the norms and practices of school reform and educational leadership by examining the contemporary conditions through which it has become possible to think of and act upon principals as 'leaders' of schools.

Although its use remains marginal in the broader literature, a poststructuralist perspective is useful for this kind of examination (Niesche and Gowlett, 2015). Poststructuralist studies criticise essentialist notions of leadership and are instead concerned with leadership and leading as a socially and politically constituted practice inextricably tied to relations of power (Blackmore, 2006; Gillies, 2013; Gunter, 2009; Niesche, 2011). An important insight of these studies is that principals are the object of political and governmental activity because the position they hold in schools makes them mediators and translators of government policy. With the effectiveness of policy enactment at the local level reliant on steering school principals to policy objectives, the various discourses of educational leadership are deployed as a governmental strategy to secure political reform of schools (Fitzgerald and Savage, 2013; Gunter, 2009; Wright, 2011). This chapter utilises these insights to examine the political dimension of leadership and principalship. Informed by Michel Foucault's (2002, 2007, 2008) use of notions of problematisation, practices, power, neo-liberalism, government and subjectivation, I outline an approach to the analysis of leadership as practices of government and self-government. My objective is to demonstrate how these concepts can be used to explore the relationship between neo-liberalism, education reforms and leadership as a practice of school reform that fashions the subject of neo-liberal government. I make specific reference to the Independent Public Schools initiative in Western Australia, where the reform of principalship is currently occurring as a result of the increased independence and discretion of selected public schools.

Regimes of practices and rationalities

The conceptual approach taken to engage with the political dimension of educational leadership is drawn from the work of Foucault (1991, 2008) and the scholarship that has developed from his research (Dean, 1999; Rose, 1999). A large part of Foucault's research sought to explore the relationships between power, knowledge, subjectivity and society's institutions. His studies of the clinic, hospitals and prisons popularised the study of modern institutions using notions of the panopticon, discipline, practices, power and truth. Foucault's creative deployment of these notions offered a more radical rendering of social organisations and power than many of his contemporaries. For example, he does not comprehend modernity as dominated by either universal logics or a dominating and repressive power (Blake and Masschelein, 2007). Foucault eschewed functionalism, the modernist *telos* of Western progress; and the Weberian and criticalist notion of instrumental reason as foundational principles of modern institutions and social relations (Dean, 1994). Foucault instead has a particular interest in practices, their immanent rules and their constitutive effects.

Foucault describes how the target of analysis of his study of prisons 'wasn't "institutions," "theories" or "ideology," but *practices* – with the aim of grasping the conditions which make these acceptable at a given moment' (Foucault, 1991, p. 75). Practices are not the personal characteristics of individuals or actions produced by personal characteristics. Foucault understands practices to be 'the places where what is said and what is done, rules imposed and reasons given, the planned and the taken for granted meet and interconnect' (Foucault, 1991, p. 75). These places are historically constituted 'organized or routinized ways of doing things that manifest an immanent logic or reason of their own' (Dean, 1998, p. 185). Foucault contends that 'types of practice are not just governed by institutions, prescribed by ideologies, guided by pragmatic circumstances – whatever role these elements may actually play – but possess up to a point their own specific regularities, logic, strategy, self-evidence and "reason"' (Foucault, 1991, p. 75). Practices do not emerge outside of the work of thought, as knowledge is immanent to practices and what people do. Foucault's analytical focus is therefore on practices and the systems of thought or the element of reasoning that are immanent to practices (or discursive practices) and which become entrenched, normalised and often seemingly beyond contest (Bacchi, 2012).

For Foucault, practices embody the interplay of the two elements of 'rules imposed' and 'reasons given'. The knowledge embodied in practices is shaped by bodies of expertise and scientific and professional protocols, but not these alone. Knowledge also emerges from the contact point of forms of knowledge with 'the always incomplete task of the organisation and ordering of conduct and bodies within spaces and temporalities' (Dean, 1998, p. 187). The regimes of practices (such as how one teaches, cares or leads) in specific institutional contexts are inscribed with a body of rules, norms and regulative codes for what one does, and these are tied to the production of true discourse legitimating forms of action. In other words, institutional practices are 'penetrated by all sorts of schemas, programmes, diagrams, maps and plans and marked by degrees of systematization and calculation' (Dean, 1998, p. 186). The 'dimension of these "regimes of practices" that Foucault wishes to analyse is one in which we find all the more or less explicit, programmatic attempts to organize institutional spaces, their administrative routines and rituals and the conduct of human actors in specified ways' (Dean, 1998, p. 185). The examination of institutions, like schools, must recognise the regulatory schemas that attempt to shape conduct, organisations and their reform and therefore the rules that shape the codification of these domains and their objects.

The emergence of and transformation to institutional practices and regimes of practices is tied to 'problematisations', a term Foucault uses in two ways (Bacchi, 2012; Foucault, 1984). First, *problematisations* describe his method of analysis, which is to examine how an issue is questioned, analysed and understood at specific times and under specific conditions. Second, Foucault uses the term to refer to the historical processes that produce objects for thought and action. It signifies the process and relations of rendering things (behaviours, phenomena, processes, practices) uncertain, unfamiliar and problematic and how these things are therefore shaped as objects for thought. Foucault (1984, p. 389) suggests that this 'development of a given into a question, this transformation of a group of obstacles and difficulties into problems to which the diverse solutions will attempt to produce a response, this is what constitutes the point of problematisations and the specific work of thought'. Instead of construing problems and institutional change as products of brute reality or ideology, the notion of problematisation focuses on how these result from the intellectual processing of reality and the use of specific practices or systems of knowledge in that process. Pertinently, the specific reasoning that renders something problematic, as in Foucault's studies of madness and sexuality, shapes how that thing is made intelligible, codified and generally understood. The form of any description renders objects amenable to certain forms of intervention. For example, neo-liberalism's problematisation of state bureaucracies as inefficient, inflexible, unresponsive and lacking entrepreneurship opens the bureaucratic apparatus to enterprising and market-based interventions. Therefore, as Foucault observes, critical analysis should try to 'see how the different solutions to a problem have been constructed; but also how these different solutions result from a specific form of problematization' (Foucault, 1984, p. 389).

This process of problematisation is ineluctably tied to government. This is a notion more fully developed in the neo-Foucauldian governmentality literature. Broadly speaking, government 'is a problematizing activity: it poses the obligations of ruler in terms of the problems they seek to address' (Rose and Miller, 1992, p. 181). In the domain of governmental practices, the processes of problematisations are shaped by political rationalities. Political rationalities are the regularities that emerge in political discourse around the 'formulation and justification of idealised schemata for representing reality, analysing it and rectifying it' (Rose and Miller, 1992, p. 178). These have a characteristically moral, epistemological and idiomatic form, which means they elaborate on the right distribution of duties, power and the ideals of government; employ certain systems of reason and knowledge to constitute, understand and represent reality and the objects to be governed; and use a characteristic vocabulary to render reality thinkable. In short, political rationalities 'are morally coloured, grounded upon knowledge, and made thinkable through language' (Rose and Miller, 1992, p. 276). As a 'relatively systematic, explicit, discursive problematization and codification of the art or practice of government' (Dean, 1994, p. 187), political rationalities 'accord the activity of politics its intelligibility and possibility at different times; it is these problematizations that shape what are to be counted as problems; what as failures and what as solutions' (Rose, 1993, p. 285). It is in this sense that Bacchi (2010) describes policy and policy-making as an activity of problematising rather than simply problem-solving. She observes that 'Governing takes place *through* particular problematisations' (Bacchi, 2012, p. 5).

Given the abstractness of these ideas, it is worth considering a tangible example – the practices of school reform. School reform is tied to the forms of intelligibility that render aspects of the domain of education visible and problematic. Over the past few decades, criticisms of education systems and schools have been influenced by the political rationalities of neo-liberalism about the purported problems confronting education – there have been innumerable 'crises'. This is discussed below, but it is worth reiterating the point that problematisations provide 'the conditions in which possible responses can be given; it defines the elements that will constitute what the different solutions attempt to respond to' (Foucault, 1984, p. 389). So, when examining education reform as regimes of practices, we must pay close attention to the intellectual (expertise and bodies of knowledge) and political resources that make the domain of schooling problematic at this particular time, such that the practices of decentralisation, contractualisation, marketisation and leadership emerge as apparently necessary for improving education systems.

Neo-liberal reform

This chapter uses a notion of neo-liberalism informed by the above conceptual perspective. It reflects a focus on the technical character of neo-liberalism as an art of government (e.g. its practices), which distinguishes it from neo-liberalism's treatment as a political philosophy and its critique in terms of its ideological conditions; for example, as a 'free-market, small government' ideology beginning with the New Right, Thatcher and Reagan (Barry et al., 1996). Foucault's discussion of neo-liberalism occurs within the context of his genealogy of the modern administrative state and his use of the notion of governmentality. Governmentality, or the rationalities that shape governmental practices (governmentalities), marks an historical transformation in how power is exercised in modern administrative states (Foucault, 2007, 2008). The term signifies a transformation from a sovereign model of rule to one concerned with governing the population of free individuals to the ends of the population's health, wealth and wellbeing, specifically through the rational know-how produced of that which is to be governed. Governmentality has become the 'common grounds for all modern forms of political thought and action' (Rose et al., 2006, p. 86), including neo-liberalism. For Foucault, neo-liberalism as a political practice emerges early in the twentieth century in response to social liberal forms of government commonly associated with the welfare state and the reformation of post-World War Two Germany (Foucault, 2008). The emphasis of Foucauldian analysis is on neo-liberalism as a political mode of thought and action that equates political freedom with economic freedom.

Unlike critiques that often construe neo-liberalism as an anti-statist agenda of marketisation and deregulation harking back to nineteenth-century liberalism, the Foucauldian treatment of neo-liberalism situates it firmly in the territory of governmental rationality and practices. Neo-liberalism involves an active form of government and regulation, and therefore 'the retreat from the State' is also itself a positive technique of government; we are perhaps witnessing a 'degovernmentalization of the State' but surely not 'de-governmentalization' per se' (Barry et al., 1996, p. 11). So, while neo-liberalism problematises an array of domains and their regimes of practices according to 'rules' of freedom, autonomy, choice, competition and entrepreneurship, competition and regulated markets are actively instantiated by political and governmental authorities. In so doing, neo-liberalism submits once non-economic spheres such as education, health care and social services to a regulatory 'permanent economic tribunal' (Foucault, 2008, p. 247). Human behaviour and social relations are rendered intelligible according to economic criteria and categories, therefore rendering human conduct amenable to being acted upon (or governed) economically, as competitive enterprises.

Over the past few decades, neo-liberalism has profoundly shaped liberal democratic countries, especially in Australia, the USA and the UK. Institutions and technologies of government have been problematised as inflexible, unresponsive and encumbered by the inefficiency and self-interestedness of their bureau-professional organisation (Clarke et al., 2000). In education, the social democratic discourses of equality have been challenged for 'legitimacy' by the discourses of standards, quality, choice and competition. As Hindess (1997, p. 26) observes, 'what had once been seen as non-economic spheres... are increasingly regarded as sources of economic inefficiency whose performance leaves room for improvement'.

Blame for education systems' supposed failings are commonly laid at the feet of education bureaucracies, teachers, teacher unions and the policies of the Left (Ball, 1994; Chubb and Moe, 1990). Education's professional enclosures have been penetrated by the neo-liberal governmentalities of entrepreneurship, innovation, choice, autonomy, accountability, performance and competition through direct policy interventions and the activities of government and non-government agencies (e.g. National College for School Leadership in England). These have not only problematised prevailing practices but also instituted new intelligibilities and means for educators to view, think about and enact teaching, managing, and leading (Gewirtz, 2002; Grace, 1995). In Australia and the UK, a 'reform' movement has coalesced around the governance practices of decentralisation, self-management, contractualisation, marketisation and performance monitoring (Gewirtz et al., 1995; Du Gay, 2000). It is in relation to these wider practices and strategies of neo-liberal government that leadership has become a prominent category for thinking about improving schools (Evers and Lakomski, 2013; Gunter, 2009).

The subject of neo-liberalism

At stake in this discussion of practices, problematisations and political rationality is the formation of the subjects of government. This is because problematisations are ineluctably tied to the knowledge and practices through which we come to question, know and act upon others and ourselves. This evinces the process of subjectivation. Here, individuals are constituted and constitute themselves as certain kinds of governable subjects through knowledge and the 'whole range of practices that constitute, define, organize, and instrumentalise the strategies that individuals in their freedom can use in dealing with each other' (Foucault, 1997, p. 300). The know-how of education reform, which includes the knowledge, theories, concepts and practices of corporate management and leadership, constitutes regimes of practices of government and self-government insofar as their knowledge and practices are taken upon the self to govern others and the self. In this exercise of power over him- or herself, 'the subject constitutes itself in an active fashion through practices of the self' (Foucault 1997, p. 291), and through such practices the individual becomes 'tied to his own identity by a conscience or self-knowledge' (Foucault, 2002, p. 331).

Such practices of self-formation implicate individuals in relations of political and social power. Individuals not only make sense of their lives through these practices, but because practices contain two dimensions – 'rules imposed' and 'reasons given' – they also impose on their existence historically contingent rules and norms. So, when a school principal takes upon him or herself the practices and knowledge of contemporary educational leadership, they constitute themselves through practices that are 'also games of truth, practices of power' (Foucault, 1997, p. 290). Today, the rational schema of neo-liberalism shapes these games of truth. Neo-liberal problematisations and practices enjoin principals and teachers to normalise themselves by subjectifying themselves to the rules of acceptability and the reason of neo-liberalism. Inscribed into everyday practices and knowledge, the rules and norms of neo-liberalism (like entrepreneurialism and self-responsibility) shape people's practices, perceptions, behaviour and speech. Consequently, the neo-liberal government of the state is accomplished through practices of self-formation or the practices of self-government. It is in this sense that Foucault locates 'the ethics of the government of the self on the same plane as the government of others and the state' (Dean, 1994, p. 196).

Leadership and reforming education systems

This section explores how the practices of school reform have introduced new practices and forms of reasoning into schools. It links neo-liberal problematisations of education to the transformation of practices and principal subjectivities. This section uses data from the author's research to illustrate its ideas (Gobby, 2013, 2015). Briefly, the study involved semi-structured interviews with two principals of two secondary schools in Western Australia (WA) on the topic of a reform initiative known as the Independent Public Schools (IPS) programme. IPS is a governance reform that increases school autonomy by devolving from the state education department a range of decision-making responsibilities, although schools must opt in and are only accepted if they can demonstrate their capacity to self-govern. The two principals interviewed, Bridgette and John (pseudonyms), lead two IP schools in a low–mid socioeconomic southern metropolitan suburb of Perth, WA.

The IPS programme emerges, at least in part, from the problematisation of and the perceived dangers posed by the practices of bureaucratic governance. These problematisations can be found in public documents and commentaries. Prior to and during the reform, the Department of Education (DOE) promoted the programme as freeing principals from 'suffocating red tape' (Government Media Office [GMO] 2009), while the state premier and education minister commented that bureaucracy 'prevents imaginative leadership' (GMO, 2009). Principals also invoked this anti-bureaucratic reasoning. Bridgette said there is too much proceduralism represented by 'red tape' and a 'lack of strategic direction' for school decision-making, while John spoke derisorily about those principals who appeared dependent on the DOE, suggesting he was not the 'sort of person who needs to know there is someone there all the time you are in contact with'. The principals particularly disliked the centralised control of budgets and resource allocation, the centralised system for the placement of staff and the central policies and procedures that needed to be followed and negotiated to 'get things done' (Bridgette). IPS promised to empower schools and communities by enabling them to 'shape their own future' (DOE, 2010). These problematisations of school governance are a condition of possibility for transforming the practices of principals. As prescriptions are derived from the diagnosis of ailments, IPS introduces new practices into schools that attempt to overcome the purported problems of bureaucratic constraint, inflexibility and unresponsiveness. The initiative accords principals responsibilities that enable them to run their schools as relatively independent enterprises, what John describes as 'more of a private enterprise'. Under the guidance of a school board, IP schools are given responsibility for allocating resources from a one-line budget, recruiting and employing staff, determining a school's staffing profile, entering into contracts and managing school maintenance.

The contract is one practice related to this problematisation. Contractualisation is associated with school self-management and neo-liberal government (Gobby, 2015). According to Du Gay (2000, p. 65), contractualisation 'typically consists of assigning the performance of function or an activity to a distinct unit of management – individual or collective – which is regarded as being accountable for the efficient (i.e. 'economic') performance of that function or conduct of that activity'. Schools in the IPS programme enter into a three-year delivery and performance agreement (DPA) with the state DOE. The DPA document outlines key responsibilities, targets and strategies of the school, along with the department's responsibilities, including the resources provided. Responding to the perceived problem that bureaucratic governance stifles school improvement, contractual relationships fostered by such agreements putatively liberate principals from interventionist and unresponsive 'bureaucratic' authorities. Schools are expected to self-govern in a field of relatively autonomous and often competing education providers, with the contract providing the conditions for innovation and responsiveness to these local markets. While the contract fosters freedom from constraint, it induces a relationship of obligation and self-responsibility. Contractualism shifts accountability for performance from the education bureaucracy and political sphere to the school, with principals and teachers being monitored and judged against the targets of the contract. In other words, the contract is a technology of self-government that, according to Du Gay, enacts neo-liberalism by inciting in individuals 'a certain entrepreneurial form of relationship to themselves as a condition of their effectiveness' (Du Gay, 2000, p. 65). So, despite their perceived 'autonomy', which the principals spoke glowingly about, principals are nevertheless caught up in subjectifying relations of power. The interviews conducted with the principals elicit descriptions of these relations of power in terms of the practices and the rationalities inscribed in them.

The principals spoke about being engaged in regimes of practices like strategic thinking, business planning and managing the conduct of staff to the ends of the organisation. This exemplifies how principals are valued and increasingly value themselves for 'their ability to fabricate an entrepreneurial identity for themselves and a distinct identity for their school' (Keddie et al., 2015, p. 87). John, who was into his second year as an IPS principal, said the autonomy accorded by this contractual relationship means, 'You can be as entrepreneurial or as conservative as you want. But what it does allow you to be is as entrepreneurial as you want'. John's entrepreneurial identity is shaped by the rationalities and practices of the education market, an indication of 'the normalization of market rationalities in schools and of the extent to which leaders are imbricated with mark pressures that require them to imagine and understand their school in market terms' (Savage, 2013, p. 90). John continues, 'We try to do things to make us more appealing.

You know, we are a modern school, we market ourselves very heavily so that people understand Westside High, where we are now, is completely different to where we were 7 years ago'. Here, the performance contract is a technology of power that attaches the principal to a corporate and entrepreneurial identity (Gobby, 2013).

The contractual nature of school governance also changed Bridgette's activities and self-perception. She viewed the school as a corporate entity that was forming collaborations as well as competing with other schools 'on choice'. She also declared that ultimate responsibility for the school's performance rested with her: 'I have been left in a lot of ways to be my own performance manager'. Like John, Bridgette takes responsibility for monitoring, managing and optimising the performance of her school. In so doing, these practices transform the identities of the principals. Both principals are disciplined by their view of themselves as dynamic, problem-solving and strategic innovators who are accountable for the smooth and optimal running and performance of their schools.

In the IPS reform, power is not operating strictly, or only, in a top-down, hierarchical manner. It is operating through the responsibilising practices exercised in the autonomy of the performance agreement. And this is why leadership is important. The central bureaucratic management of the education system associated with the welfare state required principals to be effective administrators of the policies and procedures of centralised education departments. Now, decentralised and contractualised school systems require principals who can exercise autonomy innovatively, effectively and responsibly. This increased individual discretion relies on principals possessing the knowledge, practices and techniques to manage their schools and to govern themselves. Increasingly, it is the expertise of leadership rather than management and administration that invests this autonomy with its practices and norms (Bates, 2010). Leadership is construed here as an expertise of human conduct. Utilising Rose's (1996) notion of expertise, leadership is an expertise insofar as the field contains people who claim special competence in the administration of people, and it contains a body of knowledge, techniques and procedures that claim to rationally organise and manage people. It is not unlike the expertise of economists, psychologists, political scientists and social policy experts. Such expertise is crucial to society because these make liberal government possible. Their claim to a positive, normative and objective know-how makes expertise a resource through which governments can exercise their power (with legitimacy), and individuals responsibly conduct themselves and others. This is the case with leadership, which, through professional learning courses, popular leadership books and professional standards frameworks has become 'linked to and embedded in technical means for the shaping and reshaping of conduct and in practices and institutions' (Dean, 1999, p. 18).

The Australian professional standards framework

The bureaucracy and other governing agencies mobilise the normative expertise of leadership as a tool of government. Statutory bodies like the Australian

Institute for Teaching and School Leadership (AITSL) and the National College for School Leadership in the UK have established and promoted professional standards and professional learning programmes (Gunter, 2009). The professional standards frameworks operate as 'systematic and calculated – if contingent and aleatory – endeavours to optimise the performance of teachers and school leaders by deploying techniques which seek to activate and regulate their self-governing capacities or freedom' (O'Brien, 2014, p. 2). In interview, for example, John says that while principals must be innovative and must 'find solutions' to problems, principal autonomy is also guided. Autonomy for John is 'an enabler, but you've got standards, you've got expectations or what you should be doing, you have the AITSL standards, what the principals should be'. Here, the AITSL standards are considered as an authoritative account of how principals should think and act. Moreover, in thinking and acting according to these standards, the principal cultivates a normative identity ('what the principals should be'). John continues by declaring, 'leadership is the key to any success'. John uncritically views the knowledge, concepts and practices of leadership as the principal's tools for exercising autonomy in a way that will solve problems and achieve the goals of improved performance. In short, 'success' is viewed as predicated on the principal adopting the reasoning and practices of leadership.

By taking upon themselves the prevailing know-how of leadership, principals like John utilise and implement new regimes of leadership practices, making themselves into 'leaders' or, more pertinently, reforming leaders (Gunter, 2009). This term signifies that the form of leadership inscribed in competency and professional standards frameworks reflect prevailing political aspirations, language and rationalities, which have promoted self-governance, accountability, and leader-centric and individualistic explanations of effective school functioning and performance. In this political context, individualistic, managerial, entrepreneurial and decisional models and practices of leadership have displaced cooperative, dialogic and democratic regimes of management based on teacher professional discourses (Blackmore, 2006). Given these transformations, it might be considered unsurprising to hear John say, 'I run the school like a business, the students are our clients, my shareholders. It's a business'. Employing the practices of corporate management and leadership evinces the growing acceptance of neo-liberal political problematisations of the bureaucratic model of education, the enfolding upon the self of the reasons and rules inherent in such problematisations and the fabrication and employment of practices tied to an uncompromising culture of competition and performativity (Ball, 2003).

Conclusion

This chapter has explored a set of Foucauldian notions and their use in the examination of school reform and educational leadership. Problematised through the discourses of neo-liberalism, education systems are becoming decentralised, contractualised and competitive. Principals in increasingly autonomous schools, like the IP schools discussed above, are engaging in regimes of practices that include contracts, business planning and school marketing. In doing so, principals are imposing new rules and norms upon themselves. It is through these self-forming practices and their normative rules and reasons that new kinds of principal subjectivities are cultivated. The figure of the autonomous, innovative and entrepreneurial principal has displaced the figure of the principal as an administrator of central policies and procedures and, some would argue, an educational leader. The expertise of educational leadership is a part of this transformation of the educational field. To question educational leadership in the fashion of feminist, critical and poststructuralist scholars means interrogating the power, social and political relations constituting it. As a result, this chapter has suggested that the theories, concepts and practices of the mainstream leadership field are deployed in neo-liberal programmes of government (e.g. professional standards), and that principals employ the discourses of leadership to make sense of their new work conditions and themselves. The discourses of leadership constitute one of an array of regimes of rationalities and practices penetrating the sphere of schooling through which principals actively fashion 'leaderly' subjectivities that are indexed to prevailing political and social norms. This chapter has outlined concepts and discussed real-world examples that help render visible this process of subjectivation, whereby political power operates through the practices that principals use to render their selves into responsible and disciplined subjects of neo-liberal government. In the context of increasingly politicised education systems, this ought to be a focus of continued enquiry.

References

Bacchi, C., 2010. Policy as discourse: What does it mean? Where does it get us? *Discourse: Studies in the Cultural Politics of Education*, 21(1), pp. 45–57.

Bacchi, C., 2012. Why study problematizations? Making politics visible. *Open Journal of Political Science*, 2(1), pp. 1–8.

Ball, S., 1994. *Education reform: A critical and post-structural approach*. Buckingham: Open University Press.

Ball, S., 2003. The teacher's soul and the terrors of performativity. *Journal of Education Policy*, 18(2), pp. 215–228.

Barry, A., Osborne, T. and Rose, N., 1996. Introduction. In A. Barry, T. Osborne and N. Rose, eds., *Foucault and political reason* (pp. 1–18). London: University College London Press.

Bates, R. J., 2010. History of educational leadership/management. In P. Peterson, E. Baker and B. McGaw, eds., *International encyclopedia of education* (3rd ed. pp. 724–730). Oxford: Elsevier.

Blackmore, J., 2006. Social justice and the study and practice of leadership in education: A feminist history. *Journal of Educational Administration and History*, 38(2), pp. 185–200.

Blake, N. and Masschelein, J., 2007. Critical theory and critical pedagogy. In N. Blake, P. Smeyers, R. Smith and P. Standish, eds., *The Blackwell guide to the philosophy of education*. Oxford: Blackwell.

Chubb, J. and Moe, T., 1990. *Politics, markets and America's schools*. Washington: The Brookings Institute.

Clarke, J., Gewirtz, S. and McLaughlin, E., 2000. Reinventing the welfare state. In J. Clarke, S. Gewirtz and E. McLaughlin, eds., *New managerialism new welfare?* London: Open University Press.

Dean, M., 1994. *Critical and effective histories: Foucault's methods and historical sociology.* London: Routledge.

Dean, M., 1998. Questions of method. In I. Velody and R. Williams, eds., *The politics of constructionism.* London: SAGE. (pp. 182–199).

Dean, M., 1999. *Governmentality: Power and rule in modern society.* London: SAGE.

Department of Education [DOE], 2010. *Unlock your school's future: Information for principals and school councils.* Perth: Western Australian Department of Education.

Du Gay, P., 2000. Entrepreneurial governance and public management: The anti-bureaucrats. In J. Clarke, S. Gewirtz and E. McLaughlin, eds., *New managerialism new welfare?* London: Open University Press. (pp. 62–81).

Evers, C. W. and Lakomski, G., 2013. Methodological individualism, educational administration, and leadership. *Journal of Educational Administration and History,* 45(2), pp. 159–173.

Fitzgerald, T. and Savage, J., 2013. Scripting, ritualising and performing leadership: interrogating recent policy development in Australia. *Journal of Educational Administration and History,* 45(2), pp. 126–143.

Foucault, M., 1984. Polemics, politics and problematizations. In P. Rabinow, ed., *The Foucault reader: An introduction to Foucault's thought.* Harmondsworth: Penguin Books.

Foucault, M., 1991. Questions of method. In G. Burchell, C. Gordon, C. and P. Miller, eds., *The Foucault effect: Studies in governmentality.* Chicago: University of Chicago Press.

Foucault, M., 1997. *Ethics, subjectivity and truth. The essential works of Michel Foucault, 1954–1984.* Volume 1. New York: The New Press.

Foucault, M., 2002. The subject and power. In J.D. Faubion, ed., *Essential works of Michel Foucault, 1954–1984, Volume 1: Power.* Harmondsworth: Penguin Books. (pp. 326–348).

Foucault, M., 2007. *Security, territory, population: Lectures at the Collège de France 1977–1978.* Hampshire: Palgrave MacMillan.

Foucault, M., 2008. *The birth of biopolitics: Lectures at the Collège de France 1978–1979.* Basingstoke: Palgrave MacMillan.

Fullan, M., 2011. Change leader: Learning to do what matters most. San Francisco, CA: John Wiley and Sons.

Gewirtz, S., 2002. *The managerial school: Post-welfarism and social justice in education.* London: Routledge.

Gewirtz, S., Ball, S. and Bowe, R., 1995. *Markets, choice and equity in education.* Buckingham: Open University Press.

Gillies, D., 2013. *Educational leadership and Michel Foucault.* New York: Routledge.

Gobby, B., 2013. Principal self-government and subjectification: The exercise of principal autonomy in the Western Australian Independent Public Schools programme. *Critical Studies in Education,* 54(3), pp. 273–285.

Gobby, B., 2015. Putting 'the system' into a school autonomy reform: The case of the independent public school programme. *Discourse: Studies in the Cultural Politics of Education,* 37(1), pp. 16–29.

Government Media Office (GMO), 2009. *New era for public education in Western Australia.* 12 August, Government of Western Australia, Perth.

Grace, G., 1995. *School leadership: Beyond education management: An essay in policy scholarship*. London: The Falmer Press.

Gunter, H., 2009. *Leadership and the reform of education*. Bristol: The Policy Press.

Gunter, H. and Fitzgerald, T., 2008. The future of leadership research? *School Leadership and Management: Formerly School Organisation*, 28(3), pp. 261–279.

Hargreaves, D., 2011. *Leading a self-improving school system*. Nottingham, UK: National College for School Leadership.

Hindess, B., 1997. A society governed by contract? In G. Davis, B. Sullivan and A. Yeatman, eds., *The new contractualism?* South Melbourne: Macmillan Education Australia. (pp. 14–26).

Keddie, A., Mills, M. and Pendergast, D., 2015. Fabricating an identity in neo-liberal times: Performing schooling as 'number one'. *Oxford Review of Education*, 37(1), pp. 75–92.

Lakomski, G., 2005. *Managing without leadership*. Oxford: Elsevier.

Leithwood, K., Day, C., Sammons, P., Harris, A. and Hopkins, D., 2006. *Seven strong claims about successful school leadership*. Nottingham, UK: National College of School Leadership.

Niesche, R., 2011. *Foucault and educational leadership: Disciplining the principal*. London: Routledge.

Niesche, R. and Gowlett, C., 2015. Advocating a post-structuralist politics for educational leadership. *Educational Philosophy and Theory: Incorporating ACCESS*, 47(4), pp. 372–386.

O'Brien, P., 2014. Performance government: Activating and regulating self-governing capacities of teachers and school leaders. *Educational Philosophy and Theory*, 47(8), pp. 833–847.

Rose, N., 1996. *Inventing our selves: Psychology, power and personhood*. Cambridge: Cambridge University Press.

Rose, N., 1999. *Powers of freedom: Reframing political thought*. Cambridge: Cambridge University Press.

Rose, N. and Miller, P., 1992. Political power beyond the state: Problematics of government. *British Journal of Sociology*, 43(2), pp. 173–205.

Rose, N., O'Malley, P. and Valverde, M., 2006. Governmentality. *Annual Review of Law, Society and Science*, 2, pp. 83–104.

Savage, G., 2013. Governmentality in practice: Governing the self and others in a marketized education system. In D. Gillies, ed., *Educational leadership and Michel Foucault*. New York: Routledge. (pp. 87–105).

Wright, N., 2011. Between 'bastard' and 'wicked' leadership? School leadership and the emerging policies of the UK Coalitional Government. *Journal of Educational Administration and History*, 43(4), pp. 345–362.

7 Performatively resignifying leadership

Christina Gowlett

Introduction

Educational leadership, like many other areas of research, has recurring habits of thought (Gronn, 2003; Kelly, 2008; Niesche, 2013). In some ways, this can be highly productive, but it is also limiting as it draws boundaries around scholarship, and it is sometimes hard to shift those boundaries. Like Rasmussen and Allen (2014), I believe 'queer concepts have an important role to play in places where, at first glance, they appear to have no place or purchase'. I subsequently wish to unsettle the educational leadership field by cross-fertilising it with theory from Judith Butler, a well-known queer theorist.

Butler's work originates from gender and sexualities research, but that is not the focus of this chapter. A key aspect of Butler's work, one that I think is fruitful for the area of educational leadership, is the un-anchoring (without reifying) of normative categories and the consequent illumination of their instability. What does this mean? Butler uses a version of ontology and epistemology that rejects the metaphysical anchoring of phenomena. In other words, 'things' (like bodies, words, identity categories and objects) do not have inherently determinate boundaries. She embraces uncertainty. This significantly calls into question the dominant Cartesian belief between subject and object and the dominant assumption that there is an integrity to what is being observed, 'awaiting representation' (Butler, 1990, p. 4). Crucially then, phenomena do not pre-exist (even those phenomena with a long history of sedimentation). Instead, Butler posits that phenomena are brought into being when they operate in a way that is recognisable. When a social practice is enacted, it is conferred with recognisability based on the bank of social norms in operation. Quite famously, Butler (1990) uses the example of a body putting on lipstick, and the popular assumption by many, when they see that action, to label the body as female, since women are predominantly associated with the act of putting on make-up. These actions that incite recognisability are called performatives, and this process of becoming recognisable is consequently called 'performativity'. When phenomena function in a way that is partially recognisable but not fully, then this is a mutated iteration of the initial social practice, and this is called performative resignification. These mutated and transgressive iterations of social norms productively highlight different 'modes of living' (Jackson and Mazzei, 2012, p. 81). Discussing these different modes of living is important because it incites the possibility of expanding both the ontological and epistemological terrain. It expands what is seen to count and be conferred as recognisable and thus accepted socially. Significantly, though, how might Butlerian thinking be useful in the field of educational leadership research?

By positing the idea that phenomena do not pre-exist, Butler helps us to question 'leadership' as the principal object of analysis in educational leadership research. Put simply, if we enter the field of educational leadership research without any preconceived idea about what it is, then how do we research it? Butler helps us to lose epistemological and ontological certainty, in its various shades, about leadership. This does not necessarily mean the death of leadership research. Instead, it opens up a fruitful debate about (a) what normative ideas have come to exist about leadership and how they have come to exist; (b) how ideas about leadership mutate; and (c) what role scholars play in forging dominant ideas and understandings about leadership.

My engagement with Butler in the case study below provides an example of how her ideas are useful for exploring mutated forms of leadership in schools. Education, like many aspects of society, is currently obsessed with the use of data – what Lingard (2011) labels 'policy as numbers'. There has been much discussion about the use of data in schools by school leaders in response to external accountability pressures, often to the detriment of student learning. This idea is not new and, as I have argued elsewhere (Gowlett, 2015), has become quite enduring, with much research consequently being focused on the various ways data is being used for accountability purposes and not student learning (see Steiner-Khamsi, 2004; Stobart, 2008; Taubman, 2009; Rezai-Rashti, 2009; Lingard, 2010, 2011). I am not suggesting that this research is not important – it most certainly is. I am, however, concerned that the social practice of leaders using data in schools has become too closely associated with externally generated performance indicators. Even the research on school-based data usage that *is* concerned with improving student learning, and thus individualising it, appears to operate within a prism that accepts externally created yardsticks of performance success and is driven by them. For example, Sharratt and Fullan (2012) advocate for schools to use a more individualised approach to data usage by putting 'faces on the data'. Again, I am certainly not suggesting that individualising data usage is bad. I am, however, suggesting that a recurring habit of thinking within educational leadership is the association of data usage with externally generated measures of success. The school I talk about below identifies its own goals, generates appropriate data to justify working towards those goals and then makes this align with external performance measures. This is different to schools starting with externally generated goals, unpacking data to help them align with external performance measures and then enacting interventionist strategies to achieve external measures of success. The latter is driven by the external, while the former is driven by the internal. There are, therefore, different logics of practice at play. There is a nuanced difference between being driven by external measures and aligning with external measures.

The more we talk about schools using data driven by external measures of performance *without* including the transgressive stories – the stories that illustrate how data aligns with external accountability measures, but is not generated by those same measures – the more we as researchers create a narrow range of ontological possibilities for school leaders to gravitate towards. Stories of transgressive and mutative data usage are stories of hope and possibility. They aid us in the construction of new social horizons. It is important to expand/mutate/disrupt and hence embrace the instability of what school leadership is and can be.

Informed by such an approach, in what follows, I analyse how a school leader – a director of student achievement at a secondary school located in a low socio-economic area in Queensland, Australia – uses data in unexpected ways, and by doing so, resignifies what 'doing data' can mean. Instead of using data solely for external accountability, the director of student achievement *generates* data to (a) instigate more inclusive pedagogical practices; (b) create school-specific support programmes for local families; (c) strategically give students hope about their future to counteract negative public perception about the school and its student population; and (d) begin conversations about student welfare. I argue that the director of student achievement uses external performance measures as leverage to gain traction for more localised school issues. I initiate this argument in two moves. First, I describe the school context and the way data is used. Second, I bring in Butler to analyse my description. I delay using Butler until after I have described the school context because I feel it enables a more robust analysis of the intricacies taking place within the school. Butlerian concepts are highly interconnected, and explaining one aspect without the other may mislead the reader. I break with the convention of simultaneously describing and analysing data with the hope of providing a fuller and hopefully more meaningful point of entry for Butlerian concepts into educational leadership research.

The case study school: Clawburn State High School

Clawburn State High School is located in an economically and socially disadvantaged area of Queensland. The area in which the school is located has a reputation for being 'rough'. The school is known (although far less now) for a high rate of student absences and poor results on external measures of schooling success. It has approximately 400 student enrolments, with students from an array of cultural backgrounds. Clawburn is a complex school. It often receives new migrant students who have recently settled in Australia, since housing in the area is much cheaper compared to other parts of urbanised Queensland; and many students do not use English at home. The school also has a large percentage of its student population living independently, in foster care or with extended family. The social issues that students often face are many and varied. In response to an increase in external accountability pressures, namely the improvement of student results on external measures, the school created a leadership position – director of student achievement – and a teacher already working at the school, 'Lyn', was promoted to the position. What is interesting about Lyn is the *way* in which she works with data.

I researched Clawburn State High School in 2013 as part of a previous post-doctoral project. The project focused on examining the various ways in which secondary schools were helping students to make decisions about their future. I recruited Clawburn to my project because of its eclecticism and poor public image. On external school measures of success, Clawburn did not perform well, but it was also facing a challenging set of circumstances because of the variety of social issues present at the school. I interviewed the school principal first and then a variety of staff members involved with formally helping students to plan for their future, one of whom was Lyn, the director of student achievement for the senior school. The following sections draw from my formal interview with Lyn, my brief conversations with her every time I visited the school (which was eleven times in total) plus my observations of Lyn *in situ* when she was talking with students and/or staff about the progress of the senior students at Clawburn. I draw from a case study to help generate a more nuanced understanding of data usage by leaders in schools. Working from the small outwards does, as Thomson et al. (2010) argue, help draw attention to other types of patterns of analysis, ones that are often side-lined because of their idiosyncratic nature.

When I asked Lyn about herself and her employment at Clawburn, she gave the following response:

> I have been here for twenty plus years, but this is my second year as Director of Student Achievement…I look after the year ten, eleven and twelve students. Part of what I do is around tracking them for their Queensland Certificate of Education,[1] looking at OP[2] (Overall Position) predictions, so where their OP might fall and what the implications of that are around subject changes and subject choices for the best outcomes for students. So that's sort of the main part of my role with them….a big part of my job is about managing outcomes. And it's not just for the school and our data but it's for them as well.

When I first heard Lyn describe her job, I was immediately sceptical. I had already been in a number of schools researching the ways in which they managed post-schooling outcomes, and I had read the academic literature about the use of this information for predominantly external accountability reasons. Alarm bells immediately started to ring. Upon reflection, my reaction was based on the social norm that had built up around the use of data in schools – I was becoming guilty of the very act I now caution against. I was judging Clawburn from a prism of preconceived intelligibilities, and this only 2 minutes and 32 seconds into my interview with Lyn.

Using data to reflect on pedagogy

As my interview with Lyn progressed, it became more apparent that Lyn's role was not solely concerned with using data for external accountability purposes. While accountability to external bodies was certainly a part of Lyn's job description, so too was expanding the learning opportunities made available to students as they progressed into the senior years of schooling. As Lyn outlines:

> I get to see all data that is generated by the school....this means I also get to rejig how that data is looked at and used. Take student assessment results. We have 59 students in year 11, and I get to see all their semester results. These student results are generated in an alphabetical list format....Part of my job involves sitting down with students who are not performing well, failing, and asking them why. Last semester I had to chat with 16 of our year 11 students, all of which had failed at least one subject during the semester. When I chatted with them, I mean *really* chatted with them, most spoke about not understanding how to do research. The majority had failed an assignment that required them to go away and find information. They were struggling with how to break down research questions and find relevant information about the topics they had chosen. Because of this, I decided to chat with the Social Sciences Head of Department, since the subjects many of them failed were Ancient History, Geography and English, to see if we could improve the way we were teaching these kids to research. When we looked at the students' senior profiles in each of the subjects they failed, it was definitely research related assessment tasks that were letting them down. The Head of Department decided to dedicate two faculty professional development afternoons to discussing how the faculty could improve their pedagogical approach to teaching research skills. That conversation has now started other conversations in other faculties.

This extract illustrates how Lyn is using results data to reflect upon teaching practices within the school. Lyn uses it to begin conversations with both students *and* staff to improve student access to learning.

School specific support programmes for local families

Clawburn School faces an eclectic range of student issues, many of which impact on students' access to educational opportunity. At Clawburn, the possibility of tertiary study is affected by a range of complex issues, one of which is knowing how to qualify for access to further study. Lyn outlines the complexities of this in the extended extract below:

> A large proportion of our students have many barriers to just knowing about how to qualify for entry into university....we have a large section of students whose parents and/or siblings have never been to university, it's completely new.... I certainly don't mean that in a derogatory way. It just means that the parents need help as well as the students in navigating a system they are unfamiliar with. Take pre-requisites. If you haven't had a relative who's been to uni, or known someone who has, then it's actually pretty hard to know

how to navigate putting in an application and making sure you have all the pre-requisites, or knowing how to shift across courses....then there's being able to pay....We have a number of students that want to attend university, but the fees are prohibitive. We've also been in the situation when students on temporary visas, and we haven't known they were on temporary visas, have wanted to attend university, to find out once they have been granted a place that they can't actually qualify for deferred payment of their fees because they don't have permanent residency, and international student fees are even higher. We found all of this out by actually talking to the students and their parents. That's where we started. I make a point of talking to students and then creating numbers data to show my principal so she can go away to district office and make an argument for extra money to support these students. I know it's expected that the numbers data comes first, because god knows data is only numerical (said sarcastically) but data can also be conversational, although it doesn't gain as much attention. So I did it the other way around, and I'm proud to say that we now run immigration information sessions so families can learn how to apply for permanent residency in advance.

There are several points of interest here. First, Lyn uses what she calls 'numbers data' to draw attention to issues within the school and generate support for them. This indicates the higher traction that quantitative data seems to have despite, as she critically points out, the merit of qualitative approaches such as talking with students and parents. Second, and very importantly, Lyn values different types of data and uses them in a contextual way. She makes data work for her instead of allowing herself to be worked by external data measures.

Using (qualitative) data to give students hope

Clawburn School suffers from a negative public image. It has a long history of performing badly on external assessment measures, and the general perception is that the students are 'no hopers'. This public image seems to endure despite existing information to the contrary. Having been at the school for 20 years, Lyn is privy to counter-narratives, and she uses them to help boost student morale:

I know we've had our fair share of misfits, but so too have other schools. We have students with very complex needs and it isn't OK for our kids to be made to feel like they're no hopers just because they come here. I've been here a long time and have heaps of stories about students doing well, so a couple of years ago, I decided to put together some information to share on assembly....there's one ex student who didn't do well at school, but after he left, he invented a trolley locking system and it's used in many shopping centres now, and he's really wealthy. I show them how many students may not go on to uni straight after they leave here, but how many do eventually, so I show them that there are a number of ways to get there. Quite a few do. It just takes longer sometimes. I show them how an ex student who had a baby while she was here at school is now working as a nurse, and there are many more stories like these. I do it to counteract the bad press.

I attended one such assembly and the presentation was impressive. As we walked out, I heard many students talking excitedly about the information. It created possibility and hope about the future. I heard two students discussing how they were not aware that people could go to university when they were older. They thought it was something people only did straight out of school. I heard another group discussing moving away to attend university, and if they did, the possibility of house sharing. The local area had only a satellite campus, and if they moved closer in, they would be able to access three universities instead of just one, hence opening up their study options. Lyn's presentation created a 'buzz' about the future.

Using data to have conversations about student welfare

Lyn told me quite often that the problem with using solely numerical data was the fact it was often collected too late. She often mentioned how schools were really good at identifying issues only after they had become a problem. Lyn said 'semester results tell you that there *has* been a problem, but we need to better identify when there *is* a problem, and work to resolve it'. Lyn kept a spreadsheet containing all the individual assessment item results for students in years 10, 11 and 12. She said this was 'simply the starting point to keeping track of student welfare'. When I asked her to elaborate on this more, Lyn said:

> I use this information to have conversations with staff about how our kids are going in school generally. We have a staff meeting every four weeks that is focused on discussing the welfare of our kids. I call it a meeting focused on discussing student results, since I do use their results to start the conversation, but the meeting is actually about unpacking how the kids are going in general. I like to catch the kids, if I can, before they fall.

I attended two of these data meetings. Lyn began them by pulling up a spreadsheet on a data projector with all student names and results to date by year level. One by one, Lyn asked how each of the students is going, and every teacher from each of their subjects provided a response. The teacher responses often included information about attendance, motivation in class, behaviour in class and other matters relevant to the general welfare of the student.

These data meetings focus on developing a more holistic picture about the student. Take 'Sam' as an example. Sam was in his final year of schooling and had recently become independent. His mother and father had divorced a year previously and, up until six months before the meeting, he had been living with his mother. His mother, however, had gone on a trip to New Zealand and had not come back. Sam had been left by himself. Sam had a part-time job, but the money he earned was not enough to pay for his rent and living expenses. He had no extended family that could care for him, and he was six months away from finishing his senior year. He was already 17 years of age, so not far from turning 18 (legal adult age in Australia). The school became aware of his situation when he started missing school in order to take on more work shifts to pay for his rent. His situation was identified quickly, and importantly, it was being monitored by the school. In the meeting I attended, Sam's teachers were giving an update about his progress. The school had helped him fast track an application for independent adult status, which gave him access to social security support, which in turn helped him return to school. His teachers were taking turns in helping him catch up on work. Although Sam did not take home economics as a subject, one of the home economics teachers was helping Sam learn to cook simple and nutritious meals. She was also teaching him how to meal plan and organise a grocery budget. Sam had recently mastered making a frittata, and there was a huge round of applause when the home economics teacher announced that.

I use Sam's story to illustrate the information spoken about in these data meetings run by Lyn, but his story, albeit one of the more extreme, was not unique. I witnessed many similar stories. These face-to-face conversations may not be possible in larger schools, but the point is that Lyn uses numerical data in a way that best suits the context of her school. This type of data usage may be seen to work from the presumption that student results determine student welfare issues. In other words, 'bad results = social problems'. In some contexts, this presumptive logic may be at play, but Lyn is also aware of the limitations of this approach:

> I know our conversational model about results data sort of works from the idea that there are only welfare issues when students aren't performing well, which isn't always the case. Students can be doing really well, but still be having issues, and students might also be performing badly and have no issues at home. In fact, it might be issues at school that they're having, issues with their teachers that are affecting them, and not necessarily showing up in their results. I think our model does help to also capture some of that other stuff too since I encourage staff to talk about anything – good, bad or anything in between that is of relevance to our students. It's interesting when there is a stark difference between how the student is behaving in one subject compared to another. Take Mandy. In the last meeting her Maths A teacher said she wasn't attending, but all her other teachers said that she was. This flagged an issue, so I followed up. Mandy told me she really liked Maths A, she was even doing well, but she hated being asked to help Joel all the time, so she started skipping it. Joel is having a lot of difficulty in the subject so the teacher has been using Mandy to help explain things to Joel, and Mandy was sick and tired of it. Her Maths teacher had created a dependency. Joel was now coming to Mandy all the time for help with his other subjects and Mandy just wanted to hang out with her friends.

Lyn consequently had a conversation with Mandy's maths teacher to find a solution. The teacher needed help in supporting Joel. That one conversation, beginning in the data meeting, set off a chain of further conversations, resulting in Mandy, Joel and their teacher being provided with more support. As Lyn outlined, 'support isn't just about supporting students. Sometimes it's about supporting teachers to support students, and our data meetings open up that conversation'.

Performatively (re)signifying leadership with data

> Is there a way to submit provisionally and critically to such norms, and to do so in ways that change the norms themselves? Is it possible to inhabit the norms in order to mobilize the rules differently?
>
> (Butler, 2006, p. 532)

The above provocation by Butler incites us to think about possibility within constraint. The use of what Lyn calls 'numbers data' is a current and dominant educational trend and is inculcated in what Mayer-Schönberger and Cukier (2014) delineate as the more systemic 'datafication' of our society. There is no shortage of scholars discussing the current push for school leaders to use data (Ozga, 2009; Lingard and Sellar, 2013; Goldstein and Moss, 2014; Hardy, 2015) and discussion about education 'policy as numbers' is well documented (see Lingard, 2011). Seemingly less popular, however, are transgressive and mutative stories about school leaders 'doing data differently' (Gowlett, 2013, p. 199).

Through a Butlerian prism, desire (action) is generated by a need for recognition. We gravitate towards certain social practices because they confer the possibility of acceptance. Butler (1997, p. 7) explains it simply with the phrase, 'I would rather exist in subordination than not exist'. In other words, action is not premeditated but instead pushed along by the necessity to be recognised and validated. People are pulled towards taking certain actions because they hold out the possibility of acceptance. When a practice becomes entrenched as a social norm, the gravitational pull increases because the possibility for social acceptance rises as well.

At any one time, however, we are subject to a variety of gravitational pulls, and this creates a 'complex constellation' of actions (Youdell, 2005, p. 253). As Butler (1990, p. 145) outlines: 'discourses present themselves in the plural, coexisting within temporal frames, and instituting unpredictable and inadvertent convergences from which specific modalities or discursive possibilities are engendered'. In other words, the convergence of simultaneous gravitational pulls makes it possible for social practices to be enacted in modified and mutated ways.

This messiness of how we come to act, or as Butler (1990) names it, the process of 'performative subjectification', is useful for making sense of how social norms are modified, or in Butlerian terms, 'performatively (re)signified' (1997, p. 15) as well.

Possibility for reworking dominant social practices consequently exists within the very terms that one is simultaneously constrained by. The multiplicity of subjecthood, in the form of the messiness of trying to meet convergent social practices at once, is the arena for altering the very constraints being adhered to. This is visible through the actions of Lyn as a school leader charged with the responsibility of improving student achievement. This is clear in the following extract from my interview with Lyn:

> It's all about data but for us it's also about balancing that with the welfare of our students. The current mood is all about numbers data. You get nowhere unless you use numbers and have numbers to back you up. The only form of evidence that seems to count is numbers, and no one in district or central office listens to you unless you use numbers data. So that's what we're doing. We're conforming to what is expected of us by district office, and we're accountable to them, but we're also conforming to what is expected of us as educators, and that's to take care of the welfare of our students and members of our community. I use numbers data to fulfill both those expectations. I know it isn't what most people are doing, but finding a way to fulfill both pressures helps me sleep at night.

Here Lyn is expressing how she is caught between two strong gravitational pulls. On the one hand, she is expected to be using what she calls 'numbers data' to justify her actions within the school, and she is aware of the limitations of that approach. On the other hand, Lyn is flagging the expectation that she support her school community constituents, which is often better facilitated without the use of numbers and instead via more qualitative means of evidence and support. Lyn's actions are not seemingly dominated by external measures of success. She acknowledges that she needs to be seen to be working towards external accountabilities, and 'numbers data' helps to facilitate this, but the gravitational pull towards helping students in a more organic way is very strong. What has emerged is a mutated hybrid. Lyn uses data, as she is expected to do, so she conforms to that leadership norm. However, Lyn is simultaneously charged with the responsibility of caring for Clawburn's student population due to her leadership position. These are two competing and seemingly antagonistic interpellations. Given the current emphasis on using 'numbers data', she facilitates upholding the welfare of students by using such. This makes her actions an acceptable form of leadership in the eyes of district office while also fulfilling the expectation of student welfare.

Lyn's mutated use of data is recognisable through both the prism of the district office and what they see leadership to entail *and* the school community's expectation that Lyn lead the school in improving student access to educational opportunity. Lyn's actions are a good example of what Butler (2004, p. 4) labels 'different modes of living'. Lyn is operating within the constraints of recognisable leadership practice. She is inhabiting the norms of data usage by school leaders, but also reconfiguring what those norms can mean and look like. Lyn consequently (re)signifies leadership practice using data.

Theoretical and methodological musings about using Butler to ~~think about~~ do leadership research

This chapter sits within a book dedicated to questioning the use of the word leadership in examining organisational practices within schools. What does thinking with Butler add to this discussion? Butler's work originates from a contextual paradigm familiar with open-endedness. Queer theory – or what I have elsewhere called 'queer(y)ing' – is a mode of inquiry that interrogates border and boundaries (Gowlett, 2014) without the need to instantiate a new norm. As Atkinson and DePalma (2007, p. 67) highlight, queer theory, of which Butler is a prominent advocate, is good at 'keeping questions open when faced with the temptation of easy certainties'. In this respect, using Butler to queer(y) leadership is not really about the use of the term. It is more about the methodological mindset being used to think about leadership.

While Butler's work has been critiqued for placing a large degree of emphasis on linguistic action instead of being grounded in the material,[3] I feel a defence to this claim is more evident when weaving her work into new settings away from gender and sexualities research. For example, I have used the word *leadership* in this chapter, but if I was to delete that word from my writing here, the chapter would not be significantly affected. It would still be focused on examining the social practices associated with data usage in schools and how one person working within a secondary school context mutates away from common expectations regarding how data ought to be used. For me, the issue is not whether the term *leadership* is appropriate or not, since I embrace its instability and uncertainty. I understand that for some, leadership may denote a hierarchical structure and hence delimit in advance who and what we explore in schools to manage them. I agree; it can. The same, however, can be said for any term. Instead, the issue for me is how certain actions and terms become all-encompassing and dominate the field. What is necessary, therefore, is a mode of enquiry that looks for mutations of social practice. This means exploring what the norms are and then discussing the resignified versions of them as well. Butler's unanchoring of dominant logics of thinking is useful for doing just that.

Notes

1 This is the senior certificate of education in the Queensland context.
2 OP stands for *overall position* and is the current senior ranking system for entry into university.
3 See Jackson and Mazzei (2012) for a discussion about this.

References

Atkinson, E. and DePalma, R., 2007. Exploring gender identity; queering heteronormativity. *International Journal of Equity and Innovation in Early Childhood*, 5, pp. 68–82.

Butler, J., 1990. *Gender trouble: Feminism and the subversion of identity*. London: Routledge.

Butler, J., 1993. *Bodies that matter: On the discursive limits of sex*. New York: Routledge.

Butler, J., 1997. *The psychic life of power: Theories in subjection*. Stanford: Stanford University Press.

Butler, J., 2004. *Undoing gender*. London, New York: Routledge.

Butler, J., 2006. Response. *British Journal of Sociology of Education*, 27(4), pp. 529–534.

Goldstein, H. and Moss, G., 2014. Knowledge and numbers in education, *Comparative Education*, 50(3), pp. 259–265.

Gowlett, C., 2013. Doing data differently: Disrupting the dominant intelligibilities surrounding performance data and the impact on secondary schooling. In S. Eacott and R. Niesche, eds., *Empirical leadership research: Letting the data speak for themselves* (pp. 199–214) Niagara Falls, NY: Untested Ideas Research Center.

Gowlett, C., 2014. Queer(y)ing and recrafting agency: Moving away from a model of coercion versus escape. *Discourse*, 35(3), pp. 405–418.

Gowlett, C., 2015. Queer(y)ing new schooling accountabilities through MySchool: Using Butlerian tools to think differently about policy performativity. *Educational Philosophy and Theory*, 47(2), pp. 159–172.

Gronn, P., 2003. Leadership: Who needs it? *School Leadership and Management*, 23(3), pp. 267–290.

Hardy, I., 2015. Data, numbers and accountability: The complexity, nature and effects of data use in schools. *British Journal of Educational Studies*, 64(4), pp. 467–486.

Jackson, A. J. and Mazzei, L., 2012. *Thinking with theory in qualitative research: Viewing data across multiple perspectives*. London: Routledge.

Kelly, S., 2008. Leadership: A categorical mistake? *Human Relations*, 61(6), pp. 763–782.

Lingard, B., 2010. Policy borrowing, policy learning: Testing times in Australian schooling, *Critical Studies in Education*, 51, pp. 129–147.

Lingard, B., 2011. Policy as numbers: Ac/counting for educational research. *Australian Educational Researcher*, 38, pp. 355–382.

Lingard, B. and Sellar, S., 2013. 'Catalyst data': Perverse systemic effects of audit and accountability in Australian schooling. *Journal of Education Policy*, 28(5), pp. 634–656.

Mayer-Schönberger, V. and Cukier, K., 2014. *Big data: A revolution that will transform how we live, work and think*. Boston: Mariner Books.

Niesche, R., 2013. *Deconstructing educational leadership: Derrida and Lyotard*. London and New York: Routledge.

Ozga, J., 2009. Governing education through data in England: From regulation to self-evaluation. *Journal of Education Policy*, 24(2), pp. 149–162.

Rasmussen, M. L. and Allen, L., 2014. What can a concept do? Rethinking education's queer assemblages. *Discourse: Studies in the Cultural Politics of Education*, 35(3), pp. 433–443.

Rezai-Rashti, G., 2009. The neo-liberal assault on Ontario's secondary schools. In C. Levine-Rasky, ed., *Canadian perspectives on the sociology of education*. Oxford: Oxford University Press.

Sharratt, L. and Fullan, M., 2012. Putting FACES on the data: What great leaders do! Thousand Oaks, CA: Corwin.

Steiner Khamsi, G., ed., 2004. *The global politics of educational borrowing and lending*. New York: Teachers' College Press.

Stobart, G., 2008. *Testing times: The uses and abuses of assessment*. London: Routledge.

Taubman, P., 2009. *Teaching by numbers: Deconstructing the discourse of standards and accountability in education*. New York: Routledge.

Thomson, P., Hall, C. and Jones, K., 2010. Maggie's day: A small scale analysis of English education policy. *Journal of Education Policy*, 25(5), pp. 639–656.

Youdell, D., 2005. Sex–gender–sexuality: How sex, gender and sexuality constellations are constituted in secondary schools. *Gender and Education*, 17(3), pp. 249–270.

8 Thinking beyond leadership as a service to policy

'Seeing things big' in a dialogic 'public space'

Bev Rogers

Introduction

What has been called the 'Romance of Leadership' (Meindl et al., 1985) is a deep-seated faith in the idea of a 'leader' or 'leadership' as *the* causal entity that renders 'complex problems meaningful and explicable' (Gronn, 1996, p. 12). Such a causal attribution is implicit in the preoccupation of countries such as England, New Zealand, the USA and Australia with school 'leaders' and 'leadership' *of* schools (Fitzgerald and Savage, 2013). The leadership industry in these countries is largely influenced by what Thomson, Gunter and Blackmore (2014, p. xi) call the Transnational Leadership Package (TLP), which includes prescriptions of a 'one best way' of leading, leadership and being a leader, a series of meta-analyses that attempt to establish the link between teacher quality and student achievement and an assumption that the role of the leader is to advance policy. Terms such as *leaders* and *leadership* now dominate policy discourses that sanction the means for education reform. The location of causal imputation is evident in the way policy texts have scripted school leaders to *transform* and *deliver* in ways that not only claim to achieve the mandated outcomes (Fitzgerald and Savage, 2013) but also establish that the outcomes are the result of the 'leadership' enacted.

This way of talking about leadership, which now permeates education, pressures leaders 'towards the purpose of serving policy' (Atkinson, 2004, p. 111). Within the context of *Teacher Standards* in Australia and the *Australian Professional Standard for Principals*, leadership is constructed by government policy as 'visioning', 'ensuring commitment', 'evening out differences', 'limiting uncertainty' and 'improving consistency' in 'delivering educational services' (*Australian Institute for Teaching and School Leadership* [AITSL], 2011, p. 6). Leadership is therefore offered as a tactic for orchestrating teacher performance, with leaders increasingly assumed to be acting as an agent for the state. Such 'leadership *of* schools' is no less than the 'downward delegation of the managerialist project' (Fitzgerald and Savage, 2013, p. 135), constructed as the solution to the improvement of student achievement and teacher quality through the individualised management of performance within regimes of accountability largely focused on standardised tests. The education, leadership, management and administration (ELMA) field is increasingly dominated by a 'business model of transformational leadership…with the emphasis on the headteacher as a charismatic local leader bringing about radical change through the implementation of national reforms' (Gunter, 2014, p. 23).

From this view, the school is viewed as a controllable, stable entity with an accompanying strong sense of ownership and identification of and by the principal with its success or otherwise. When leadership is seen as an instrument for attaining outcomes, a pervasive technical rationality is focused on the 'performance' and 'improvement' of the school as an entity, often enacted through the 'performance management' of staff. This makes it more likely that the school principal acts to promote harmony rather than risking opening up conflicting views and promotes standard-*isation* of what it means to be a 'good' teacher through implementation and 'delivery' rather than dialogue. Within this frame, differing views may be seen as 'resistance'. A sense of 'failure' is reflected in any absence of harmony with a nagging doubt for principals about their effectiveness.

We need to question why the predominant view of leadership being presented at this time maintains leadership as the management of consensus around agreements for 'delivery', through which, the school as an entity 'performs'. This leadership of schools is what Greene (1995, pp. 10–11) identifies as 'the vision that sees things small', which takes a technical view from the vantage point of the system preoccupied with accountability measures and management procedures, 'while it screens out the faces and gestures of individuals, of actual living persons'. Greene argues that we can also see the world (seeing things big) from the view that brings us into close contact 'in the midst of what is happening', where people are not viewed as 'mere objects or chess pieces' but in their integrity and particularity (Greene, 1995, p. 10). Leadership as it is currently conceived is a benign form of thinking from the view of a system with all of its manipulation of others justified by system ends – seeing things small.

Johnson et al. (2016, p. 143) argue that 'one of the most persistent issues confronting governments, education systems and schools today: the attraction, preparation and retention of early career teachers' is significantly impacted upon by the 'damaging effects of top-down policies that…marginalise and silence early career teachers' (Johnson et al., 2016, p. 9). One of the ways the authors suggest that leadership might be rethought in this context is in reconceiving notions of participatory democracy based on the realities of teachers' daily lives, by opening up 'scrutiny and debate' the dominance of neoliberal thinking (Gunter, 2014, p. 87). Rather than the detached system view, the ways in which 'teachers negotiate the damaging effects of the political, managerial and technical interventions on their emotional and professional labour' (Johnson et al., 2016, p. 4) requires that school principals and head teachers 'see things big' (Greene, 1995, p. 10). The juxtaposition of big and small thinking may be possible by learning 'how to move back and forth' (Greene, 1995, p. 11), but this requires a view of leadership beyond the detached system view of it as a service to policy. In developing an argument for another view of *educational* leadership, I argue that current dominant views of leadership are instrumental and de-politicised, enacted through engendering a space of compliance. I mobilise the ideas of the political philosopher Hannah Arendt in relation to 'public space' and plurality as a provocation to re-think educational leadership. In addition to her ideas about plurality, natality and public space, I also mobilise Arendt's ideas about the origins of the separation of 'rule' from 'execution', so embedded in neoliberal ideologies and policies, which lays the ground work for examining her concepts of plurality and public space to allow a reimagining of educational leadership as a collective practice of 'seeing things big'. Arendt describes this as the *power* of acting 'in concert' (Arendt, 1958) in a space of ongoing dialogue.

Hannah Arendt

Hannah Arendt is generally seen as one of the most influential political philosophers of the twentieth century. A resurgence of Arendt's work since the 1990s has informed a renewed interest in the relationship of action to agency (Calhoun and McGowan, 1997), with a growth in the number of writers in education using her work, (e.g. Duarte, 2001; Gordon, 2001; Gunter, 2014; Schutz, 1999; Wiens, 2000). Gunter (2014, p. 1) identifies the 'impressive intellectual legacy that continues to act as a provocation to think about current human predicaments in fresh and challenging ways'. Arendt's life's work lay in trying to understand totalitarianism from the view of actual experiences and also conceptually, since she was 'trying to find bulwarks against [totalitarianism] and reflecting on these difficulties and complexities in doing so' (Canovan, 1992, p. 197). Bernstein (2010) argues that Arendt's service to our thinking is to highlight that although we are not living in a totalitarian society, the temptation to appeal to 'totalitarian solutions' is still very much with us. With resources from Arendt's analysis of totalitarianism, the existing view of leadership can be seen as 'a form of tyranny' because 'it works through the ordinariness of every day practice in ways that can be handled, seem sensible, but makes teachers complicit in a form of practice that is disconnected from learning' (Gunter, 2007, p. 3). In *The Human Condition*, Arendt identifies a political component to 'the solution', whereby citizens feel a collective responsibility for others and the common world, which can only be 'realised' in free discussion with others (Canovan, 1992, p. 184).

In *The Human Condition*, Arendt (1958) conceives of power being actualised when words are used to disclose realities rather than veil intentions, and when word and deed come together in establishing relations and creating new realities rather than being used to violate or destroy. Through the focus on leadership as a causal attribution for successful outcomes, Arendt would argue that we have lost the power of acting 'in concert' without force, manipulation or violence. If we reconceive educational leadership in the context of understanding better the political and ethical capacities of leaders and teachers to work together as respected partners, we might understand educational leadership as being about recognising plurality through fostering a dialogic, democratic and moral community. Leadership for education might then be seen more as a shared responsibility, recognising that 'human meaning is not achieved in solitary singularity, either of ideas or people, but in the complex interactions of both in dialogical situations' (Wiens, 2000, p. 304).

Current instrumental and de-politicised practice of leadership

Arendt uses the term *power* to talk about collective action generated when people gather together to act in concert. 'Arendt distinguishes power from domination…and violence…[to locate it] within the open and common world of human speech and action' (Dixon, 2014, p. 65). In Arendt's conception, the power of acting in concert is rooted in plurality and natality – a diversity of perspectives and the capacity to begin anew in the space of dialogue and gathered actions. In speech and action, people 'appear' to each other, disclosing who they are (Arendt, 1958). Arendt also identifies the *in-between* – the capacity for dialogue to relate and bind unique individuals together around common projects but also to separate them. With the plurality of perspectives, a public space is created where 'only in public can individuals achieve a coherent *position* by relating their own opinions to those expressed by others in that space' (Schutz, 2001a, p. 99). It is actors acting together *with* other actors that generates power (Dixon, 2014). Such power generated from action in concert is not possible without a space that supports dialogue, thinking and judgement as well as an ongoing investigation into how to avoid the splintering or destruction of that space.

In *The Human Condition,* Arendt (1958) separates *labour, work* and *action,* carefully defining their meanings in an attempt to shed light on the three forms of activity she thought fundamental to the human condition. The central political activity is defined as action and therefore separated conceptually from 'doing-as-making' with which it is usually confounded, confusing *praxis* with *poiesis* (Baehr, 2003, p. xxix) and collapsing action into work. 'Labour is the activity which is tied to the human condition of life, work the activity which is tied to the condition of worldliness, and action the activity tied to the condition of plurality' (Rogers, 2016, p. 233). Whilst Arendt acknowledged that action can be informed by moral principles, these operate 'as forces that are disclosed in action, not as limiting conditions' (Disch, 1997, p. 151), because moral action is not about applying decontextualised principles (or silencing 'truths' as she saw them). For Arendt, the acceptance of the plurality of the human condition provides a foundation for human coexistence.

According to Arendt, action is uncertain, irreversible and without a single author, yet in organisations, we are tempted to find 'a substitute for action in the hope [for, and]…escape [from] the haphazardness and moral irresponsibility inherent in plurality of agents' (Arendt, 1958, p. 220). The attempt to replace *acting* with *making* (or action with work) manifests in 'an activity where one man…remains master of his doings from beginning to end' (Arendt, 1958, p. 220), in an attempt to do away with plurality. Arendt points to the misreading of reality when we forget that starting action is not theoretical and controlled by reason but actually 'uncertain and unpredictable whether…let loose in the human or the natural realm' (Arendt, 1958, pp. 231–232). With a preoccupation with ends (a technical rationality), we think there is a way of constraining action so that we know what has been done and can attribute a single author to the act.

The view of the single leader is tied to a technical rationality in which relationships with teachers are seen as one of management, surveillance and control, not only partly fulfilling the needs of managerial logic but also as a way of defending the vulnerability of the principal. The accompanying discourse of technical rationality – for example, in performance management – is oriented to techniques of teaching that have become ends in themselves. The technologies of regulation and control (e.g. documentation of evidence against particular *standards*, which is a common form of performance appraisal) shape how teachers see the 'good' teacher through performance management and their expected role in processes of agreement to 'whole-school' practices.

When principals orchestrate such whole-school agreements, the logic of practice internalises an avoidance of conflict and disagreement, since this can get 'out of hand' and 'potentially can count against [the principal]' (Thomson, 1999, p. 17). Not involving staff in some way is considered ineffective, but then so is opening up conflict that promotes demonstrations against 'corporate loyalty' (Thomson, 1999, p. 17) or 'school loyalty'. A 'failure to convince staff of the merits of a particular project or position' (Thomson, 2001, p. 18), of a particular direction being right, is seen as a personal failure, and every effort is made to avoid this by orchestrating the performance of staff agreement to the 'delivery' of means to achieve policy outcomes. Resistors to such agreement (Evans, 1996) are viewed as 'rebellious children' in an otherwise 'happy family' (Thomson, 1999, p. 15). School principals then focus on producing the imaginary of collaborative reform, which demonstrates both corporate loyalty, school loyalty and successful leadership. The idea of leadership thereby

> functions as a means for engendering compliance with dominant goals and values and harnessing staff commitment, ideas, expertise and experience in realizing these.
>
> (Woods, 2004, p. 4)

Rather than being seen as entailing the collective meaningful action of moral beings, such participation is instrumental and de-politicised. The principal's efforts to dominate through the prior management of conflict (Southworth, 1995), produces a 'contrived collegiality' (Hargreaves, 1999) that 'does not recognize legitimate differences in teachers' views' (Hayes et al., 2004, pp. 523–524). Underpinning the orchestration of agreements with staff is a view that, from the principal's standpoint, the school is 'their own', and its success is intimately connected to how they view themselves and their project.

> Whether they were successful principals or not, is connected to how they mobilised the teaching staff, in particular, to enact the vision they had for the school...Whilst the circumstances and processes were vastly different, each

principal created a story of *their* school, told differently and incorporating different levels of participation, which included a 'logic of practice' for the leadership *game* (Bourdieu, 1990) they played...They took for granted that their role involved primarily deploying these skills in the interests of mobilising harmony in one direction, which they determined for the school.

(Rogers, 2016, p. 106, emphasis added)

Efforts towards mobilising harmony in one direction implies an attempt to bring certainty and security to the messiness of working together in a school. Improvement and performance are situated as individual responsibilities with the naming and shaming of individual success or failure (Thomson, 1999) so that evidence can be presented to identify the success of 'leadership' or its lack. 'Wholly absent is any recognition of the complex, messy and contested environment of schools and school leadership' (Fitzgerald and Savage, 2013, p. 130). Our efforts to substitute the certainty the 'right direction' for the messiness of being in 'the midst of what is happening' attempts to substitute 'seeing things small' for 'seeing things big' (Greene, 1995, pp. 10–11) – substituting the detached system view of commanding 'mere objects' for the close up view of the participant within sight of 'the faxes and gestures of...actual living persons' (Greene, 1995, p. 11). To substitute in this way, according to Arendt, denies the reality of the uncontrollable arena of actions and re-actions and tempts us to substitute *making* and *fabrication* for the uncertainty of action. Arendt argues that this leads to the misreading of leadership as sovereignty.

Such a need to cling to the solid-ness of a concept of leadership, when what we experience is actually the result of many unpredictable interactions, reveals the domination of prediction and control being reinforced at a time when 'we live in the midst of unrelenting evidence of how things are not only transient, but contingent upon other things as conditions' (Newland, 2009, p. 95). What emerges is a relentless complexity of many interdependent conditions, in which we cannot locate a single cause. The attempts to locate leadership as a reason for desirable outcomes denies both the ethical and political capacities to act together and the capacity to recognise the power of acting in concert (Dixon, 2014, p. 66) with its consequent loss of a public space of dialogue. Without a public space, 'the loss of power is the loss of our capacity to act with others in a way that generates, sustains, and discloses a common world'.

Leading separate from action

Our world, Arendt repeatedly emphasised, is simply too complex and multifaceted to be captured by a single point of view (Schutz, 2001b, p.140). This is in contrast with the dominant tendency in Western philosophy

to privilege and valorise unity, harmony, totality and thereby to denigrate, suppress, or marginalize multiplicity, contingency, particularity, singularity.

(Clark et al., 1998, p.789)

Rather than what is 'common' to the human condition being a single view, a single way of seeing the world, Arendt identified that the common world we share exists as a result of the differences we reveal in dialogue. Paradoxically, we get 'commonality' as a result of nurturing difference (Calhoun and McGowan, 1997) through dialogue. Arendt discovered in Kant's work the notion of the common world

> that lies *between* human beings, keeping them distinct and relating them, a shared world in which they can appear and be recognized as unique beings.
> (Kohn, 2001, p. 3, emphasis added)

For Arendt, the hallmark of the idea of sovereignty is the suspicion of action (as defined by Arendt), not the 'will to power' and the desire to substitute fabrication for action, the notion that we live together 'only when some are entitled to command and others forced to obey…[– there are] those who rule and those who are ruled' (Arendt, 1958, p. 222). In the attempt to replace acting with making, Arendt (1958, p. 224) attributes to Plato the establishment of a scheme that allows for many 'to 'act' like one man (sic) without even the possibility of internal dissension…through rule'.

Arendt's approach to understanding how making and fabrication came to substitute for action involved an historical analysis of the Greek and Latin words meaning 'to act', which presents an interesting perspective on the historical roots of our conceptions of leadership. Over time, the meanings of the two words meaning 'to act' changed: in Greek, *archein* (to begin, to lead, to rule) and *prattein* (to pass through, to achieve, to finish), corresponding to the Latin words *agere* (to set in motion, to lead) and *gerere* (to bear) (Arendt, 1958, pp. 177, 189). In each case, the word that designated the achievement – *prattein* and *gerere* – became the accepted word for action in general, whereas the words designating the beginning of the action became specialised – *archein*, meaning 'to rule', 'to lead' and *agere* meaning 'to lead' (p. 189). Arendt (1958, p. 229) thus identified, through tracing back, the beginnings of the separation of 'to lead' and 'execution' that is now embedded in dominant views of leadership. According to Arendt, Plato identified with the person in command, the vision or 'idea' of the image or shape – (*eidos*) of the product-to-be and the means to execute it through the deployment of action by others, interpreted as 'making' and 'fabrication' in *work*. For Arendt, the separation of 'vision' from execution or implementation/delivery, so common in modern times, is associated with the view that 'all means, provided they are efficient are permissible and justified to pursue something defined as an end'.

Understanding the public realm – Arendt's public space

The idea of the *common world* enabled Arendt to understand the crisis of the twentieth century – the denial of plurality – as a crime against humanity: 'the refusal of totalitarian regimes to share the world with entire races and classes of human beings' (Kohn, 2001). Arendt identified the 'thoughtlessness' – the 'inability to *think* … from the standpoint of somebody else' (Arendt, 1963, pp. 48–49) and the loss of public space (Arendt, 1968, p. 242) as crucial to the denial of plurality.

Schutz (2001a) identifies three tensions that arise in sustaining action in a public space. First, public spaces cannot exist without objects of common concern, which allow participants to locate themselves with respect to other participants. If people cannot see where they can contribute or if participants are unwilling to risk exposing their perspectives to others, the plurality of the space disappears. Second, assertions of incontestable truth and certainty, which seek to coerce others, also collapse the space, since if someone claims 'the truth', there is no reason to listen to the opinions of others. Arendt (1958, p. 244) cautions against efforts to control and dominate a space of dialogue through the misuse of agreements that 'cover the whole ground of the future' mapping out a path 'secured in all directions'. Agreements 'secured in all directions' are the kind of whole-school agreements that are commonly used to standardise a school's approach (literacy, for example) and typically do not represent discussion with a diversity of views. Third, the unpredictability of acting 'in concert' leads some to seek out ways to stabilise and control these processes. Since some predictability and stability is needed, Arendt (1958, p. 244) describes 'islands of predictability…in which certain guideposts of reliability are erected' in the form of agreements or promises for action. Arendt identifies the processes of *forgiving* and *making and keeping promises* as contributing to the force that keeps the public space in existence.

The *public-ness* of Arendt's 'public space' is not as a result of the mere *presence* of other people but as a result of the accessibility, intersubjectivity and the 'web of human relationships' (Arendt, 1958, p. 183) in that space – the *in-between* that 'simultaneously "relates and separates men"' (Hayden, 2009, p. 99). In such a space, all speech and action can be 'discussed, debated, and judged by everyone' (Hayden, 2009, p. 99) because we share a common space through appearing to each other in speech and action. The intersubjective *common* 'reality' is shared not because we each have a duplicate version of what is 'real' but because it is constituted by 'co-presencing…[and] is created and sustained through the sharing of a world built up between a plurality of persons…who speak and act together as equals' (Hayden, 2009, p. 99). The intersubjective 'reality' is a result of sharing what is *in-between*.

There are two types of *in-between*. The action by which a person reveals *who* and not merely *what* he or she is in the public realm is intangible (Arendt, 1958, p. 188) because 'direct interaction and dialogue between people manifest the transience and spontaneity of joint political action itself, as well as the distinctness and uniqueness of acting and speaking agents' (Hayden, 2009, p. 101). This is fragile. In the modern era, we substitute an enlarging of the private for the public realm where the 'only thing people have in common is their private interests' (Arendt, 1958, p. 52). In modern times, we therefore experience a depoliticisation of the public realm.

Arendt's entire project was to have people understand the implications of human plurality, which 'she deemed to be the need to act for, with and [on] behalf of others and in so doing, for the sake of one's own humanity' (Wiens, 2000, pp. 239–240). Human plurality has a two-fold character (Benhabib, 2003) – without equality, persons cannot understand one another or plan for a common future; without distinction, there is no need for speech and action. Arendt constantly reiterated in her writings that our fullest and most reliable knowledge of reality can only be gained from the plural perspectives of many persons and viewing issues from all sides. Arendt's identification of the power of acting 'in concert', in an educational context, opens up possibilities for things to be other than the 'harm being done to children' (Greene, 1997, p. 1) in our current version of 'dark times'. The relational focus of pedagogy, which relies on working with students as active partners in the educational process, can only be supported by teachers 'who are themselves trusted and respected partners in the educational process', which is both 'conceived and implemented in dialogue with teachers' (Hart et al., 2004, p. 266).

The importance of public space for acting 'in concert'

Arendt understood public spaces as places of recognition where we reveal our distinct voice, not as a pre-thought-out position but in relation to others – a self emerges *as part* of a community activity, not *prior*. In such a space, individuals make a unique contribution, which is unpredictable, because they are neither totally autonomous nor acting as a collective 'mass' (Arendt, 1958). Plurality is nurtured, fostered and protected for the 'sense of the real that is at stake', which is 'the precondition of our ability to belong to each other, to care for our lives together, and, finally, to act deliberately together' (Curtis, 1997, p. 47).

A public space for teacher dialogue, following Arendt, is a space between people, created by discourse in seeking reciprocal understanding through recognising and engaging with difference rather than a conflict waged from 'fixed positions' in adversarial debate. The pedagogic nature of a teacher public space is revealed in the potential for teachers to engage in deep reflection on practice, which is not possible when working alone, when engaged in social dialogue or in conversations that simply re-count teaching activities (Penlington, 2008). Being involved in dialogue means mediating between different perspectives, enabling each participant to 'see things differently' and be changed by this experience (Burbules, 1993, p. xii).

Penlington (2008, p. 1314) identifies some of the characteristics of dialogic conversations, consistent with Arendt's views. These include being free to question one another so that different viewpoints are taken into account, within which there is an optimum level of conflict or dissonance. For this to happen, teacher dialogues move beyond *re-counting* teaching activities to discussing the *reasonableness* of teaching practices in ways that consider the effects on students. Combined with trust, dissonance in views prompts reflection and discussion rather than defending positions in a back-and-forth movement between polar positions. Dialogue has no 'method' or 'blueprint' but is rather a direction for pedagogical exploration, not a map (Burbules, 1993). The process of dialogue might be seen as an educational voyage to be re-visited regularly rather than a destination or an endpoint. Consistent with Arendt's views, dialogue in a public space recognises each teacher's distinctive contribution and creativity as well as the potential for working together, without coercion, to establish promises and 'islands of security' (Arendt, 1958, p. 237) within projects of common concern.

This seems to be the kind of 'empowering and democratic school culture' (Johnson et al., 2016, p. 10) in which professional learning communities based on 'trust, respect and care built on relationships rather than control, manipulation and fear' can be supported in 'relational schools' (Johnson et al., 2016, p. 141). Educational leadership in such schools may be seen in cultivating plurality in a dialogic teacher 'public space', which resists the temptation to coerce or force people into agreement through a disposition to control but rather respects and trusts educators, allowing 'the space within which to exercise sound professional educational judgements' (Smyth, 2006, p. 317). Such spaces might be opened up in moments when 'seeing things big' – the faces of actual living persons (Greene, 1995) acting 'in concert' – becomes central to leadership in schools (Fitzgerald and Savage, 2013).

Conclusion

Through the focus on leadership as a causal attribution for successful outcomes, Arendt would argue that we have lost the power of acting 'in concert' without force, manipulation or violence. In Arendt's conception, the power of acting in concert is rooted in plurality and natality – a diversity of perspectives and the capacity to begin anew in the space of dialogue and gathered actions. Such action 'in concert' is not possible without a space that supports dialogue, thinking and judgement as well as an ongoing investigation into how to avoid the splintering or destruction of the space.

Current dominant views of leadership are largely instrumental and de-politicised, shutting down the public space through the management of consensus in the service of policy. This leadership of schools is a form of performance scripted by policy texts to transform and deliver outcomes of policy, and it is primarily concerned with efficiency and accountability (Fitzgerald and Savage, 2013). Aligned with practices of managerialism, this view of leadership takes a detached view of reform from the vantage point of the system and is one of the concerns identified in the work of Johnson et al. (2016, p. 10) in regard to its contribution to issues for early-career teachers. One of the identified contributing factors to a more pedagogically engaged form of teacher resilience is the cultivation of dialogic spaces within a more 'empowering and democratic school culture'. As Arendt points out, the elimination of plurality through the separation of knowing and doing, so embedded in dominant views of leadership, is tantamount to 'the abolition of the public realm itself' (Arendt, 1958, p. 220). Or, as she also put it, 'The end of the common world has come when it is seen only under one aspect and is permitted to present itself in only one perspective.' (Arendt, 1958, pp. 57–58).

The view of educational leadership put forward here seeks to interrupt neo-liberal versions of leadership through examining how educational leadership might be linked more to working with teachers to develop 'a humane pedagogy' (Greene, 1997) in a space where the views and contributions of each teacher matter. This is a space where taking into account a range of perspectives means that one has to listen and acknowledge difference and that the enlarged understanding of the world developed with others is 'unavailable to any of them from their own perspective alone' (Young, 1997, p. 361).

References

AITSL, 2011. *Australian professional standard for principals.* AITSL, Victoria: MCEECDYA Secretariat.

Arendt, H., 1958. *The human condition.* Chicago: The University of Chicago Press.

Arendt, H., 1963. *Eichmann in Jerusalem: A report on the banality of evil.* New York: Viking Press.

Arendt, H., 1968. *Truth and politics: Between past and future.* New York: Viking Press.

Atkinson, E., 2004. Thinking outside the box: An exercise in heresy. *Qualitative Inquiry,* 10(1), pp. 111–129.

Baehr, P., 2003. Editor's introduction. In P. Baehr, ed., *The portable Hannah Arendt.* New York: Penguin Books, vii-liv.

Benhabib, S., 2003. *The reluctant modernism of Hannah Arendt.* Lanham, Maryland: Rowman and Littlefield.

Bernstein, R. J., 2010. Is evil banal? A misleading question. In R. Berkowitz, J. Katz and T. Keenan, eds., *Thinking in dark times.* New York: Fordham University Press, pp. 131–136.

Bourdieu, P., 1990. *The logic of practice.* Stanford: Stanford University Press.

Burbules, N. C., 1993. *Dialogue in teaching: Theory and practice.* New York: Teachers College Press.

Calhoun, C. and McGowan, J., 1997. Introduction. In C. Calhoun and J. McGowan, eds., *Hannah Arendt and the meaning of politics* (pp. 1–24). Minneapolis: University of Minnesota Press.

Canovan, M., 1992. *Hannah Arendt: A reinterpretation of her political thought.* Cambridge: Cambridge University Press.

Clark, C., Herter, R. J. and Moss, P., 1998. Continuing the dialogue on collaboration. *American Educational Research Journal,* 35(4), pp. 785–791.

Curtis, K. F., 1997. Aesthetic foundations of democratic politics. In C. Calhoun and J. McGowan, eds., *Hannah Arendt and the meaning of politics* (pp. 27–52). Minneapolis: University of Minnesota Press.

Disch, L., 1997. Please sit down, but don't make yourself at home: Arendtian 'visiting' and the prefigurative politics of consciousness-raising. In C. Calhoun and J. McGowan, eds., *Hannah Arendt and the meaning of politics* (pp. 132–165). Minneapolis: University of Minnesota Press.

Dixon, W., 2014. When power is lost. *The Journal of the Hannah Arendt Center for Politics and Humanities at Bard College*, 2, pp. 64–66.

Duarte, E., 2001. The eclipse of thinking: An Arendtian critique of cooperative learning. In M. Gordon, ed., *Hannah Arendt and education: Renewing our common world*. Boulder, Colorado: Westview Press.

Evans, R., 1996. *The human side of school change: Reform, resistance, and the real-life problems of innovation*. Market Street, San Francisco: Jossey-Bass.

Fitzgerald, T. and Savage, J., 2013. Scripting, ritualising and performing leadership: Interrogating recent policy developments in Australia. *Journal of Educational Administration and History*, 45(2), pp. 126–143.

Gordon, M., 2001. Introduction. In M. Gordon, ed., *Hannah Arendt and education: Renewing our common world*. New York: Westview Press.

Greene, M., 1995. *Releasing the imagination: Essays on education, the arts, and social change*. San Francisco: Jossey-Bass.

Greene, M., 1997. Teaching as possibility: A light in dark times. *Journal of Pedagogy, Pluralism and Practice*, 1(1), pp. 1–11.

Gronn, P., 1996. From transactions to transformations: A new order in the study of leadership? *Educational Management Administration and Leadership*, 24(7), pp. 7–30.

Gunter, H., 2007. Remodelling the school workforce in England: A study in tyranny. *Journal for Critical Education Policy Studies* [Online], 5(1). Available at http://www.jceps.com/?pageID=articleandarticleID=84

Gunter, H., 2014. *Educational leadership and Hannah Arendt*. London: Routledge.

Hargreaves, D. H., 1999. The knowledge-creating school. *British Journal of Educational Studies*, 47(2), pp. 122–144.

Hart, S., Dixon, A., Drummond, M. J. and McIntyre, D., 2004. *Learning without limits*. Maidenhead, England: Open University Press.

Hayden, P., 2009. *Political evil in a global age: Hannah Arendt and international theory*. London: Routledge.

Hayes, D., Christie, P., Mills, M. and Lingard, B., 2004. Productive leaders and productive leadership. *Journal of Educational Administration*, 42(5), pp. 520–538.

Johnson, B., Down, B., Le Cornu, R., Peters, J., Sullivan, A., Pearce, J. and Hunter, J., 2016. *Promoting early career teacher resilience*. London: Routledge.

Kohn, J., 2001. *The world of Hannah Arendt* [Online]. New York: Hannah Arendt Center, New School University [Accessed November 11, 2012].

Meindl, J. R., Ehrlich, S. B. and Dukerich, J. M., 1985. The romance of leadership. *Administrative Science Quarterly*, 30(1), pp. 78–102.

Newland, G., 2009. *Introduction to emptiness*. Boston, MA: Snow Lion Publications.

Penlington, C., 2008. Dialogue as a catalyst for teacher change: A conceptual analysis. *Teaching and Teacher Education*, 24, pp. 1304–1316.

Rogers, B., 2016. *Educational leadership: Cultivating plurality in a 'public space'*. Saarbrücken, Germany: LAMBERT Academic Publishing.

Schutz, A., 1999. Creating local 'public spaces' in schools: Insights from Hannah Arendt and Maxine Greene. *Curriculum Inquiry*, 29(1), pp. 77–98.

Schutz, A., 2001a. Contesting utopianism: Hannah Arendt and the tensions of democratic education. In M. Gordon, ed., *Hannah Arendt and education: Renewing our comon world*. Boulder, CO: Westview Press.

Schutz, A., 2001b. Theory as performative pedagogy: Three masks of Hannah Arendt. *Educational Theory*, 51(2), pp. 127–150.

Smyth, J., 2006. The politics of reform of teachers' work and the consequences for schools: Some implications for teacher education. *Asia-Pacific Journal of Teacher Education*, 34(3), pp. 301–319.

Southworth, G. W., 1995. *Looking into primary headship: A research based interpretation*. London: Routledge.

Thomson, P., 1999. Reading the work of school administators with the help of Bourdieu: Getting a 'feel for the game'. *Australian Association for Research in Education and New Zealand Association for Research in Education Joint Conference*. Melbourne, Australia.

Thomson, P., Gunter, H. and Blackmore, J., 2014. Series Foreword. In H. Gunter, ed., *Educational leadership and Hannah Arendt*. London: Routledge.

Wiens, J. R., 2000. *Hannah Arendt and education: Educational leadership and civic humanism*. Doctor of Philosophy thesis. Simon Fraser University: Burnaby, BC V5A 1S6, Canada.

Woods, P. A., 2004. Democratic leadership: Drawing distinctions with distributed leadership. *International Journal of Leadership in Education*, 7(1), pp. 3–26.

Young, I. M., 1997. Asymmetrical reciprocity: On moral respect, wonder and enlarged thought. *Constellations*, 3(3), pp. 340–363.

Commentary

Questioning postmodernism: Does it have something to offer leadership fields?

Robert Donmoyer

My task here is to comment on the chapters included in the part of this book labelled 'Postmodernist Perspectives on Leadership'. The plan is to use the chapters to explore the relevance of postmodernism for 'questioning leadership' as well as its utility for leadership/administration-oriented fields generally.

Definition matters

The term *postmodernist* is slippery. Its use has been traced back to the last decades of the nineteenth century. Since then, the term has been employed to characterise a variety of human activity and thought in an array of fields and professions, every-thing from literary criticism to architecture. Within leadership- and administration-oriented fields, the term normally refers to (a) French poststructuralist thought during the second half of the twentieth century – for example, the work of scholars such as Foucault, Derrida and Lyotard – or (b) scholarship in other parts of world and/or to twenty-first-century century academic work strongly influenced by the writing and thinking of twentieth-century French poststructuralists.

The French-poststructuralist definition clearly is appropriate for the first three chapters in Part 2. Both Niesche's and Gobby's chapters, for example, are rooted in the work of one or more of the French poststructuralists listed in the prior paragraph, and the third chapter by Gowlett draws upon the work of Judith Butler. Butler is an American queer theorist, not a French postmodernist, but most queer theorists, including Butler, have been influenced by the work of Foucault (Halperin, 1995).

Definition difficulties do arise when attention shifts to Part 2's final chapter. Here, the author, Bev Rogers, focuses on Hannah Arendt's endorsement of public dialogue. Arendt was a German-born political theorist who did work in both her native country and in the USA prior to the time theorists like Foucault, Derrida and Lyotard took centre stage in international academic discourse. Ultimately, despite Rogers' valiant attempt, it would be difficult to make the case that Arendt's earlier twentieth-century work anticipated, in significant ways, the ideas French poststructuralists articulated during the latter part of the twentieth century. Arendt scholar Seyla Benhabib (2003), in fact, characterised Arendt as a reluctant *modernist*, not as a prescient *postmodernist*.

This definition problem should not cause great concern. After all, the scholarly agendas pursued by, say, Foucault and Derrida are at least as different as they are similar. Furthermore, a hallmark of postmodernist thought is the rejection of tightly defined linguistic boundaries. Lyotard's concept of postmodernism, in short, is rather elastic, and though it would be difficult to stretch the meaning of the term to include the work of Arendt, her work can be used to highlight what postmodernist perspectives ignore.

A note on positionality

Positionality refers to the perspective and assumptions a writer/researcher makes and the stance he or she takes while examining phenomena. Before proceeding, I should acknowledge my own stance in this respect.

Let me start by acknowledging that I am not a French-poststructuralist 'groupie'. For better or worse, I was socialised by a culture that counts the pragmatism of Dewey, James and Pierce as its indigenous philosophy and thinks of Mark Twain's book about an unschooled but street-savvy boy as the great American novel. Every time I read the work of French poststructuralists/postmodernists, I find myself thinking of Jonathan, a down-to-earth character in the first theatrical comedy written and produced on US soil, Royal Tyler's *The Contrast*. During one of Jonathan's encounters with a pretentious European character – an Englishman with an erudite vocabulary who periodically breaks into French, for no apparent reason – Jonathan asks, 'What means this outlandish lingo?' As I read the work of French social theorists, I frequently find myself asking Jonathan's question.

Many of my friends in the US academy easily transcended their cultural socialisation and embraced French poststructuralist/postmodernist thought with gusto. I have tried not to reject French poststructuralist thought out of hand and, especially, not to let discomfort with form – or ethnocentrism more generally – blind me to any important substantive points that postmodernists might make. However, I have not been able to get past the gnawing feeling that postmodernist thought – with its frequent emphasis on never-ending critique and sometimes myopic focus on text at the expense of attending to the material world – has little to contribute to applied, action-oriented fields that focus on leadership/administration. Writing this commentary is an opportunity to reconsider this assumption by focusing on work that is explicitly about educational leadership.

Chapter commentaries

Zombie ~~Leadership~~, a différend *and deconstruction*

Richard Niesche begins his chapter by declaring that leadership is a concept that will not die and comparing the concept to zombies, that is, the fictional living dead. Niesche notes that, in zombie lore, the only way to kill zombies is to cut off their heads, and he announces that his goal is to 'cut off the head of zombie

~~leadership~~'. He compares this goal to Foucault's talk, in his analysis of power, of the need to cut off the king's head. Foucault, of course, used the decapitation metaphor to dramatise his belief that power is not the property of individuals but rather something that is embedded within relationships.

Niesche begins his attempt at intellectual decapitation by invoking Lyotard's concept of a *différend*, that is, what results when a dispute cannot be resolved rationally or empirically because there is no rule or standard operating procedure to use to compare and assess rival positions. The positions are, in essence, incommensurable,[1] and the space between incommensurable positions is what Lyotard calls a *différend*.

Niesche uses Lyotard's notion of a *différend* to distinguish between two approaches to challenging the notion of leadership: 'A first response is the idea that we must do away with or not mention the word *leadership*....[A] second response...[involves] engaging with and using the term in order that its problematisation (Foucault, 1996a) and deconstructions (Derrida, 1997) can be seen' (p. 74). Niesche indicates that he opted for the second strategy – hence his use of Derrida's strategy of crossing out a key term to signal that the term is problematic but necessary – and proceeds to employ the work of two quite different French poststructuralists, Foucault and Derrida, to challenge the concept of what he refers to as '*~~leadership~~*'.

Niesche first focuses on Foucault's notion of problematisation. He notes that the term, for Foucault, refers to studying the history of problems in specific fields, including how problems come to be characterised as problems at different times. In the field of educational leadership, Niesche suggests, problematisation

> would entail exploring the practices that construct leadership as a concept to be used in describing the link between the individual and organisational processes and outcomes. Such an approach is not concerned with building models of good practice or good leadership but rather examining how leadership is mobilized in different ways in the formation of particular truths and also questioning the assumptions underlying such discursive practices.
>
> (p. 76)

Niesche does not actually apply Foucault's problematisation strategy to make sense of the practice(s) of educational leadership. He simply explains what Foucault means by this term and what the term might mean, generally, in the educational leadership field. He concludes his discussion of problematisation by asserting (but not demonstrating) the importance of problematisation 'for opening up spaces of contestation and discussion rather than closing down debates through the identification of leadership as specific adjectival models and other forms of representation such as standards' (p. 77).

Niesche takes somewhat more of a demonstration tack with Derrida's notion of deconstruction. After describing what deconstruction is (a close reading of a text intended to expose contradictions of logic) and is not (a method or set of rules to be applied), Niesche offers a limited demonstration of the contribution that deconstruction can make to educational leadership. First, he indicts current discourse in the educational leadership field:

> Thinking with Derrida in educational ~~leadership~~ is no easy task, for scholarship in the field is largely concerned with articulating what ~~leadership~~ is and particularly what "good" leadership can be....This search for an objective truth leads to a closing down of what ~~leadership~~ can be.
>
> (p. 80)

Then he attempts to make the case that this 'closing down of what ~~leadership~~ can be' is problematic because, among other problems, it leaves unexamined

> the Western metaphysical binary whereby *leader* is conceptualised as a form of presence as being, while *follower* is conceptualised as a form of lack in relation to leader. It is through the relation with leaders that followers are signified through this particular subordinate relationship.
>
> (p. 80)

Niesche argues that this sort of binary thinking undergirds even what many believe are more democratic models of leadership, such as distributed and transformational ~~leadership~~. To transcend the traditional leader/follower binary, Niesche asserts, we must abandon the search for definitive models of leadership, even ostensibly democratic ones. Instead, we must engage in something akin to Derrida's notion of deconstruction. We must engage in deconstruction – and, presumably, also a version of Foucault's problematisation – Niesche reminds us, because 'we have to cut off the head of zombie ~~leadership~~' (p. 82).

The chapter's contributions

There are at least two potentially valuable general contributions embedded in this chapter. First, it seems important for anyone engaged in educational decision making to understand the notion of incommensurability, that is, the notion embedded in Lyotard's concept of a *différend*. Decision makers – whether they are leaders with positional power or simply members of an organisation who want to exercise leadership more informally on a particular issue at a particular time – need to understand they cannot assess or even conceive of alternative options as long as their thinking is bounded by a particular way of framing a problem. They also cannot understand why some people might disagree with their proposals, a necessary (though, of course, not sufficient) condition for making the sort of Arendt-like public dialogue championed in Rogers's chapter productive.

Second, it is important for decision makers to be sensitised to the Western tendency to engage in binary thinking and the limitations of binary thought. They should be alerted, for example, to the status and power differentials that Niesche claims are covertly embedded in the ordering of terms in a binary. Becoming aware of the binaries we often take for granted also is a first step to moving beyond either/or thinking and developing truly novel options to consider.

Of course, in both cases, there are sources other than French postmodernist thought that provide similar insights. Decades before postmodernists wrote about binary thinking, for example, John Dewey wrote about human beings' penchant for dualisms, a reasonable facsimile for postmodernists' binaries. Dewey's work did not make claims about the significance of the ordering of terms in a dualism, but Dewey did demonstrate how seemingly antithetical concepts in the education field could be creatively synthesised (see e.g. Dewey, 1938). In other words, he suggested what might be done to transcend the limitations of dualistic or binary thinking, a topic that tends to be overlooked when deconstruction is treated as an end in itself.

Also, years ago, long before I had encountered Lyotard's notion of a *différend*, I demonstrated the phenomenon of incommensurability by using real-world examples from the education field. I noted, for example, that two leading scholars in the field had endorsed antithetical approaches to classroom management and discipline and demonstrated that this occurred because the two scholars had based their recommendations on different bodies of 'empirical' literature rooted in incommensurable *a priori* assumptions. Both scholars' recommendations might make sense under certain circumstances and to accomplish certain purposes, I argued; but to make such assessments, one must transcend a single frame of reference (Donmoyer, 1996).

If one prefers explications of the incommensurability notion rooted in formal theory rather than real-world examples, there is Donald Schön's (1979) discussion of the importance of problem framing and generative metaphors in organisational and policy decision making and his demonstration that different frames and metaphors are often incommensurable. Also, Kuhn's talk about incommensurable paradigms in the physical sciences has made its way into popular culture and has been applied to highlight incommensurable thinking in a wide variety of popular-culture contexts (Donmoyer, 2006).

In short, it is not at all clear that we really need to employ Lyotard's rather arcane talk about a *différend* for those in the field of educational leadership/administration to understand that some concepts and practices are incommensurable. We also may not need to engage in Derrida's metaphysics-oriented process of deconstruction to expose binary/dualistic thinking. Still, it is good to have a number of 'roads to Rome', and presumably, for some individuals, postmodernist thinking and practices may be the preferred 'route' for developing such understanding.

Contributions to questioning leadership

Niesche is much less successful in using postmodernist thinking and analysis strategies to 'question leadership'. His limited attempt at deconstructing the concept does not suggest, to me at least, that the notion of leadership is so horribly problematic that it is necessary to draw a line through the term whenever one uses it. Ultimately, he relies on a clever metaphor (i.e. zombie ~~leadership~~) and declamations about the need for intellectual decapitation to make his case. Such tactics are no substitute for more tightly constructed argumentation.

I am particularly concerned with Niesche's propensity for cartoon-like portrayals of the leadership literature. In recent years, there have been significant attempts to disassociate the notion of leadership from the idea of positional power and to re-conceptualise leadership as a relational process rather than as a property of individuals (see e.g. Komives et al., 2007). Even the social psychology-inspired 'new psychology of leadership' (Haslam et al., 2011) that maintains the traditional leader/follower distinction suggests that so-called followers have much more power over leaders than is suggested by Niesche's portrayal of leadership as a 'top-down flow of power in which the leader is constructed as the primary instigator of change' (p. 80).

Could the problem here be Niesche's embrace of Foucault as an intellectual role model? Connolly (1985), after all, has noted that Foucault's goal was '*to incite* us to listen to a different claim *rather than to accept the findings of an argument*' and '*to excite* in the reader the experience of discord between the social construction of normality and that which does not fit neatly within the frame of these constructs' (p. 368, emphasis added). Might Niesche's failure to attend to recent leadership literature, his endorsement of a vision of the functioning of power that is at best incomplete and his reliance on talk of 'zombie ~~leadership~~' in lieu of presenting convincing arguments about the need to question leadership be by-products of his desire to emulate Foucault's goals to incite and excite? This certainly is a hypothesis worth considering.

There is, however, at least one other possible explanation for the failure to present a tightly argued case for questioning leadership: It is difficult to conceive how a convincing case could be made simply by deconstructing text; some reference to the empirical world would seem to be required to demonstrate any problems associated with our current infatuation with leadership. Of course, Foucault's problematisation strategy is an empirical inquiry strategy of sorts, but Niesche only describes the strategy and hints at what it might accomplish; he does not provide even a limited demonstration of its use. Fortunately, the following chapter by Gobby offers a case that was constructed by using a facsimile of Foucault's problematisation strategy, and Gowlett provides an even more intriguing empirically grounded case study. Discussion now turns to these chapters.

Problematisations, practices and subjectivation: Educational leadership in neoliberal times and performatively resignifying leadership

As Niesche does in his chapter, Gobby invokes the constructs and procedures of Michel Foucault, including Foucault's notion of problematisation. As already noted, Gowlett has a somewhat different reference point in the queer theory of Judith Butler. Both authors, however, share similar starting assumptions about the tenuousness of all efforts to definitively categorise and demarcate the social world.

Gobby, for example, explicitly challenges 'essentialist notions of leadership', and Gowlett indicates she is invoking Butler not because chapter 7 is about sexuality, but because

> Butler uses a version of ontology and epistemology that rejects the metaphysical anchoring of phenomena. In other words, 'things' (like bodies, words, identity categories and objects) do not have inherently determinate boundaries. She embraces uncertainty.
>
> (p. 99).

Gowlett goes on to unpack other key concepts in Butler's thought, and Gobby does not simply rehash what Niesche said about Foucault's notion of problematisation. Unfortunately, space restrictions dictate that I forgo a more detailed recounting of these theoretical discussions and focus instead on each chapter's empirical case material in an effort to ferret out evidence of the role that postmodernist thought can play in questioning leadership and in leadership/administration fields generally.

Gobby's case

Gobby focuses the empirical portion of his chapter on an Australian school reform initiative, the Independent Public Schools (IPS) programme. The programme frees participating schools from implementing policies and procedures developed by a central authority in exchange for school leaders' agreement to meet, over a three-year period, performance targets specified in a Delivery and Performance Contract. The two school principals Gobby interviewed to create his case were enthusiastic about the IPS programme and happy to be free of bureaucratic red tape. Gobby, however, offers a somewhat more nuanced storyline about the freedom the IPS programme provides:

> While the contract fosters freedom from constraint, it induces a relationship of obligation and self-responsibility. Contractualism shifts accountability for performance from the education bureaucracy and political sphere to the school, with principals and teachers being monitored and judged against the targets of the contract. In other words, the contract is a technology of self-government that…enacts neoliberalism.
>
> (p. 93)

Gobby's account of the IPS programme lacks the epic scope of Foucault's historical accounts of social phenomena such as punishment and imprisonment, but the storyline about the transformation of school principals from administrators straitjacketed by policies developed outside their schools into entrepreneurial school leaders who assume personal responsibility for producing contractually specified outcomes is quite reminiscent of Foucault's historical writing, especially his account of the movement from a reliance on torture as a mechanism for social control to self-imposed psychic control.

What is important here is that Gobby's Foucault-like storyline is less about questioning the current infatuation with leadership and more about providing an explanation for why this infatuation is occurring. Furthermore, the explanation provided focuses on a factor emanating from the societal rather than the school level: neo-liberal ideology.

Understanding the societal forces that get played out in schools undoubtedly can be helpful in developing more informed and thoughtful educational policy over the long haul. Such understanding, however, has little to offer principals concerned with what to do on Monday morning. After school principals like the two Gobby studied are designated school leaders rather than administrators, should they abandon the sort of systems thinking administrators in the past were encouraged to employ? Should they attend less to creating, assessing and, if necessary, modifying organisational structures and pay more attention to the interpersonal aspects of their jobs? Or is some sort of balancing act required?

Gobby's storyline does not attend – much less suggest answers – to such questions, and it is unlikely that other empirical work inspired by Foucault's problematisation strategy would ever focus on such micro-level matters. After all, once one has resolved to cut off the king's head, why should one bother to generate knowledge that might help a decapitated leader do his or her job better? In short, whether individuals tapped to head organisations should function as traditional administrators, new-age entrepreneurial leaders or some sort of amalgamation of the two is a question that is not likely to matter much to Foucault disciples in the education leadership and administration fields.

Furthermore, anyone engaged in empirical work that is inspired by Foucault's problematisation strategy and his somewhat pre-ordained storylines is unlikely to focus closely enough on the context ostensibly being studied even to generate the sort of contextually grounded data that would help answer questions about the consequences of playing the principal role as an entrepreneurial leader, a traditional manager/administrator or in some other way that somehow synthesises these two ideal typical conceptions of the principal role. It is hardly surprising, in other words, that a Foucault-inspired scholar like Gobby ends up playing a different game than the questioning-leadership game that is the announced focus of this book.

Gowlett's case

In the theoretical as opposed to the more empirical parts of her chapter, Gowlett announces that she is not really interested in whether the term leadership is appropriate or not because, like postmodernists generally, she embraces any term's 'instability and uncertainty.' She writes,

> I understand that for some, leadership may denote a hierarchical structure and hence delimit in advance who and what we explore in schools to manage them. I agree; it can. The same, however, can be said for any term. Instead, the issue for me is how certain actions and terms become all-encompassing and dominate the field.

(p. 109)

Clearly, in the above quotation, Gowlett is articulating the postmodernist party line. In the discussion of her empirical work, however, Foucault's influence is difficult to decipher. Rather than employing a reasonable facsimile of Foucault's problematisation strategy, Gowlett appears to have employed a relatively traditional qualitative research design, that is, a design that is not oriented towards accounting for 'how certain actions and terms become all-encompassing and dominate the field' but rather is focused on documenting the often idiosyncratic and unexpected elements of the particular context being studied.

Gowlett's design netted a transgressive story (her characterisation) about the actions of one school leader and the impact these actions had. Furthermore, despite Gowlett's announcement that she is not interested in the task of questioning leadership, there is the semblance of an answer to the question about the utility of the current infatuation with leadership embedded in the data-based story Gowlett tells. Gowlett's story is about a particular school's director of student achievement. The director refused to mindlessly accept the measures of student achievement developed externally and simply do what she was expected to do with these measures while playing the director-of-student-achievement role. Gowlett documents how the director supplemented and even at times (at least for a time) substituted internally generated performance measures of achievement (including qualitative measures) for measures that were externally created in an effort to respond to the needs of the school's students and parents. Near the end of her discussion, Gowlett argues that more stories about leaders engaging in transgressive behaviour are needed.

Now, there certainly are societal forces at work in the transgressive tale Gowlett tells, but the main focus is on a protagonist who 'kept her head', so to speak, and was not mindlessly controlled by dictates from the external environment. Consequently, the chapter suggests that a savvy and assertive school leader (in this particular case, the school's director of student achievement) can, indeed, make a difference in a school. Implicit in all of this is at least a clandestine endorsement of contemporary culture's infatuation with leadership.

Of course, Gowlett also demonstrates that the school leader she focused on made a difference by attending to and modifying existing standard operating procedures. The case, in short, provides an implicit argument for balancing the current infatuation with leadership with a more traditional emphasis on the structural and policy dimensions of schools, an argument made in other parts of this book.

So, is Gowlett's empirical contribution to the process of questioning leadership (despite her stated lack of interest in the question) evidence that postmodernist thought has something to offer fields leadership-related fields? Not necessarily. The important question is: What is postmodern here? Gowlett, for example, did not employ a postmodernist-inspired research design to do her empirical work. Consequently, it is a bit difficult to attribute Gowlett's contribution to the questioning leadership discussion to postmodernist thought.

To be sure, while interpreting her data, Gowlett did invoke Judith Butler's queer-theory variant of postmodernism on two occasions, but the points highlighted almost certainly could have just as easily been made without reference to Butler's work. Of course, Gowlett's bottom-line argument is that Butler's thinking is important because it reveals the instability and uncertainty of language. Again, today, that insight is rather self-evident. Without even thinking about Butler, for example, I knew that I needed, at the outset of this paper, to stipulate what the term postmodernist refers to in this commentary.

So, Gowlett's discussion of Butler's version of postmodernism, though interesting, ultimately appears to be largely window dressing. The window dressing is not innocuous, however. In fact, it undercuts Gowlett's contribution to the questioning leadership discussion because, even though she endorses the need for 'transgressive stories' about leaders' activities, she also dismisses the whole idea of leaders and leadership because the terms are characterised by 'instability and uncertainty'. What Gowlett and many other postmodernists fail to realise is that those who emphasise the need to 'question leadership' are not talking primarily about questioning the word but rather the behaviours and actions the word signifies. While it is true that different people often will mean somewhat different things when they use the term *leadership* and that even individuals may alter their definitions in different contexts, Gowlett's own story of a school leader engaged in transgressive behaviour indicates that the instability and uncertainty of terms is not so great that it is impossible to ask and empirically answer questions about the impact the current infatuation with leadership may have.

Thinking beyond leadership as a service to policy: 'Seeing things big' in a dialogic 'public space'

Rogers begins Part 2's final chapter sounding very much like a postmodernist: 'Leadership is...[today] offered as a tactic for orchestrating teacher performance, with leaders increasingly assumed to be acting as an agent for the state' (p. 112). For an antidote, however, Rogers turns to the work of Hannah Arendt. As already noted, stretching the definition of *postmodernism* to accommodate Arendt's work is problematic.

To be sure, Rogers makes a valiant attempt to use Arendt's work to critique many of postmodernists' favourite targets (neo-liberalism, for example), but in the end, Rogers endorses Arendt's vision of a society where 'citizens feel a collective responsibility for others and the common world, which can only be "realized" in free discussion with others' (p. 114). *Différend*-obsessed postmodernists would have to view Arendt's faith in the power of dialogue as modernist romanticism. Consequently, the Rogers chapter is not ideal for exploring the contributions postmodernist thought can make to leadership-related fields. It seems more appropriate to use the chapter as a kind of foil that demonstrates what is lost if leadership fields uncritically embrace postmodernist thinking.

What is lost is the hope that dialogue can 'disclose realities rather than veil intentions' (p. 114). I, personally, have clung to this hope throughout my career. My first funded research project was an exploration of a programme evaluation strategy built around an Arendt-like conception of dialogue (Donmoyer, 1991). More recently, I have argued that dialogue is the only hope for making research more than a political weapon, given that empirical studies emanating from incommensurable paradigms normally prescribe different solutions to educational problems (Donmoyer, 2014).

My attempts at facilitating 'dialogue across differences' (Burbules and Rice, 1991) remind me that Arendt's notion of dialogue is, indeed, more than a little romantic, and I understand that most current school leaders are not well equipped to practise the sort of dialogical leadership Rogers champions. Still, I am not willing to let brute politics and mindless managerialism carry the day, and I am not content with merely documenting and/or critiquing such processes.

Conclusion

Here I have searched the chapters in Part 2 of this book for evidence of what postmodernist thinking can contribute to the educational leadership and administration fields. The evidence identified is not impressive. Undoubtedly, this less-than-positive result has much to do with what Lyotard calls a *différend*: I am concerned with utility, but utility concerns are not front and centre in postmodernist work. I make no apologies for invoking the utility criterion. For me, interest in utility is a defining characteristic of leadership-oriented academic work. When this interest is absent, we are doing sociology or philosophy; it is hard to claim we are engaged in scholarship for an action-oriented enterprise like leadership.

Note

1 Lyotard, on occasion, used the land-right claims of indigenous groups in Australia to illustrate a *différend*. Indigenous groups' claims are often based on tribal law, while the claims of the European settlers who now occupy tribal land are rooted in existing governmental jurisprudence. The claims, consequently, are clearly incommensurable, and there is no shared rule that can be applied to settle the rival claims.

References

Benhabib, S., 2003. *The reluctant modernism of Hannah Arendt*. Lanham, MD/ Oxford: Rowman and Littlefield Publishers, Inc.

Burbules, N. and Rice, S., 1991. Dialogue across differences: Continuing the conversation. *Harvard Educational Review*, 61(4), pp. 393–416.

Dewey, J., 1938. *Experience and education*. New York: Macmillan.

Donmoyer, R., 1991. Postpositivist evaluation: Give me a for instance. *Educational Administration Quarterly*, 27, pp. 265–296.

Donmoyer, R., 1996. The concept of a knowledge base. In F. Murray, ed., *The teacher educator's handbook*. San Francisco: Jossey-Bass.

Donmoyer, R., 2006. Take my paradigm...please! The legacy of Kuhn's construct in educational research. *The International Journal of Qualitative Studies in Education*, 19(1), pp. 28–29.

Donmoyer, R., 2014. What if educational inquiry was neither a social science nor a humanities field? Revisiting Joseph Schwab's 'The Practical' in the aftermath of the science wars. *Educational Policy Analysis Archives*, 22(8), pp. 1–16. http//epaa. asu.edu/ojs

Halperin, D., 1995. *Saint Foucault: Toward a gay hagiography.* Oxford: Oxford University Press.

Haslam, A., Reicher, S. and Paltow, M., 2011. *The new psychology of leadership: Identity, influence, and power.* Hove/New York City: Psychology Press.

Komives, S., Lucas, N. and McMahon, T., 2007. The relational leadership model. *Exploring leadership*, pp. 73–113. San Francisco: Jossey-Bass.

Schön, D., 1979. Generative metaphor. A perspective of problem-setting in social policy. In A. Ortony, ed., *Metaphor and thought.* Cambridge: Cambridge University Press.

Part III

Select issues in leadership theory and practice

9 (Re)positioning the distributed 'turn' in leadership

Howard Youngs

Introduction

For a number of decades now, 'leadership' has been both an assumed answer to and cause of organisational and societal problems. Its popularisation has led to many definitions, yet the issue of ambiguity in definitions in leadership literature raised nearly 40 years ago by Pfeffer (1977) still remains (see Alvesson and Spicer, 2014). Since the start of the millennium, interest in distributed, shared, collaborative and collective conceptualisations of leadership has gathered momentum, adding to leadership's popularisation, particularly in the field of education. This distributed 'turn' is attractive due to the implied democratic, inclusive flavour of the related nomenclature. It can also appear as an antidote to the romanticism that Meindl, Ehrlich and Dukerich (1985) claim is associated with heroic leader-centric models of leadership 'dominated by views of leaders as exceptional individuals' (Gronn, 2011, p. 438). Evidence of this distributed 'turn' lies in the rapid increase of associated publications (Bolden, 2011) and the assertion of distributed leadership as a new direction in the leadership field (Grint, 2011; Contractor et al., 2012).

The aim of this chapter is to question whether this 'turn' adequately furthers our understanding and theorising of practice constructed as leadership, particularly in the context of educational organisations, and it asks, is it time to reposition thinking concerning distributed leadership and similar conceptualisations of leadership? To inform this questioning, Bourdieu's sociological tools of fields and capital are utilised alongside Goffman's notion of deference. The parameters for applying these tools are discussed first. The second section provides an articulation of the theoretical context within which the distributed turn has occurred in the leadership field and how New Public Management (NPM) has contributed to knowledge production in the education field that emphasises functional constructions of distributed leadership rather than critical ones (Gunter et al., 2013). Thirdly, examples of practice labelled as leadership from two 20-month organisational case studies are described and then analysed with the aforementioned sociological tools. The purpose of this is to argue for an alternative approach to analysing practice described as leadership so the distributed turn is repositioned as complementary to a leader-centric view rather than as a reactionary alternative to it.

Fields, capital and deference

Within a Bourdieusian framework, the social world is made up of multiple and overlapping fields in which forms of capital are distributed amongst different agents according to their determined social position(s) (Bourdieu, 1998; Thomson, 2005). Bourdieu (1991, pp. 230–231) describes the social field as:

> a multi-dimensional space of positions such that each position can be defined in terms of a multi-dimensional system of co-ordinates whose values correspond to the different pertinent variables. Agents are thus distributed, in the first dimension, according to the overall volume of the capital they possess and, in the second dimension, according to the composition of their capital – in other words, according to the relative weight of the different kinds of capital.

In her critique of education policy in England, Thomson (2005) illustrates how the application of Bourdieu's concept of fields reveals how the interplay of the economic field, with its emphasis on market advantage; and the political field, with its use of bureaucratic controls, can dominate and shape what is deemed to be of worth in the education field. This domination then impacts on how leadership is viewed, as appointed leaders such as school principals are positioned by the state as the official conduits of education reform. A leader's positioning in the social space of an educational organisation can be interpreted in Bourdieu's first dimension as agents having more capital than others and sets up a dualism between official formal leadership and non-official informal leadership. This assumed dualism will be revisited later in this chapter as a restraining element to understanding practice labelled as leadership.

An agent's positioning in the social world is not only based on the volume of his/her capital, which, according to Bourdieu (1998) is the most important aspect, but is also determined by the composition of capital and the relative weight of each form. Bourdieu (2004, p. 15) explains that the capital agents possess in a field 'takes time to accumulate' and classifies forms of capital as economic, cultural, social and symbolic in nature. Thomson (2005, p. 742) provides a succinct explanation of each form evident in the writings of Bourdieu, namely 'economic (money and assets); cultural (e.g. forms of knowledge; taste, aesthetic and cultural preferences; language, narrative and voice); social (e.g. affiliations and networks; family, religious and cultural heritage); symbolic (things which stand for all of the other forms of capital, including credentials)'. Bourdieu (1998, p. 102) argues that symbolic capital is a capital of recognition that permits an agent to 'exert symbolic effects' in line with collective expectations, which results in others obeying and accepting the agent's exertion 'without even posing the question of obedience' (Bourdieu, 1998, p. 103). Consequently, Bourdieu (1998, p. 104) argues that 'the structure of the distribution of symbolic capital tends to present a rather great stability'; in other words, the recognition and deference given to those with dominant volumes of symbolic capital is unlikely to change. Here, there is a possible conundrum, for what if the recognition of capital wanes while an agent is still deemed to be in an official leadership position[1] or when an agent recognised as an official leader voluntarily steps back while still retaining his or her official position in order to create space for other agents not in official leadership positions to gain more symbolic capital and status? This latter possibility is presented in the examples from the case studies that follow, where deference was given to agents not in official leadership roles.

Goffman's (1956) notion of deference can be used to help understand how capital is acquired and perceived. Goffman (1956, p. 477) defines *deference* as 'activity which functions as a symbolic means by which appreciation is regularly conveyed to a recipient of this recipient, or of something of which this recipient is taken as a symbol, extension, or agent'. Even though an individual may desire or deserve deference, they are not able to bestow it on themselves; only others can do this (Goffman, 1956; Sauder et al., 2012). As was explained earlier, others may bestow deference on an agent who has more capital, particularly in its symbolic form as described by Bourdieu, so that the structures of perception are unlikely to change, particularly towards those in official leadership positions. In a similar manner, this perspective could be interpreted to mean that only those with larger volumes of capital are able to defer it on others. Limiting deference so that it maintains the *status quo* of symbolic capital means that any understanding of practice labelled as leadership must be framed as a leader–follower construct and limits agents who engage in this practice only to those who hold an official leadership position. In other words, what we have here are leader-centric models of leadership. The distributed turn has broadened the focus of practice labelled as leadership beyond those in official leadership positions, and so in this chapter deference is also used in such a way as to help understand why some people may ascribe the term *leader* to others even if they are not in an official role of leadership. Using deference beyond the limitation of maintaining the *status quo* provides the opportunity to understand forms of leadership practice beyond formal leadership roles.

The context of the distributed 'turn'

The concept of leadership, particularly in its individualistic form, is often established around an ontology of leader, followers, organisational goals and goal-related decision-making. This ontology is reflected in the prominent leadership theories prior to the distributed turn. Two such theories that came to prominence in the 1980s were transformational and charismatic leadership, which Parry and Bryman (2006) argue have been over-exposed in the wider leadership field. In response to this over-exposure of leader-centric theories, Gronn (2011) argues that in the literature there has been a reaction towards favouring alternative distributed conceptualisations. The majority of leadership studies do not subject leadership to much critique, and the construction of actors is rarely scrutinised as to whether they reflect actual social relations in leader-centric studies (Alvesson and Spicer, 2014). The notion of distributed leadership suffers from a similar lack of scrutiny, particularly in relation to power, micropolitics and why it has become a popular feature of the leadership landscape, particularly in education (Youngs, 2009), where it has been susceptible to a 'managerial colonisation' (Thrupp and Wilmott, 2003).

To understand how this colonisation has come about, Thomson's (2005) critique of education policy through a Bourdieusian framework illustrates how the economic field, with its emphasis on market advantage, when combined with the fiscal issues in the political field and the need to generate new 'stories' within the field of media, has created conditions conducive to the three fields having an impact on the field of education. This is illustrated particularly through the political field, where the state has introduced controls over other fields such as education through the implementation of New Public Management (NPM), not just in England, as illustrated by Thomson (2005), but also in nations where governments have focused on efficiency, performance and accountability agendas in the education field. NPM has provided a means to standardise schools as low-trust organisations (Thrupp and Willmott, 2003; Bottery, 2004); shape and control teachers' work as managed professionals (Smyth, 2001; Wright, 2001; Codd, 2005); emphasise line management (Thrupp and Willmott, 2003); and reduce leadership to a rational and technical form (Bottery and Wright, 2000). NPM, with its emphasis on effectiveness, efficiency and economy – where *economy* means doing more with less (Sachs, 2003) – has uncritically positioned leadership, or what O'Reilly and Reed (2010) describe as *leaderism*, as the unquestioned enabler of reform wherein leaders are reified as the authors of reform. The distributed turn fits conveniently into this reform environment as a solution to any subsequent work intensification through a wider division of (leadership) labour and the implied notion of shared decision-making so teachers are positioned as implementers of the reforms. Consequently, distributed leadership is 'promoted as part of the discursive armoury of official policy making' (Gronn, 2009, p. 384), but this has become a slippery and elastic concept that is used loosely across the field of education (Hartley, 2007; Torrance, 2009). Some examples that illustrate the breadth of terms used to classify distributed leadership include concertive action (Gronn, 2002); formal distribution (MacBeath, 2005); representational (Harris, 2006); planful alignment (Leithwood et al., 2007); classical, where existing organisational clusters are used (Thorpe et al., 2011); collaborated, collective and coordinated distribution (Spillane, 2006); opportunistic and cultural (MacBeath, 2005); emergent (Hargreaves and Fink, 2006; Harris, 2006; Thorpe et al., 2011); spontaneous (Leithwood et al., 2007); and autonomous (Harris, 2009). This list is not exhaustive.

The elasticity evident in notions of distributed leadership is also clearly illustrated in Gunter et al.'s (2013) mapping of distributed leadership based on their review of 90 texts wherein distributed leadership was the main focus. The resultant four positions identify how, why and for whom knowledge is produced in relation to distributed leadership. The four positions are functional-descriptive, functional-normative, critical and socially critical. The 'functional approaches focus on removing dysfunctions from the system' (Gunter et al., 2013, p. 559), and so these research studies tend not to critique or recognise how NPM has shaped and regulated practice. The irony here is that NPM is a hierarchical approach in which official leaders are assumed to have more capital than other agents. Consequently, 'distributed leadership literature is littered with contradictions' (Lumby, 2013, p. 588) that espouse distribution yet also rely on leader-centric perspectives of leadership (Gronn, 2011). The existence of distributed leadership within hierarchical structures also makes it an inherently political concept (Maxcy and Nguyen, 2006; Hartley, 2010) and supports Gronn's (2011) argument that hybrid configurations of orchestrated (official) and emergent (non-official) forms of leadership practice co-exist and occur simultaneously in organisations. Chreim (2015, p. 539), in her research of leadership teams, also suggests that 'distributed leadership models might present ambiguous spaces that can be negotiated and shared, appropriated, or vacated by the interactants'. The multiplicity and combining of these forms suggest that neither individualistic leader-centric models nor the distributed 'turn' can adequately provide a realistic view of leadership practice by themselves. This raises the question as to whether the concept of leadership is part of the problem here, particularly if it is constrained to an ontology of leader, followers, organisational goals and goal-related decision-making aligned to NPM. Therefore, analytical tools are required to reposition studies of practice labelled as (distributed) leadership into the critical and socially critical positions mapped by Gunter et al. (2013, p. 557), so questions are raised about 'how professionals go about their work within a high accountability context' and 'about knowledge claims' so alternative approaches can be promoted.

Examples of practice labelled as leadership

Case studies of practice

A case-study research design was used to observe practice in two urban secondary schools in Auckland, New Zealand,[2] over a 20-month period. A qualitative approach was employed since it was felt that this would be more likely to contextualise leadership practice (Conger, 1998; Bryman, 2004), with observation being more likely to reveal informal unofficial sources of leadership (Bryman, 2004). Both schools were structured around subject-based departments and had in place pastoral care systems across each year level of students, which went up to the final year of schooling, usually when students turned 18. Heads of departments had responsibility for the subject-based teams, whereas a dean was responsible for co-ordinating pastoral care support across one year level. All deans were also members of department teams, and a small number were also heads of department.

Data were collected mainly through 36 observations of meetings and interactions and supported by 13 individual and group interviews with a staff-wide questionnaire administered near the end of the fieldwork in each school. Most participants were either senior or middle leaders who also taught the students. Observation took place while each school implemented their own school-based mentoring system aimed at raising student achievement through one-on-one staff-led 'academic counselling', where a holistic rather than a silo subject-based approach was employed to planned staff–student interactions.

From the resulting data, distributed forms of leadership practice were identified that often overlapped with each other. The forms included role-based responsibilities being officially *distributed through* organisational curriculum and pastoral care structures, often *in parallel* to each other as a division of labour; participants *stepping up*, either cognitively with organisational-wide thinking in one school or in behaviour through practicing by example in the other; official leaders *stepping in* to orchestrate practice amongst others; the *stepping back* of those with organisation-wide or team-based roles of responsibility to allow individual and group practices to emerge; and *boundary-spanning* practices within groups, where an individual not in an official agenda-holding role would engage with others, resulting in a wider participation amongst group members.

At times, those whose roles were at the top level of their organisation's hierarchical structure influenced the ensuing distributed forms of leadership practice or relied on existing structures to reinforce distribution, whereas at other times, top-level role holders were not needed to sanction other forms of individual and collective leadership practice that emerged. The key point here is that if a leader–follower concept had been applied as the only starting place whereby to understand practice labelled as leadership in each school, then not all distributed forms of leadership would have been identified. There is a lot more going on in organisations where 'substitutes for leadership are apparently prominent' (Kerr and Jermier, 1978, p. 377). Five examples from the case-study schools are used here to illustrate this without referring to labels of *leader, follower* or *goals*. This is done deliberately so that practice described as *leadership* can be illustrated without reverting to a leader-centric ontology or the term *distributed leadership*, especially as the label *follower* is not part of the vocabulary of those who worked in these schools.

In school A, when it came to trialling the school-based mentoring system, implementation was left to deans who each co-ordinated pastoral care across a year level in the school. It was assumed by staff that the deans as a collective group, rather than subject-based heads of department, would step up to do this because they had a reputation for 'getting things done'. A common saying was 'leave it to the deans'. In contrast, this could not have occurred in school B because the deans as a collective group were not viewed in this way. In school A, emergent practice from the deans as a collective group was expected, and no-one questioned this.

In school B, the initial group of mentors who trialled the mentoring system across one year level were those who individually had 'taken responsible risks', regardless of whether they had official organisation-wide, subject-based or pastoral care responsibilities. Such individuals had a reputation for stepping up and getting things done and so staff accepted them in this new mentoring role. Similar to the first example, the approach described in this second example would not have worked in school A, where this reputation was associated with the deans as a collective group rather than a range of individuals.

In the third example, near the end of the trial period in school B, students from another year level approached their dean and asked if they too could have some mentoring. She was not one of the trial mentors and was also a subject-based head of department. Without checking with the principal, deputy principals and other mentors, she put in place a mentoring system through other staff in parallel to the one being trialled. When the principal, deputy principals and mentors of the other year level discovered this, they accepted this without question, as if it was expected she would take the initiative without checking with those further up the hierarchy first.

The fourth example from school A was based on comparing the order and frequency of verbal participation in group settings as well as taking note of the focus of the ensuing discussions in each observation. *In situ* sociograms, supported by calculating the co-efficient of variance for each participant related to how many times they participated verbally[3], revealed that two heads of departments consistently engaged with a wider group of participants well ahead of any others in attendance over the period observations were carried out. As with the previous examples, no-one questioned this level of proactive engagement, even though these two individuals did not have official school-wide or agenda responsibilities for the group. Both illustrated boundary-spanning behaviour beyond their own subject and department as they encouraged others to 'step up' out of subject and department-based silo thinking to school-wide thinking. The manner in which they did this was non-threatening due to the open-ended questioning approach used to encourage discussion.

Finally, the fifth example is based on a synthesis of data from both schools. At times, the focus of a group observation was solely the school-based mentoring initiative. At other times, the focus was on implementing a revised curriculum or the day-to-day operations of the school. At a group level, the *in-situ* sociograms and the resultant combined co-efficient of variance for each meeting revealed some degree of difference with the distribution of overall participation. When the focus of a meeting was solely on the school-based mentoring initiative, the degree of verbal participation was distributed more evenly across the whole group when compared to meetings that had a school operations focus. This occurred even if the membership of the group largely stayed the same across the two forms of meetings. When the context was mentoring, all mentors (which included the principal and deputy principals in school B), irrespective of their official role in the school, positioned and accepted each other has having equal responsibility with the other mentors. When the context changed, assumptions related to the degree of official school-wide responsibility changed according to the focus of an agenda. It was as though without any need to discuss it, participants understood that the 'rules of the game' changed depending on the focus of a meeting where participants adjusted their participation according to how those in official roles of leadership positioned themselves.

These five examples provide a sample of all of the findings from a broader study that sought to describe day-to-day practice usually labelled as leadership by the participants over a sustained period of time. However, they do not explain why the practice played out as it did, and sociological tools from Bourdieu (1990, 1991, 1998, 2004) and Goffman (1956) make a deeper understanding possible. Central to this was the variable of time so that history became a key component in understanding the observed practices, which were then discussed later with participants through individual and group interviews. This allowed 'for the incorporation of the dynamic aspects of social life, in which status ascribed to forms of capital changes over time' (May and Powell, 2008, p. 128).

Interpreting the examples of practice

In school A, the collective group called 'the deans' had over many years accumulated deference from other staff as they 'got things done', so when the need came for a group to step forward and co-ordinate a new mentoring initiative, it came as no surprise that it was the deans who picked this up. Their reputation amongst the staff reinforced and added to the symbolic capital they already had. In comparison, had school B attempted to use the same implementation process as in school A, the trial in school B may not have been as successful because the deans in school B, as a collective group, did not have sufficient symbolic capital to warrant staff giving them the degree of deference exhibited in school A.

In school B, adequate volumes of cultural and social capital existed, not with an official group linked to the organisation structure and hierarchy but with specific individuals who over a period of time had been shown deference, especially by those in senior official roles of leadership, because they took responsible risks in attempting to enhance the conditions of student learning. 'Taking responsible risks' was an established discourse in school B espoused by the official leaders, so again it was of no surprise to staff when the selected trial mentors were announced. The parallel mentoring development in another year level illustrates how both the role-based authority of the dean and the bestowing of deference by senior leaders and other staff provided the dean with an uncontested space where she responded to the request for mentoring made by students in her year level. She had sufficient authority to draw on from her role to initiate some action and did not need to check with the principal and others because of the deference bestowed on her over the previous years as illustrated in how the principal and others celebrated this form of emergent responsible risk-taking practice. In a similar way, the two boundary-spanners in school A had also developed sufficient levels of capital through the deference shown to them by both official leaders and others in the group. Both were viewed by other staff as having credible amounts of social and human capital due to their years of acceptable service.

Finally, when the focus of group interactions was on the mentoring initiative, the degree of participation broadened compared to other contexts in which the focus centred on day-to-day operations. In both schools, those in these mentoring groups who were situated in official roles further up the organisational hierarchy chose, most of the time, not to draw on their symbolic capital. They repositioned themselves as unofficial leaders who were known as mentors in this context, so the 'rules of the game' were adjusted by the group because they all wanted to take shared responsibility for the trial mentoring system. In other settings, the groups reverted back to another 'set of rules' where those in official roles resumed their practice as official leaders.

The interpretation of practice discussed in this section adds further evidence to the argument that we do not need to start with leaders, followers and goals or a typology of distributed leadership as a default framework for understanding practices labelled as 'leadership', even if these practices involve people appointed to organisational roles labelled as executive, senior or middle leaders. It also illustrates why the transferability of practice from one organisation to another may be problematic due to the different histories of practice and the associated distribution of capital that exist across agents in organisations. The dualism evident in dividing actors as official formal leaders and unofficial informal leaders is also not helpful, as the examples illustrate that actors do not always need to be bound to this dualism. To suggest that this divide is fixed, with official leaders always having a greater volume of capital, means there would be limits on the volume of capital an actor could have, thus limiting emergent practice labelled as leadership.

Conclusion

As the practice labelled as leadership is always shifting from a sociological perspective, such shifts undo the adequacy of conceptualisations of leadership that rely solely or mainly on official roles. It does not matter in this respect whether the conceptualisations are individualistic, leader-centric ones, or whether they are associated only with the distributed 'turn' in leadership. The examples illustrated here also support the argument that any understanding of the distributed turn cannot be achieved without reference also to role-based and leader-centric perspectives of leading. The leader-centric approach and the distributed turn need to come together as an alternative configuration that blends the two, albeit within a critical dimension rather than a functional one. This alternative view needs to incorporate the critique of how other fields, such as the political, can colonise the field of education and normalise leadership practice as well as critique how the game is played within the social space of an educational organisation. This does not mean the end of leadership but rather adds to our understanding of the practice often labelled as such. One way of considering a way forward is to focus on the emerging leadership-as-practice approach, which is an alternative to focusing on 'the traits or behaviours of individuals' (Raelin, 2016, p. 3) and limiting leadership to the distribution of official roles in an organisation. The distributed 'turn' has contributed to broadening our view of leadership beyond an individualistic one, but it now needs to be repositioned or even replaced with a view that is practice-based first, rather than leadership-based first.

Notes

1   As an example of this, Hallett (2007) presents a case where a new school principal was deemed to have sufficient symbolic and cultural capital from the school board, yet the teachers did not provide the principal with the same recognition due to the lack of social and cultural capital afforded to the principal by the teachers.

2 A full description of each school and the broader context that informed their attempts to raise student achievement can be read in Youngs (2014).
3 For further details of this analysis, refer to Youngs (2014).

References

Alvesson, M. and Spicer, A., 2014. Critical perspectives on leadership. In D. V. Day, ed., 2014. *The Oxford handbook of leadership and organisations.* Oxford: Oxford University Press, pp. 40–56.

Bolden, R., 2011. Distributed leadership in organisations: A review of theory and research. *International Journal of Management Reviews,* 13(3), pp. 251–269.

Bottery, M., 2004. *The challenges of educational leadership.* London, UK: Paul Chapman Publishing.

Bottery, M. and Wright, N., 2000. *Teachers and the state: Towards a directed profession.* London: Routledge.

Bourdieu, P., 1990. *The logic of practice (English translation).* Stanford, CA: Stanford University Press.

Bourdieu, P., 1991. *Language and symbolic power.* Cambridge, UK: Polity Press.

Bourdieu, P., 1998. *Practical reason.* Cambridge, UK: Polity Press.

Bourdieu, P., 2004. The forms of capital. In S. Ball, ed., 2004. *Sociology of education.* London: RoutledgeFalmer, pp.15–29.

Bryman, A., 2004. Qualitative research on leadership: a critical but appreciative view. *The Leadership Quarterly,* 15(6), pp. 729–769.

Chreim, S., 2015. The (non)distribution of leadership roles: Considering leadership practices and configurations. *Human Relations,* 68(4), pp. 517–543.

Codd, J., 2005. Teachers as 'managed professionals' in the global education industry: The New Zealand experience. *Educational Review,* 57(2), pp. 193–206.

Conger, J. A., 1998. Qualitative research as the cornerstone methodology for understanding leadership. *The Leadership Quarterly,* 9(1), pp. 107–121.

Contractor, N. S., deChurch, L. A., Carson, J., Carter, D. R. and Keegan, B., 2012. The topology of collective leadership. *The Leadership Quarterly,* 23(6), pp. 994–1011.

Goffman, E., 1956. The nature of deference and demeanor. *American Anthropologist,* 58(3), pp. 473–502.

Grint, K., 2011. A history of leadership. In A. Bryman, D. Collinson, K. Grint, B. Jackson, B. and M. Uhl-Bien, eds., 2011. *The Sage handbook of leadership.* London: SAGE, pp. 3–14.

Gronn, P., 2002. Distributed leadership as a unit of analysis. *The Leadership Quarterly,* 13(4), pp. 423–451.

Gronn, P., 2009. Leadership configurations. *Leadership,* 5(3), pp. 381–394.

Gronn, P., 2011. Hybrid configurations of leadership. In A. Bryman, D. Collinson, K. Grint, B. Jackson, B. and M. Uhl-Bien, eds., 2011. *The Sage handbook of leadership.* London: SAGE, pp. 437–454.

Gunter, H., Hall, D. and Bragg, J., 2013. Distributed leadership: A study in knowledge production. *Educational Management Administration and Leadership,* 41(5), pp. 555–580.

Hallett, T., 2007. Between deference and distinction: Interaction ritual through symbolic power in an educational institution. *Social Psychology Quarterly,* 70(2), pp. 148–171.

Hargreaves, A. and Fink, D., 2006. *Sustainable leadership.* San Francisco, CA: Jossey-Bass.

Harris, A., 2006. Opening up the 'Black Box' of leadership practice: Taking a distributed leadership perspective. *International Studies in Educational Administration*, 34(2), pp. 37–45.

Harris, A., 2009. Distributed leadership, knowledge creation. In K. Leithwood, B. Mascall and T. Strauss, eds., 2009. *Distributed leadership according to the evidence*. New York: Routledge, pp. 253–266.

Hartley, D., 2007. The emergence of distributed leadership in education: Why now? *British Journal of Educational Studies*, 55(2), pp. 202–214.

Kerr, S. and Jermier, J. M., 1978. Substitutes for leadership: Their meaning and measurement. *Organisational Behavior and Human Performance*, 22(3), pp. 375–403.

Leithwood, K., Mascall, B., Strauss, T., Sacks, R., Memon, N. and Yashkina, A., 2007. Distributing leadership to make schools smarter: Taking the ego out of the system. *Leadership and Policy in Schools*, 6(1), pp. 37–67.

Lumby, J., 2013. Distributed leadership: The uses and abuses of power. *Educational Management Administration and Leadership*, 41(5), pp. 581–597

MacBeath, J., 2005. Leadership as distributed: A matter of practice. *School Leadership and Management*, 25(4), pp. 349–366.

Maxcy, B. D. and Nyugen, T. S. T., 2006. The politics of distributing leadership. *Educational Policy*, 20(1), pp. 163–196.

May, T., and Powell, J. L., 2008. *Situating social theory*. 2nd ed. Maidenhead: Open University Press.

Meindl, J. R., Ehrlich, S. B. and Dukerich, J. M., 1985. The romance of leadership. *Administrative Science Quarterly*, 30(1), pp. 78–102.

O'Reilly, D. and Reed, M., 2010. 'Leaderism': An evolution of managerialism in UK public service reform. *Public Administration*, 88(4), pp. 960–978.

Parry, K. W. and Bryman, A., 2006. Leadership in organisations. In S. R. Clegg, C. Hardy, T. B. Lawrence and W. R. Nord, eds., 2006. *The Sage handbook of organisation studies*, 2nd ed. London: SAGE, pp. 447–468.

Pfeffer, J., 1977. The ambiguity of leadership. *Academy of Management Review*, 2(1), pp. 104–112.

Raelin, J. A., ed., 2016. *Leadership-as-practice: Theory and application*. New York: Routledge.

Sachs, J., 2003. *The activist teaching profession*. Buckingham: Open University Press.

Sauder, M., Lynn, F. and Podolny, J. M., 2012. Status: Insights from organisational sociology. *Annual Review of Sociology*, 38, pp. 267–283.

Smyth, J., 2001. *Critical politics of teachers' work*. New York: Peter Lang Publishing.

Spillane, J. P., 2006. *Distributed leadership*. San Francisco, CA: Jossey-Bass.

Thomson, P., 2005. Bringing Bourdieu to policy sociology: Codification, misrecognition and exchange value in the UK context. *Journal of Education Policy*, 20(6), pp. 741–758.

Thorpe, R., Gold, J. and Lawler, J., 2011. Locating distributed leadership. *International Journal of Management Reviews*, 13(3), pp. 239–250.

Thrupp, M. and Willmott, R., 2003. *Education management in managerialist times: Beyond the textual apologists*. Maidenhead, UK: Open University Press.

Torrance, D., 2009. Distributed leadership in Scottish schools: Perspectives from participants recently completing the revised Scottish Qualification for Headship Programme. *Management in Education*, 23(2), pp. 63–70.

Wright, N., 2001. Leadership, 'Bastard Leadership' and managerialism: Confronting twin paradoxes in the Blair education project. *Educational Management Administration and Leadership*, 29(3), pp. 275–290.

Youngs, H., 2009. (Un)Critical times? Situating distributed leadership in the field. *Journal of Educational Administration and History*, 41(4), pp. 377–389.

Youngs, H., 2014. Moving beyond distributed leadership to distributed forms: A contextual and socio-cultural analysis of two New Zealand secondary schools. *Leading and Managing*, 20(2), pp. 88–103.

10 Leadership standards and the discursive repositioning of leadership, leaders and non-leaders

A critical examination

*Augusto Riveros, Paul Newton
and David Burgess*

Introduction

In this chapter, we interrogate conceptualisations of leadership in policy documents and initiatives that propose standards for the practice of leadership in education. We note that literature and policies dealing with school reform have tended to favour leadership-centred explanations of social action, advancing a leader(s)-centric vision of school reform and improvement without consideration of the multiple and diverse political, social, economic, cultural and ideological factors that converge in processes of organisational transformation (Alvesson, 2014). This is clearly evidenced in the recent emphasis that influential educational leadership literature has placed on the role of the school leader in improving student achievement (Leithwood et al., 2008; Leithwood et al., 2012), the effects of distributing leadership in improvement processes (Timperley, 2009) and the central role of teacher leadership in improving schools (Reeves, 2008). As Glatter (2006, p. 73) indicated, the discursive construction of leadership as the focal instrument of reform presents a 'danger of continuing to be trapped within the ideology of the "can-do" culture…whereby agency is always considered capable of overcoming structure'. By placing unqualified emphasis on the role of leadership in school change, defined in terms of student achievement, contemporary reform initiatives relinquish crucial questions about the social processes that intersect in the transformation of schools. Glatter's cautions about the literature's optimism regarding the leaders' capacity to overcome the systemic and structural constraints in their organisations, suggest that for such statements to be true, they must be accompanied by empirical evidence. As we will show below, the research community has been sceptical about the possibility of finding a direct connection between leadership and student achievement given the multiple factors that may influence the learning process, so assuming that we understand what we mean by *leadership*, and assuming the we can isolate the effects of this phenomenon, our evidence for this connection is, at best, indirect.

As leadership is instrumentalised in policy documents and influential texts, school actors who are discursively construed as 'leaders' become the agents of reform. In other words, the burden of school change, defined in terms of student achievement, is now placed on the 'school leaders', for they have been positioned as the agents capable of overcoming the structure and bringing about the long-sought but elusive transformation of the educational system. This repositioning of some school actors as leaders also invites an interrogation of the ways the non-leader is construed in the literature and policies. If agency for change is bestowed upon school administrators and selected school actors, for example, 'teacher leaders', then it seems safe to assume that the agency of other actors is not relevant in the accomplishment of the goals of reform; thus all is needed from them is compliance.

In order to analyse this repositioning of some school actors as the champions of school reform, we offer an analysis of the ways leadership has been conceptualised in Canadian policy documents with an emphasis on the provinces of Alberta and Ontario (Alberta Education, 2009; Ontario Institute for Educational Leadership, 2013). Further, we suggest that these articulations of leadership correspond to a view of leadership as 'a social and organizational technology' (O'Reilly and Reed, 2010, p. 961) that could result in 'limited and tightly managed professionalism of a kind that is dangerously malleable in the face of such a powerful and dominant wider context' (Hall, 2013, p. 13). In what follows, we scrutinise two prominent domains in which leadership is being discursively construed: the creation and adoption of leader competencies or standards and the emerging discourses on teacher leadership. Our examination of key policy documents and influential literature yielded four analytical themes: (a) the positioning of leadership practices as 'causal' in school improvement initiatives; (b) the re-emergence of the artificial distinction between leadership and management; (c) the legitimation as the 'leader' in detriment of the agency of the 'non-leader'; and (d) the redefinition of the goals of education in terms of student achievement, with the subsequent postulation school leadership as the means to attain this goal. We conclude with a reflection on the epistemological implications of this repositioning of leadership as an instrument of school reform.

Leader competencies, standards and teacher leadership

As noted above, recent reform initiatives have characterised leadership as an instrument to achieve the goals of reform (Department for Education and Skills [DfES], 2004; Education Services Australia, 2011; Husbands and Gleeson, 2003; Ingvarson et al., 2006; Leithwood et al., 2008; Pont et al., 2008; Volante, 2012). What Riveros (2015) has called the 'leadership turn' in education reform has been evidenced in policy initiatives that promulgate standards of leadership practice for school administrators (Alberta Education, 2009; British Columbia Principals and Vice-Principals Association, 2013; The Ontario Institute for Educational Leadership, 2013). O'Reilly and Reed (2010) have argued that these policy discourses operate by portraying public institutions as dysfunctional spaces in need of immediate intervention. In order to intervene and change the public sector, technologies of surveillance and control originated in the private sector have been mobilised into public education (English, 2012). The result is the introduction of tacit forms of managerialism that instantiate new technocratic regimes under the label of 'school leadership' (Hall et al., 2013). Through these managerialist strategies, discourses on leadership standards work to reconfigure the practices and identities of school administrators.

Ball (2003) has argued that the adoption of standards creates a performative paradox: on the one hand, standards are portrayed as guides for action that promote agency and decision making at the local level; on the other hand, practices at the local level are expected to follow centrally mandated standards, which, in principle, operate without consideration of the local context. In Ball's perspective, standards attempt to guarantee compliance through various surveillance mechanisms, such as performance measurement and accountability. Ball's insights are corroborated by Riveros's (2015) study of the adoption of leadership standards in the province of Ontario, Canada. In his study, Riveros (2015) found that 'when used as a component in processes of evaluation, recruitment and promotion, standards contribute to the regulation of practices, actions and identities in schools' (p. 10). Similarly, Eacott (2011b) has argued that the emerging phenomenon of leadership standards instantiate a neo-liberal and market-driven approach to the educational systems and to leaders' roles as deliverers of policy. As argued above, the reconstitution of school leaders' roles (e.g. through competencies) instrumentalises the school principal's work to serve the goals of reform.

Principal standards and competencies tend to focus on principals' knowledge. As such, these policy discourses reinforce the notion of leadership as a property of expert individuals. Riveros (2015) described a worrying trend in the jurisdictions where standards have been deployed: standards tend to be positioned as a *unifying theory of leadership*, that is, as the ultimate compendium of what leadership is and should be. This discursive positioning of leadership, accompanied by the incorporation of the standards in processes of evaluation and appraisal, has two unintended consequences: first, it situates leadership as an organisational phenomenon in the practices of selected individuals; and second, it defines leadership in terms of traits and specific practices. Consequently, this policy-driven characterisation of leadership limits the practitioners' spaces for critical interrogation of leadership theories and perspectives. In previous work (Riveros et al., 2012), we have argued for an understanding of leadership as situated practices, that is, as an emerging organisational phenomenon that implies coordinated forms of intentionality, the negotiation of meaning and the reconfiguration of agencies and subjectivities through practices. This perspective recognises that 'agency and understanding are situated in the interaction of bodies in the material world, rather than a view of inner mental faculties as the origin of action' (Newton and Riveros, 2015, p. 331).

One of the consequences of recasting leadership as an instrument of reform has been the redefinition of the principals' work; however, this is not the only area in which contemporary discourses on leadership operate to serve the goals of reform policies. Recent calls for distributing and sharing leadership within schools (Murphy, 2005) seem to support the notion of 'teacher leadership' (Harris, 2003). Though there exists at least 20 years of devoted scholarly work on the topic, the concept of teacher leadership remains theoretically elusive (Newton et al., 2013).

A growing body of literature and policy (Glatter, 2006; Hall et al., 2013) has suggested that teacher leadership, shared leadership or distributed leadership help in dispersing and capitalising on broader bases of agency in schools (Hartley, 2007). As suggested by many authors in the educational leadership literature (Fitzgerald and Gunter, 2008; Murphy, 2005; Reeves, 2008), teacher leadership can be deployed to pursue the achievement of system and school improvement goals. Teacher leadership, distributed leadership and shared leadership are often presented as strategies to employ within leadership competency frameworks. On the surface, these calls for the distribution of leadership appear to invite more fulsome participation and encourage a 'democratisation' of teachers' work environments. However, even in such conceptualisations of distributed, shared or teacher leadership, the questions left unanswered are: What about non-leaders? Do they also have agency? Or is agency only a property of leaders? Does equating leadership with agency permit only 'authorised' sources of agency to influence school practices and the attainment of school improvement goals?

Fitzgerald and Gunter (2008, p. 334) questioned the motivation and usefulness of teacher-leadership policies: 'of concern is that this is simply a modernized way to seduce teachers to take on additional tasks and responsibilities without the commensurate increase in their salary or time allowance'. Central to our critique is the way in which teacher-leadership discourses (to a greater extent even than distributed-leadership discourses), by their very nature, exclude some actors from full participation as agents. As a result, only the actions of actors appointed as leaders are legitimised through the teacher-leadership discourses, regardless of the rhetoric surrounding distribution and sharing of leadership (Hall, 2013). According to Fitzgerald and Gunter (2008, p. 335), 'linked then with hierarchy structure, power and authority, teacher leadership is, we would suggest, a management strategy and not a radical alternative'. In the next section, we explore the ways in which leadership is assumed to be a primary policy lever for system improvement and the assumption that causal powers can be attributed to the phenomenon of leadership in schools.

Leadership as a causal influence in school improvement initiatives

As Alvesson and Sveningsson (2000) have indicated, the popularity of the leadership discourse does little to establish its empirical adequacy as an explanation of social activity. Central to its popularity, however, is a contemporary belief in its power to initiate social change – 'Today leadership is hailed as a major explanatory factor for organizational performance' (Salovaara, 2011, p. 84). Leadership has exploded as an area of interest in diverse fields. Luminaries such as Oprah Winfrey and Bill Gates have chimed in on the subject, dozens of competing models litter book-store shelves and elementary schools deliver educational programmes based on the leadership theories of management gurus (Franklin Covey, 2015). The discourse is so ubiquitous in educational trade publications and scholarly literature that one could be tempted to assume its veracity as a conceptual and theoretical category. Whether or not leadership is an adequate explanation of phenomena in the social world, it has clearly become a primary area of leverage for school-improvement initiatives. Numerous researchers and formulators of policy start their work from the premise that 'school leadership is second only to classroom teaching as an influence on pupil learning' (Leithwood et al., 2008, p. 27), which, in our view, suggests that school leadership is instrumental to the ultimate goal of student achievement. O'Reilly and Reed (2010, p. 962) reported on the ubiquity of leadership discourses in their empirical study of publicly available public-administration documents in the UK. They provided 'evidence of an increasing rise in the language of leadership, in English-writing countries, over the past few decades'.

What seems clear from the activity surrounding leadership standards and competencies is that policy makers and governments hold the belief that leadership is a key point of leverage to redesign educational organisations. In some ways, this makes good sense. Large-scale reform and improvement can be onerous and expensive to initiate. The strategy of developing on-site policy implementers in the person of the school leader is a cost-effective way to ensure system initiatives are communicated to a larger employee population. The most compelling argument for the causal powers of school leadership has come from the oft-cited article by Leithwood et al. (2008). In this work, five sources of evidence are presented to substantiate the claim that 'school leadership is second only to classroom teaching as an influence on pupil learning' (Leithwood et al., 2008, p. 27): (a) qualitative case studies of outlier schools that demonstrate large leadership effects on student learning; (b) large-scale quantitative studies that show small but significant leadership effects on student achievement; (c) correlational studies of the relationship between leadership responsibilities and student achievement; (d) studies of leadership effects on student engagement (with 'some evidence' of the link between school engagement and achievement); and (e) studies of headteacher turnover that conclude negative effects on school initiatives. Methodologically, these studies cited as evidence generally suffer from a lack of conceptual clarity (concepts such as *student achievement, student learning, engagement* and *leadership* are notoriously elusive) are non-generalisable (in the case of qualitative case studies – which Leithwood et al. point out), correlational or attempt to link narrowly multiple complex social and systemic phenomena to student achievement. Further, as Lakomski (2005, p.9) pointed out, leadership research is empirically problematic in that methods to assess leadership often rely on 'after-the-event rationalisations of people's subjective views of leadership'. As such, the independent 'leadership' variable is in reality an interpretation, a *post-hoc* explanation that locates 'causality in one person rather than attributing it to a complex set of inter-relationships' (Lakomski, 2005, p. 4). As well, as we will discuss later, the purposes or desired ends of schooling receive no attention here. The conceptual and methodological issues in linking leadership to student achievement are significant. This did not escape Leithwood et al. (2008) and likely is the reason for referring to 'strong' claims. As they indicate in their paper, the claim that 'school leadership is second only to classroom teaching as an influence on pupil learning' (Leithwood et al.,

2008, p. 27) might be viewed as controversial. In our view, however, this has become doxa for many scholars, practitioners and policy makers.

The re-emergence of the distinction between leadership and management

There is a long-standing rhetorical distinction between school leadership and management. In Alberta, for example, policy documents reinforce an artificial distinction between leadership-related activity and management. For example, the *Alberta School Leadership Framework* (Alberta Education, 2010, p. 5) indicates that 'school leaders' workloads have become arduous as a consequence of increased managerial responsibilities related to school-based budgeting, decision-making and governance and their greater accountability for results'. This statement implies that school leaders' work has been diverted from 'leadership' by accountability and increased managerial minutiae. Furthermore, an additional implication arises that suggests that such things as school-based budgeting do not require leadership but are merely necessary evils that interfere with the work of agents in schools. It is not entirely clear that these areas might be the very areas for which agency should be exercised – although Leithwood et al. (2008) and Leithwood (2012) make exactly this case. As another example, Alberta Education (2010, p. 6) stated that 'today's school leaders are especially challenged to devote sufficient time and attention to instructional leadership as a consequence of the time and effort that managerial duties require'. However, despite the widespread distinction between leadership and management in these policy documents, it is not clear how they could be separated in any study of the actual practices of school leaders or if such separation offers useful insights about the ways in which school leaders exercise their agency. Traditionally, the distinction between management and leadership has been presented as a distinction between the technical/preservationist and the moral/creative dimensions of the administrators' work (Bush, 2008). We believe, along with Robinson (2006), that the suggestion that moral agency is only present in those activities classified as 'leadership' is troubling. The importance of, and moral and ethical consequences inherent in, questions about budget, resources, staffing decisions, collective agreements, timetables and so on ought to be treated as more than diversions from leadership.

Legitimating leaders to the detriment of non-leaders

Is leadership the same as agency? This is a central question in our work. In fact, we contend that agential activity within school systems has been equated with both the notions of 'competent' leaders and distributed or teacher leadership with inconsistent results. Previously, we have argued 'that the constitution of leadership: (a) is predicated on individualist/atomistic assumptions, (b) privileges leadership as the primary location of agency in educational organizations, and (c) constructs leaders as the sole bearers of agency in schools' (Newton and Riveros, 2015, pp. 335–336). An example of this unqualified correspondence between agency and leadership could be seen in the *Ontario Leadership Framework* (The Institute for Educational Leadership, 2013, p. 6), where there is an emphasis on personal traits associated with leadership practice: 'While many traits or personal characteristics have been associated with leaders and leadership, the framework includes only those for which there is compelling research evidence. School leader and system leader practices are enacted most effectively using these Personal Leadership Resources'. The emphasis on personal traits highlights the individualistic understanding of leadership and the role of 'school leaders' as primary agents. This is far removed from a conception of leadership as a socially situated and distributed set of practices (Gronn, 2010).

Leadership standards and competencies construct processes and relations in ways that reinforce an object–subject relationship. As we have argued in other venues (Newton and Riveros, 2015; Riveros et al., 2012; Riveros, 2012, 2015), the concept of agency and its corresponding notion of structure have been appropriated to recast leaders in the role of agents of reform, while other school actors have been positioned as the passive subjects of school reform. 'It seems, however, that these notions have often been reconstructed to fit into conventional categories of subject/object and leader/organisation. Leadership is often viewed as the exercise of a variety of political agency that rests on powerful individuals within organisational contexts' (Newton and Riveros, 2015, p. 335). Clearly, one consequence of the proliferation of leadership frameworks is the redefinition of agency in schools. We believe this invites further reflection about the nature of the dyad leader-follower, in particular about the consequences of the discursive construction 'followership' as unrecognised forms of agency in organisations. An emerging area of scholarship in leadership studies has focused on the concept of *followership* (Riggio et al., 2008; Salovaara, 2011; Thody, 2003). Proponents of followership theories portray following as an act of agency that is equally essential for organisational functioning. As Salovaara (2011, p. 86) suggested, 'follower-centric models that define followers within the subject-object framework, that is, that despite the shift of emphasis from leaders to followers, there remains a separation of these two'.

Our analysis suggests that there appear to be contradictory phenomena with respect to the portrayal of agency at play. First, leaders in the form of school principals and teacher leaders are agents, their actions are legitimised by systemic processes and, as such, the exercise of their agency is strictly controlled and constrained by the larger school system and state-level priorities. Second, other non-leader actors in schools are portrayed as passive or 'non-agents' in relation to the goals of reform – or at the very least, they are ignored within the literature or policy formulations. Non-agents have the potential to become agents if they assume the mantle of teacher leaders; however, their agency is legitimised by the system only if it is coherent with the goals of the larger system. In fact, those teachers who exercise the desired sort of agency become, by definition, 'emergent' teacher leaders. Non-agents who choose not to step up to take on predefined leadership roles are thought to be inert, and those who exercise unauthorised agency are labelled 'resistors'. Similarly, Fitzgerald and Gunter (2008, p. 332) argued that teacher leaders' roles tend to be legitimised when their activities are seen to be in alignment with organisational priorities and goals. The call for more teachers to get involved in leadership (Muijs and Harris, 2003) or to distribute leadership practices has rather more to do with implementing reforms and meeting organisational requirements than a concern for teaching and learning. Further, Fitzgerald and Gunter (2008, p. 337) stated that 'being a functional teacher leader means being on message'.

Although many of the discourses in educational leadership appear to include distributed, shared and collaborative approaches, the policy documents tend toward descriptions of the competencies or practices of individual formal leaders within a school system. The inclusion of collaborative approaches is often framed as a strategic approach to ensure the appropriate dispersion of system and government priorities. Eacott's (2011b, p. 52) views support our assertion that policies primarily position principals as the key actors in leading schools. In his words, '[d]espite the rhetoric of participation and distributed leadership in schools in the literature, legally, the ultimate accountability for the operational management of the school rests with the principal'.

Within the framework of standards and competencies, leadership practices can be seen as the result of the enactment of the desired traits and dispositions of leaders. In these documents, school leaders are characterised as the primary agents who exercise 'influence' over other school actors. Although there is mention of shared and distributed leadership practices, the policy documents and competencies frameworks we explored rarely include explicit reference to teachers, students or staff as active participants in leadership practices. As such, this characterisation of leadership practices is unidirectional and does not reflect the theorising with respect to agency that suggests that multiple agents are at work when enacting organisational realities (Gronn, 2010; Riveros et al., 2012). Similarly, Lakomski (2005, p. 7) cautioned about a study of leadership that privileges the individual over the social context in which leadership practices are enacted. As she notes, 'Continuing to focus on the individual to the exclusion of the group or groups makes the study of *informal or other leadership processes and practices* almost impossible' (Lakomski, 2005, p. 7).

As noted above, these policies and competency frameworks portray school leaders as the bearers of agency and have little to say about 'non-leaders' and *their* agency. In this way, the practices of 'school leaders' are treated as practices that differ from and are disconnected from the practices and actions of teachers, students and other actors in the school context. This represents a decontextualised approach to leadership practice (or practices) the purpose of which is to direct and manage the organisational context, not as integrated within general sets of practices within the school context (English, 2012; Thomson, 2008). As a result, and according to Lakomski (2005), this leads to a study of leadership and organisational action that is, at best, anaemic and holds no explanatory power.

Student achievement and the goals of education

Glatter (2006), citing the work of Lumby et al. (2003), has suggested that the current emphasis on leadership for student achievement, promoted by policy makers and scholars alike, has 'lost sight of the fact that learning is not solely an end in itself, but may serve other purposes also' (Glatter, 2006, p. 78). Glatter (2006) has expressed his concern that making school leadership all about achievement may have the consequence of ostracising this domain from more important and wider discussions about the ends of education. Parallel to this, many policy makers (Pont et al., 2008), have come to the conclusion that standards and competencies for school leaders may have potential to leverage the larger school system towards these unproblematised ends. Fitzgerald and Gunter (2008) argue for the connection between standards-based educational reform and school leader standards and explain the emerging fascination with competencies and standards in light of beliefs about the causal power of leadership. They point out that 'Concern by policymakers that school leadership, pupil attainment, school improvement and school effectiveness are inextricably linked has prompted the promulgation of standards for leaders and normative training programmes for aspiring and current leaders in schools' (Fitzgerald and Gunter, 2008, p. 332).

Niesche (2013, p. 144) has argued that the pervasive influence of New Public Management discourses in education has positioned leadership as a technique of governmentality that is 'being deployed as a strategy of governments, and as an answer to educational problems'. Within these discursive regimes, school leaders are not in charge of defining the nature of educational problems, nor are they seen as having the capacity to challenge or resist the imposition of the surveillance practices that come with the adoption of the many school-reform narratives.

Glatter (2006), following Owaga and Bossert (1997), has indicated that the literature's emphasis on leadership obscures the significance of the organisational as the contexts where the leadership as a phenomenon emerges. As we have noted, this reorientation towards leadership has the potential to distract our attention from key social processes that influence education and schooling. By focusing on leadership as the key phenomenon to investigate in relation to school change, researchers could end up treating it as a quality of influential actors detached from the social contexts in which such quality is manifested. In response to this concern, Glatter (2006, p. 72) has proposed a return to the macro- or meso-level of analysis, that is, a return to the organisational as the unit of analysis, which would allow researchers to understand how leadership is a 'systemic characteristic' or as an emergent phenomenon that is configured (Gronn, 2010) as part of processes of social change. In Glatter's (2006) view, the focus on leadership limits our capacity to analyse the complexity of educational institutions, in particular the interconnections between power, policy and practice. This claim has been echoed by Wright (2011), who argued that a conceptualisation of leadership as a mechanism of school reform, could de-politicise the work of school administrators. By stressing the actors' potential to influence the system under the guidance of prescribed standards, discourses on school reform transform school leaders into implementers of policies, actors whose actions and practices must conform to narratives of school reform expressed in terms of student achievement (Newton and Riveros, 2015).

Conclusion

In this chapter, we have outlined some of the issues with current policy formulations that position school leadership as the key driver of educational reform in school systems. The ubiquity of leadership discourses in public sector institutions is well documented (Hall, 2013; O'Reilly and Reed, 2010; Pont et al., 2008). Viewed uncritically, these formulations of leadership appear to provide school actors with the autonomy and conceptual resources to influence educational reform in their school contexts. We have identified, however, that there are several areas of concern in the way in which these leadership discourses have been constructed in policy. First, the characterisation of leadership practices as both 'causal' in school improvement initiatives and as unidirectional is a theoretically untenable understanding of agency, practices and leadership in light of the multiple social factors that have been documented to influence school change (Ball et al., 2012). Moreover, a causal and unidirectional understanding of the effects of leadership may be at odds with contemporary understandings of the situated nature of actors, processes and related phenomena in school contexts (Newton and Riveros, 2015; Riveros, 2012; Riveros et al., 2012). Second, the artificial distinction between leadership and management has the potential to remove school actors from involvement in important social justice decisions pertaining to the distribution and allocation of financial and material resources in schools by portraying management as neutral and irrelevant with respect to moral agency. Third, the privileging of selected school actors as legitimate 'school leaders' prompts questions about the value that leadership discourses allocate to the agency of other 'non-leader' actors within schools. Fourth, positioning student achievement as the focus of school leadership leaves unanswered questions about the ends of education.

By positioning achievement as the goal of reform, contemporary discourses on leadership avoid the critical task of interrogating the nature and purpose of educating future generations. In this regard, Eacott (2011b) points to the impotence of school leaders under the current regime to address issues of central concern with respect to schooling. As he notes, 'If school leaders are to reclaim their radical past and engage in public intellectualism, an alternate leadership habitus, one built on educational problem posing and contestation as opposed to organisational problem solving, is required' (Eacott, 2011b, p. 45). Similarly, we have argued for a more theoretically and ethically robust conception of educational leadership that emphasises the complexity of leadership as a social practice and that might have the resources to tackle the difficult issues confronting schools.

> Leadership (if it is a useful notion at all) is not the property of powerful individuals, a subsystem of organization, or a technology employed to ensure compliance with a predetermined course of action, but rather is a practice or practices situated in a social and material context.
>
> (Newton and Riveros, 2015, p. 336)

Finally, we suggest that the emergence of a discourse on leadership competencies has significant epistemological implications for the study of educational administration. The decontextualisation of knowledge, the unification of the field under standards and the delegitimation of dissent are symptomatic of a standardisation of knowledge about the administration of schools. As English (2006, p. 467) argued, 'a singular knowledge base that does not revolve around contested space in a dynamic structure creates a false picture of permanence, and when incorporated into accreditation criteria works against the production of new knowledge'. It also suggests an objectively knowable administrative world and denies that knowledge may be socially constructed (English, 2006) and socially situated (Newton and Riveros, 2015). We suggest that further discussion and critique of the implications of the dominance of these discourses on leadership in educational policy is of central importance to the work of schoolteachers and administrators.

Note

1   The Alberta Principal Quality Practice Guideline is scheduled to be replaced by a new professional practice standard for school principals some time in 2016.

References

Alberta Education, 2009. *Principal quality practice guideline: promoting successful school leadership in Alberta*. Edmonton: Alberta Education.[1] Available from: http://georgecouros.ca/blog/wp-content/uploads/2010/04/pqs.pdf

Alberta Education, 2010. *The Alberta school leadership framework*. Edmonton, Alberta: Alberta Education.

Alvesson, M., 2014. *Understanding organizational culture*. London: SAGE Publications.

Alvesson, M. and Sveningsson, S., 2003. The great disappearing act: Difficulties in doing 'leadership'. *The Leadership Quarterly*, 14(3), pp. 359–381.

Ball, S. J., 2003. The teacher's soul and the terrors of performativity. *Journal of Education Policy*, 18(2), pp. 215–228.

Ball, S. J., Maguire, M. and Braun, A., 2012. *How schools do policy: Policy enactments in secondary schools*. London: Routledge.

British Columbia Principals and Vice-Principals Association, 2013. *Leadership standards for principals and vice principals in British Columbia*. Vancouver: BCPVP.

Bush, T., 2008. From management to leadership: Semantic or meaningful change? *Educational Management Administration and Leadership*, 36(2), pp. 271–288.

DfES, 2004. *National standards for headteachers*. Nottingham: DfES.

Eacott, S., 2011a. *School leadership and strategy in managerialist times*. Rotterdam: Sense Publishers.

Eacott, S., 2011b. Preparing 'educational' leaders in managerialist times: An Australian story. *Journal of Educational Administration and History*, 43(1), pp. 43–59.

Education Services Australia, 2011. *Australian professional standards for principals*, Victoria: ESA.

English, F. W., 2006. The unintended consequences of a standardized knowledge base in advancing educational leadership preparation. *Educational Administration Quarterly*, 42(3), pp. 461–472.

English, F. W., 2012. Bourdieu's 'misrecognition': Why educational leadership standards will not reform schools or leadership. *Journal of Educational Administration and History*, 44(2), pp. 155–170.

Fitzgerald, T. and Gunter, H. M., 2008. Contesting the orthodoxy of teacher leadership. *International Journal of Leadership in Education*, 11(4), pp. 331–340.

Glatter, R., 2006. Leadership and organization in education: Time for a re-orientation? *School Leadership and Management*, 26(1), pp. 69–83.

Gronn, P., 2010. Leadership: Its genealogy, configuration and trajectory. *Journal of Educational Administration and History*, 42(4), pp. 405–435.

Gunter, H., 2012. *Leadership and the reform of education*. Bristol: Policy Press.

Hall, D., 2013. Drawing a veil over managerialism: Leadership and the discursive disguise of the New Public Management. *Journal of Educational Administration and History*, 45(3), pp. 267–282.

Hall, D., Gunter, H. and Bragg, J., 2013. Leadership, new public management and the re-modelling and regulation of teacher identities. *International Journal of Leadership in Education*, 16(2), pp. 173–190.

Harris, A., 2003. Teacher leadership as distributed leadership: Heresy, fantasy or possibility? *School Leadership and Management*, 23(3), pp. 313–324.

Hartley, D., 2007. The emergence of distributed leadership in education: Why now? *British Journal of Educational Studies*, 55(2), pp. 202–214.

Husbands, C. and Gleeson, D., 2003. Modernizing schooling through performance management: A critical appraisal. *Journal of Education Policy*, 18(5), pp. 499–511.

Ingvarson, L., Anderson, M., Gronn, P. and Jackson, A., 2006. *Standards for school leadership*, Acton: ACER.

Lakomski, G., 2005. *Managing without leadership: Towards a theory of organizational functioning*. Oxford: Elsevier.

Leithwood, K., 2012. *The Ontario leadership framework 2012: With a discussion of the research foundations*. Toronto, ON: The Institute for Education Leadership.

Leithwood, K., Harris, A. and Hopkins, D., 2008. Seven strong claims about successful school leadership. *School Leadership and Management: Formerly School Organisation*, 28(1), pp. 27–42.

Leithwood, K. A., Louis, K. S. and Anderson, S. E., 2012. *Linking leadership to student learning*. San Francisco: Jossey-Bass.

Lumby, J., Foskett, N. and Maringe, F., 2003. Restricted view: School leadership and the 'choices' of learners. Paper presented at the Annual Conference of the British Educational Management and Administration Society. Milton Keynes, UK.

Muijs, D. and Harris, A., 2003. Teacher leadership – improvement through empowerment? An overview of the literature, *Educational Management and Administration*, 31(4), pp. 437–448.

Murphy, J., 2005. *Connecting teacher leadership and school improvement*. Thousand Oaks, California: Corwin Press.

Newton, P., Riveros, A. and da Costa, J., 2013. The influence of teacher leadership in the career advancement of schoolteachers: A case study. *Journal of Educational Administration and Foundations*, 23(2), pp. 105–117.

Newton, P. and Riveros, A., 2015. Toward an ontology of practices in educational administration: Theoretical implications for research and practice. *Educational Philosophy and Theory*, 47(4), pp. 330–341.

Niesche, R., 2013. Politicizing articulation: Applying Lyotard's work to the use of standards in educational leadership. *International Journal of Leadership in Education*, 16(2), pp. 220–233.

Ogawa, R. and Bossert, S. 1997. Leadership as an organizational quality. In M. Crawford, L. Kydd and C. Riches, eds., *Leadership and teams in educational management* (pp. 9–23). Buckingham: Open University.

O'Reilly, D. and Reed, M., 2010. 'Leaderism': An evolution of managerialism in UK public service reform. *Public Administration*, 88(4), pp. 960–978.

Pont, B., Nusche, D. and Moorman, H., 2008. *Improving school leadership: Policy and practice.* Paris: OECD.

Reeves, D. B., 2008. *Reframing teacher leadership to improve your school.* Alexandria, VA: ASCD.

Riggio, R. E., Chaleff, I. and Lipman-Blumen, J., 2008. *The art of followership: How great followers create great leaders and organizations.* San Francisco, CA: Jossey-Bass.

Riveros, A., 2012. Beyond collaboration: Embodied teacher learning and the discourse of collaboration in school reform. *Studies in Philosophy and Education*, 31(6), pp. 603–612.

Riveros, A., 2015. Examining the 'leadership turn' in school reform: The translation of leadership standards into leadership practices. Paper presented at the American Educational Research Association (AERA). April, 2015, Chicago, Il.

Riveros, A., Newton, P. and Burgess, D., 2012. A situated account of teacher agency and learning: Critical reflections on professional learning communities. *Canadian Journal of Education*, 35(1), pp. 202–216.

Robinson, V. M. J., 2006. Putting education back into educational leadership. *Leading and Managing*, 12(1), pp. 62–75.

Salovaara, P., 2011. *From leader-centricity toward leadership: A hermeneutic narrative study.* Tampere, FL: Tampere University Press.

Franklin Covey, 2015. *The leader in me.* Available from: http://theleaderinme.org.

The Ontario Institute for Educational Leadership, 2013. Toronto: *The Ontario leadership framework*, TIEL.

Thody, A., 2003. Followership in educational organizations: A pilot mapping of the territory. *Leadership and Policy in Schools*, 2(2), pp. 141–156.

Thomson, P., 2008. Headteacher critique and resistance: A challenge for policy, and leadership/management scholars. *Journal of Educational Administration and History*, 40(2), pp. 85–100.

Timperley, H. S., 2009. Distributing leadership to improve outcomes for students. In K. Leithwood, B. Mascall and T. Strauss. eds., *Distributed leadership according to the evidence* (pp. 197–223). London: Routledge.

Volante, L., 2012. Educational reform, standards and school leadership. In L. Volante, ed., *School leadership in the context of standards-based reform* (pp. 3–19). Dordrecht: Springer.

Wright, N., 2011. Between 'bastard' and 'wicked' leadership? School leadership and the emerging policies of the UK coalition government. *Journal of Educational Administration and History*, 43(4), pp. 345–362.

11 Reflections on successful school leadership from the International Successful School Principalship Project

Lawrie Drysdale and David Gurr

Introduction

The 2000s have been described as the golden age of leadership (Leithwood and Day, 2007a, p. 1), yet the topic of leadership remains contentious. Some academics question the concept of leadership itself and the usefulness and relevance of locating leadership in the work of people such as school principals. While acknowledging many of the criticisms, in this chapter we reflect on 14 years of research from the International Successful School Principalship Project,[1] and in particular we report on three aspects of this research, two of which are somewhat challenging to current views of school leadership. After describing the project, we discuss the importance of context to successful school leadership and argue that while context is important, there seem to be leadership attributes that are important in most contexts, rather than, as is commonly assumed, leadership being context dependent. We then argue that the idea of heroic leadership needs to be revisited rather than abandoned, and that it needs to be updated to acknowledge the support of many in leading schools: a post-heroic view. Finally, we attempt to define school leadership by describing in some detail one of the models we have developed.

International Successful School Principalship Project (ISSPP)

The ISSPP was established in 2001 to address the need to better understand how principals contribute to school success. The initial intent of the project was to identify across countries the knowledge, skills and dispositions that school principals use in schools deemed successful. Since then, the project has also focussed on uncovering the contributions of others to school success.

The project initially involved eight countries, but through several evolutions has grown to include over 20 countries and 38 universities. The ISSPP has completed two phases (carrying out initial case studies and then revisiting these to explore the sustainability of success) and is currently embarking on the third phase, which involves conducting mixed-method case studies (interview, observation, document analysis and survey) in schools that are performing below expectations. The project has been an outstanding success in terms of productivity with research groups from more than 20 countries contributing to four edited project books, seven special issues of journals (e.g. Drysdale, 2011a), and more than 100 book chapters and journal papers. Caldwell (2014, p. xxi) has described it as 'the most comprehensive and coherent international comparative study of the principalship ever undertaken.'

Research framework

The ISSPP research has largely adopted qualitative case-study methodology that incorporates multi-perspective views of the actions and events that contribute to school success. Within the competing paradigms of qualitative research (Guba and Lincoln, 1994) the project sits within the interpretative or constructivist paradigm because it seeks to understand and describe the phenomenon of principal leadership and its influence on school success. There are also parallels between the ISSPP research and Gunter's (2001) description of four main positions for leadership studies: instrumental, scientific, humanistic and critical. The instrumental position provides leaders with models and strategies to ensure effective and desired organisational performance. Similarly, the scientific position attempts to measure and establish causality between effective leadership and organisational outcomes. The humanistic position gathers data from leaders who outline experiences and stories of their leadership in context and over time. The critical position is concerned with showing how leaders and followers can be liberated from social injustice and subjection of existing power structures by questioning and exploring the interplay between these various aspects and processes. The ISSPP fits into the humanistic and instrumental research approaches because the research seeks to use the experiences of practitioners to describe and theorise about school leadership, and from this to develop models and strategies that lead to school success (e.g. Day and Gurr, 2014; Day and Leithwood, 2007; Moos et al., 2011a; Ylimaki and Jacobson, 2011a). Through survey-based research that some groups conducted in the first phase, there is also a scientific orientation through the development of weighted pathway models that seek to link leadership with organisational outcomes (e.g. Mulford and Edmunds, 2009; Mulford and Silins, 2011). This research approach is being revisited in the project's third phase, which incorporates principal and teacher surveys about leadership and organisational outcomes. The ISSPP has not taken a critical position.

The ISSPP builds upon and parallels the research on successful school leadership in North America (such as Leithwood and Riehl's 2005 summary of the successful school leadership literature; and the many reports from The Wallace Foundation on school leadership, such as Whalstrom et al., 2010; and The Wallace Foundation, 2013), England (such as the large mixed-method study by Leithwood et al., 2006; and Day et al., 2009) and Australia (see Gurr, 2009; and Drysdale and Gurr, 2011).

Methodology

The ISSPP has been focused on exploring the leadership of principals who are regarded as being successful leaders in successful schools. This, of course, harks back to the long tradition of the effective schools literature focusing on principal leadership and reflects Lezotte's perceptive observation, 'If you know of an effective school without an effective principal, call me collect' (Cotton, 2003, p. 74). Three precepts guided the research:

- Multi-perspective data about successful principalship will provide richer, more authentic data than has hitherto been available.
- Such data is best provided by those with close knowledge of the principal, that is, teachers, students, parents, non-teaching members of the school and other community members.
- Collaborative research designed to a set of agreed common protocols across English and non-English-speaking countries will provide understandings of, and insights into, successful principalship and school improvement, which will add to existing knowledge.

The ISSPP decided to focus on *success* rather than *effectiveness* because success was seen to be a more inclusive and broader concept. Sergiovanni (1991) had previously noted that the term *successful* should be used because it communicated a broader definition of effectiveness. The effective schools movement focuses on inputs and throughputs (Sammons, 1999), whereas successful schools focus on outcomes. In order to better understand success, we wanted to investigate perceptions of success at the school level and explore the contribution of the principal to that success. In addition, there was little identifiable research on successful school leadership as opposed to effective school leadership.

The criteria for selecting schools were based on a range of evidence that demonstrated that the school had been successful during the period of the current principal and that the principal was acknowledged as successful. Whenever possible, selection was based on evidence of student achievement beyond expectations on state or national tests, principals' exemplary reputations in the community and/or school system and other indicators of success that were site-specific.

Once the schools were selected, the ISSPP sought to determine how the participants in the study defined success (which they tended to define more broadly than the project's criteria) and then to determine the extent that participants in the study could identify and confirm the principal's contribution to the school's success through reflection upon, and examples of, the principal's practice. This was followed up by asking participants to identify what they thought were the characteristics and qualities of the principals who helped them to contribute to that success and to identify others in the school who have contributed to school success.

As previously stated, the ISSPP relies on multiple perspective case studies. Primary data is collected through semi-structured interviews using a standard protocol conducted with the school principal (multiple interviews), teachers (individual and group interviews), parents (group interviews), students (group interviews) and members of the school board or council (individual interviews). Secondary data is collected through school documents, minutes of meetings, press reports, school websites, researcher ethnographic notes and so forth. For latter case studies, observations of the work of the principal and of the life of the school are also included through researcher field notes of the observations. Full methodological details are contained in Day (2014). Observational multiple perspective case studies are a robust and trustworthy way to gather information on successful school leadership.

Leadership qualities and context

Context

We know that context matters. But how much does it matter, and does it override personal factors in terms of determining success? This was a major research area for the ISSPP.

The initial ISSPP case studies represented significant contextual differences: they consisted of a range of case-study sites (primary, secondary, special school, rural and city, small and large, demographic and geographical, low and high socio-economic status), education systems and structures (centralised and decentralised, various degrees of autonomy, government and non-government) and government education policy (divergence of initiatives).

Cross-country comparisons (Drysdale, 2011b; Gurr, 2014; Gurr and Day, 2014; Gurr et al., 2006b; Leithwood, 2005; Leithwood and Day, 2007a, b; Moos et al., 2011b; and Ylimaki and Jacobson, 2011b) indicate that successful principals seem to be less contextually dependent and are able to work with and influence the context to help school success. For example, in one of our case studies (Gurr et al., 2005) the leader of a specialist school that catered for students with disabilities was threatened by new government regulations that encouraged students with disabilities to enrol in mainstream schools as the default option. The principal lobbied and worked through political and social networks to turn this around to her own school's advantage and to secure the school's survival and growth for the medium term. Day (2005a, p. 581) noted that successful school principals demonstrated the ability not to

> be confined by the contexts in which they work. They do not comply, subvert, or overtly oppose. Rather they actively mediate and moderate within a set of core values and practices which transcend narrowly conceived improvement agendas.

We can also conjecture that perhaps less successful principals are likely to be more contextually dependent; that they may be captured and held hostage by the context in which they found themselves. This is something that further ISSPP students hope to investigate.

Qualities

When exploring the many cases of the ISSPP, across the countries the findings show that the principal is the key figure in a school's success (Gurr et al., 2006b);

that there are more similarities than differences in terms of how they lead (Day, 2005b); that personal values, personalities, character traits, skills and cognitive styles are antecedents of successful principal leadership (Leithwood and Day, 2007a, b); and that it is a combination of values, qualities and skills that allow principals to 'make a difference' (Day, 2005b, p. 535). The ISSPP does not claim that these qualities are leadership, but that they do enable the principal – the designated leader – to work more effectively with organisational members to achieve the school's goals. In some respects, this revisits trait theory, although as noted by Stogdill (1974), there are no lists of traits that can be consistently identified with leaders. However, several case studies also showed the reciprocal nature of the leader–follower relationship. For example, in one New Zealand school, the principal had adopted a directive style in the initial phase of a school improvement agenda. At a later stage, staff requested that the principal adopt a collaborative style (Notman and Henry, 2011). In this case, his values, personal qualities and skills enabled him to establish relationships that allowed this to occur.

Practices

Perhaps one of the most contentious claims by the ISSPP is that it has identified a common set of values, characters and behaviours that it believes are stable and span various contexts. The ISSPP has found support for a widely known common set of leadership practices that include building vision and setting direction, understanding and developing people, designing the organisation and managing the teaching and learning programme (Leithwood and Day, 2007a). This has been used as a conceptual framework in many of the case studies for identifying successful leadership practices (see Jacobson and Ylimaki, 2011a) and confirmed in syntheses of 15 case-study findings (e.g. Gurr and Day, 2014). Gurr et al. (2006a) used the heading 'interventions' rather than practices but verified that principals worked in these four areas. Through analyses of the cases, we have now added three more practices to how we conceptualise educational leadership in our post-graduate programmes: understanding the broader context, influencing others and self-leadership (see Figure 11.1).

Gurr et al. (2006b) also identified 'capacity building' to be a common theme in all case studies. *Capacity building* is a broad term that includes a range of interventions designed to increase the ability of people and organisations to do what is expected and demanded of them. This could include professional learning, coaching, mentoring and providing the structures and conditions that facilitate improvement (Harris and Muijs, 2005; Tucker, 2001). All subsequent educational leadership frameworks and models we have developed include school capacity building as a major intervention that impacts on student outcomes (e.g. Drysdale and Gurr, 2011). What we have found is that successful principals use particular kinds of influence and intervention strategies to improve outcomes such as 'enhancing the school and professional capacity of teachers, improving the quality of instruction, redesigning the curriculum, building social capital, and providing a safe and secure environment' (Drysdale, 2011b, p. 454). Across the

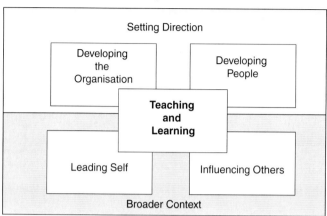

Figure 11.1 The University of Melbourne Masters in Educational Management leadership framework (2015).

ISSPP, there is sufficient evidence to develop models that seem to describe the areas in which successful principals work in many countries, and contexts within these countries, throughout the world. One such model is presented towards the end of this chapter.

Heroic and non-heroic leadership

One feature from the studies that caught our imagination was the concept of heroic leadership and how it might apply to the successful principals. We noted that a number of the principals demonstrated many of the characteristics of heroic leaders in helping the school to become successful. Heroic leadership can encompass many concepts. For the Ancient Greeks, the word hero meant 'superhuman'. It could also be seen as a continuation of Great Man Theory of leadership. Others define it as charisma (Western, 2012). Burns (1978) used the term *heroic leadership* to describe a relationship between leader and follower in which followers placed great faith in the leader's capacity to overcome impediments and crises. Generally, the leadership literature associates heroic leadership with the use of formal authority and power to direct the actions of organisational members. Much of the literature on leadership in business and education has argued against 'heroic leadership' (e.g. Burns, 1978; Gosling and Mintzberg, 2003; Manz and Sims, 1991; Murphy, 1988) as being autocratic, hierarchical, non-participative and generating dependency. They argue that today, organisations require initiative, shared responsibility and interdependency. Modern organisations are too complex and the environment too dynamic and unpredictable for one person. The alternative approach is more democratic – that of a 'quiet leader' (Badaracco

2001a, b) or 'post heroic' leader (Dutton, 1996; Huey and Sookdeo, 1994) who facilitates, collaborates, empowers and encourages ownership. Here, leadership is shared and followers are empowered to act together. Manz and Sims (1991) use the term 'Superleader' to describe a formal leader's role as facilitating followers as self-leaders where power is more evenly shared and commitment is based on ownership.

We found these archetypes to be inadequate in categorising our principals and describing leadership. Principals showed characteristics of both heroic and post-heroic stereotypes (Drysdale et al., 2014; Drysdale et al., 2011). There was no 'either/or'. If we take Adair's definition of heroic leadership, we could argue that all our principal leaders were heroic; Adair (1989, p. 227) defined a heroic leader as a person 'who exhibits extraordinary courage, firmness or greatness of soul, in the course of some journey or enterprise.' Our principals challenged the *status quo*, showed integrity in conflicting situations, put duty before self, took risks to champion a better way, showed courage in standing up to those in authority and showed uncommon commitment. In many cases, they promoted diversity in students and their families, cultivating civic capacity so that students succeeded socially and academically (Drysdale et al., 2011). At the same time, they were collaborative and empowered followers to take greater responsibility in shaping the school and its goals and priorities. They provided opportunities for personal and professional growth and helped to build strong learning communities. Most importantly, they attempted to build the talent pool of new leaders.

Successful school principals demonstrated a view of leadership in which leaders showed heroic or post-heroic features or any combination of these. The stereotypical definitions of heroic and post heroic do not explain successful principal leadership. This means we may need to redefine and recast our image of successful school principals to include a combination of factors and exemplify what they do to generate academic success for the students so that others can lead from their work.

Defining leadership through models of successful school leadership

The concept of leadership is still highly contested, and it is useful to consider some issues before we present our view of school leadership through the description of one of our models.

Consensus on a clear definition remains elusive because of competing ideas and positions (Grint, 2005). Forty years ago, Stogdill (1974) noted that there were almost as many definitions of leadership as there were people who have tried to define it. In the same decade, Burns (1978) argued that leadership needed to be separated from the leader to remove the focus on individuals, and this continues today with criticism of leader-centric research (e.g. Evers and Lakomski, 2013). Many argue that leadership and leader-centred orientations matter little to organisations. For example, Lakomski (2005, p. 1) argued that '(o)rganizations keep performing whether they have a strong leader, a weak leader, or no leader at all' and that there is little evidence to confirm a causal relationship between leadership and organisational practice. Lambert (2000, p. 1) observed that principals often come and go, while teachers are frequently the most stable component, and that because of this, 'leadership needs to be a broad concept that is distinguished from a person, role, and a discrete set of individual behaviours'. Others go further and argue that it is not possible to find specific values, behaviours or leader practices that can be identified as leadership (Alvesson and Sveningsson, 2003). Despite the criticisms just mentioned, the ISSPP has deliberately focussed on describing principal leadership and the contribution of this to school success, and in this section we show how we have used the ISSPP research to develop what for us is the best definition of school leadership.

In order to draw the research findings together conceptually, we proposed several frameworks that highlight the key dimensions and variables related to successful school leadership. Conceptual frameworks or models help make sense and explain complex ideas and relationships resulting from research. They provide a conceptual map for testing ideas and a guide to future research. They also provide a framework for practitioners to use as a guide to future action.

Gurr et al. (2006a), Gurr and Drysdale (2007), Drysdale and Gurr (2011) and Gurr (2015) have developed a series of models of successful school leadership based on a social systems approach. Our models draw on social systems theory, which shows leadership behaviour as a function of the leader who acts within an institutional role (Getzels and Guba, 1957; Getzels et al., 1968; Hoy and Miskel, 1987; Lewin, 1935). The two dimensions – the organisational dimension and the personal dimension – are conceptually independent and at the same time interactive. This is consistent with organisational behaviour theory (Luthans, 2011; Owens and Valesky, 2011; Robbins and Judge, 2011), which shows that behaviour is determined by the interplay between individuals and the social environment of their world of work. One of the criticisms of this approach is that it was derived from industrial psychology, scientific management, human relations and social science theories (Crow and Grogan, 2011) and as a result, aspects such as aesthetic, spiritual, ethical and social justice dimensions have been ignored. They assume a 'linear progression towards clarity and greater conceptual inclusiveness but tend to ignore feminist, critical theory, spirituality, and postmodern perspectives among others that have made and can make major contributions to leadership thought and practice'. (Crow and Grogan, 2011, p. 256). We argue that social systems theory still has its use in conceptualising the interaction between the leader in her or his environment and particular situation.

One of our models (Figure 11.2) shows how successful school leaders interact within a particular school context to deliver strategic interventions aimed at improving student outcomes. The model identifies both traditional outcomes (e.g. results on standardised tests and other contrived measures of attainment) and authentic outcomes (e.g. outcomes of learning that involve knowledge construction and disciplined inquiry; see Newmann et al., 2007).

The areas that can influence student outcomes are teaching and learning (Level 1), school capacity building (Level 2) and other influences (Level 3). The leader can make interventions at any level in the model, including student outcomes, where they can help determine some of the authentic outcomes and prioritise some of the traditional outcomes for the school.

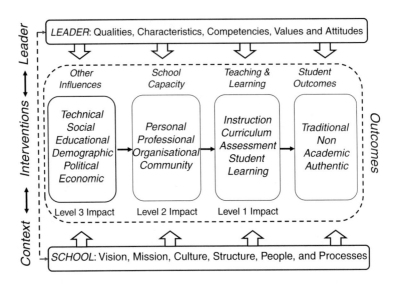

Figure 11.2 Drysdale and Gurr successful school leadership model (2011).

Level 1 interventions are focused on teaching, learning, curriculum and assessment and have the most impact on student outcomes. Within this area, the quality of instruction, the design of the curriculum, the various forms of assessment and the ability to motivate and equip students to manage their own learning directly impact on student outcomes. Level 2 interventions are focused on school capacity building (individual, professional, organisational and community capacity building). Level 2 interventions are more indirect. Level 3 interventions are 'other influences' that can impact on student outcomes. Successful school principals were found to contribute in some of these areas, such as district and system level policy development, network meetings and professional associations. The effectiveness of the interventions will be determined by the interaction between the leader and the situation or context.

Previous findings (Drysdale and Gurr, 2011; Gurr and Drysdale, 2007; Gurr et al., 2006a) showed that the most common interventions by successful school principals were in Level 2 (capacity building), although there were some principals who had a direct impact through a hands-on approach with interventions within the classroom and with students and teachers (e.g. the work of John Fleming described in Gurr, 2007; Hardy, 2006). Outside of the ISSPP research, our middle-level research suggests that these leaders tend to operate between Levels 2 and 1, with a closer relationship to directly influencing teacher practice to improve student learning (Gurr and Drysdale, 2013).

This is but one of many approaches. We recommend that school leaders adopt a portfolio approach whereby they draw upon a range of theories to inform their practice and provide a repertoire of skills and knowledge to handle particular situations.

Conclusion

In this chapter, we have outlined three findings from our research that are likely to be more controversial within the context of this book because they support the mainstream orthodoxy of leadership. Hopefully, we have acknowledged and accounted for a number of the criticisms that question the concept of leadership.

We continue to support the proposition that successful school leadership broadly, and successful principal leadership in particular, can be identified, articulated and explained in terms of how it contributes to school success; our models show how we conceptualise this. We argue that while context does matter, successful school principals demonstrate a set of personal qualities, skills and competencies and common practices that help them to adapt, influence and succeed in many contexts. While the research question was focused on individual contributions, none of the principals acted alone. Leadership was mostly distributed or shared.

We argue that principal leadership is complex and can include heroic and post-heroic characteristics. Dealing with this complexity does not entail an 'either/or' approach but rather an acknowledgement that certain situations require different leadership approaches. This challenges the narrow stereotypical definitions of heroic and post-heroic leadership. This also applies to the leadership style debate, in that our successful principals do not usually subscribe to a particular leadership style, such as transformational or instructional leadership, but rather adopt a pragmatic or portfolio approach (Gurr, 2015) whereby they construct their leadership from the best ideas. Over the course of our research on successful leadership, we have tried to make sense of the research by explaining the phenomenon of leadership and how it impacts on student outcomes through models and frameworks. The models borrow and build on previous models and research, and we presented one of our more recent models in this chapter. Our conception of successful school leadership through modelling continues to evolve, as no one model can explain it all. All models miss certain aspects, and new research can change the way we see the models to improve their veracity. However, we would strongly argue that models can provide a valuable explanation for current circumstances and also act as a support and guide to practice and further research. Our findings describe some of the complexity of schools, their environments and the leadership that guides their progress.

Note

1   ISSPP: https://www.uv.uio.no/ils/english/research/projects/isspp

References

Adair, J. E., 1989. *Great leaders.* Guildford, UK: Talbot Adair.

Alvesson, M. and Sveningsson, S., 2003. The great disappearing act: Difficulties in doing 'leadership'. *Leadership Quarterly*, 14(3), pp. 359–381.

174   *Lawrie Drysdale and David Gurr*

Badaracco, J., 2001a. *Leading quietly: An unorthodox guide to doing the right thing.* Boston: Harvard Business School Press.

Badaracco, J., 2001b. We don't need another hero. *Harvard Business Review*, 76(8), pp. 120–126.

Burns, J. M., 1978. *Leadership.* New York: Harper and Row.

Caldwell, B. J., 2014. Forward. In C. Day and D. Gurr, eds., *Leading schools successfully: Stories from the field* (pp. xxi–xxii). London: Routledge.

Cotton, K., 2003. *Principals and student achievement: What the research says.* Washington: ASCD.

Crow, G. M. and Grogan, M., 2011. The development of leadership thought and practice in the United States. In F. W. English, ed., *The SAGE handbook of educational leadership, advances in theory, research and practice* (2nd ed., pp. 255–272). Thousand Oak, California: Sage Publications.

Day, C., 2005a. Sustaining success in challenging contexts: Leadership in English schools. In C. Day and K. Leithwood, eds., *Successful school leadership in times of change* (pp. 59–70). Toronto: Springer.

Day, C., 2005b. Introduction to ISSPP, *Journal of Educational Leadership*, 43(6), pp. 533–538.

Day, C., 2014. *ISSPP research protocol manual.* Nottingham, UK: The University of Nottingham.

Day, C. and Leithwood, K., eds., 2007. *Successful school leadership in times of change.* Dordrecht, the Netherlands: Springer.

Day, C. and Gurr, D., eds., 2014. *Leading schools successfully: Stories from the field.* London: Routledge.

Day, C., Sammons, P., Hopkins, D., Harris, A., Leithwood, K., Gu, Qing, Brown, E., Ahtaridou, E. and Kington, A., 2009. The impact of school leadership on pupil outcomes. *Research Report DCSF-RR108.* London: Department for Children, Schools and Families.

Doherty, J., Gurr, D. and Drysdale, L., 2014. The formation and practice of a successful principal: Rick Tudor, headmaster of Trinity Grammar School, Melbourne, Australia. In C. Day and D. Gurr, eds., *Leading schools successfully: Stories from the field* (pp. 85–97). London: Routledge.

Drysdale, L., 2011a. Introduction to the Special Issue 'New evidence on successful school principal leadership: case studies from four countries'. *Leadership and Policy in Schools*, 10(4), pp. 371–374.

Drysdale, L., 2011b. Evidence from new cases in the International Successful School Principalship Project. *Leadership and Policy in Schools*, 10(4), pp. 444–455.

Drysdale, L. and Gurr, D., 2011. The theory and practice of successful school leadership in Australia. *School Leadership and Management*, 31(4), pp. 355–368.

Drysdale, L., Goode, H. and Gurr, D., 2011. The heroic leader – myth or reality: Findings from current research of successful school principals. Paper presented at the *European Conference on Educational Research*, Berlin, September 13–16, 2011.

Drysdale, L., Bennett J., Murakami, E., Johansson, O. and Gurr, D., 2014. Heroic leadership in Australia, Sweden, and the United States. *International Journal of Educational Management*, 28(7), pp. 785–797.

Dutton, G., 1996. Leadership in the post heroic age. *Management Review*, 85(10), October, p. 7.

Evers, C. W. and Lakomski, G., 2013. Methodological individualism, educational administration, and leadership. *Journal of Educational Administration and History*, 45(2), pp. 159–173.

Getzels, J. W. and Guba, E. G., 1957. Social behaviour and the administrative process. *School Review*, 65(4), pp. 423–441.

Getzels, J. W., Lipham, J. M. and Campbell, R. F., 1968. *Educational administration as a social process: Theory, research and practice*. New York: Harper and Row.

Gosling, J. and Mintzberg, H., 2003. The five minds of a manager. *Harvard Business Review*, 81(11), pp. 54–63.

Grint, K., 2005. *Leadership: Limits and possibilities management, work and organisations*. Houndmills, Basingstoke UK: Palgrave Macmillan.

Guba, E. G. and Lincoln, Y. S., 1994. Competing paradigms in qualitative research. In N. K. Denzin and Y. S. Lincoln, eds., *Handbook of qualitative research* (pp. 105–117). Thousand Oaks, CA: Sage.

Gunter, H., 2001. Critical approaches to leadership in education. *Journal of Educational Enquiry*, 2(2), pp. 94–108.

Gurr, D., 2007. We can be the best. In P. Duignan and D. Gurr, eds., *Leading Australia's schools* (pp. 124–131). Sydney: ACEL and DEST.

Gurr, D., 2009. Successful school leadership in Australia. In N. Cranston and L. Erlich, eds., *Australian educational leadership today: Issues and trends* (pp. 369–394). Brisbane: Australian Academic Press.

Gurr, D., 2014. Successful school leadership across contexts and cultures. *Leading and Managing*, 20(2), pp. 75–88.

Gurr, D., 2015. A model of successful school leadership from the International Successful School Principalship Project. *Societies*, 5(1), pp. 136–150.

Gurr, D. and Drysdale, L., 2007. Models of successful school leadership: Victorian case studies. In C. Day and K. Leithwood, eds., *Successful school leadership in times of change* (pp. 39–58). Dordrecht, the Netherlands: Springer.

Gurr, D. and Drysdale, L., 2013. Middle-level school leaders: Potential, constraints and implications for leadership preparation. *Journal of Educational Administration*, 51(1), pp. 55–71.

Gurr, D. and Day, C., 2014. Thinking about leading schools. In C. Day and D. Gurr, eds., *Leading schools successfully: Stories from the field* (pp. 194–208). London: Routledge.

Gurr, D., Drysdale, L. and Mulford, B., 2005. Successful principal leadership: Australian case studies. *Journal of Educational Administration*, (43)6, pp. 539–551.

Gurr, D., Drysdale, L. and Mulford, B., 2006a. Models of successful principal leadership. *School Leadership and Management*, 26(4), pp. 371–395.

Gurr, D., Drysdale, L., Clarke, S. and Wildy, H., 2014. High needs schools in Australia. *Management in Education*, 28(3), pp. 86–90.

Gurr, D., Drysdale, L., Swann, R., Doherty, J., Ford, P. and Goode, H., 2006b. The International Successful School Principalship Project (ISSPP): Comparison across country case studies. In L. Smith and D. Riley, eds., *New waves of leadership* (pp. 36–50). Sydney: ACEL.

Hardy, R., 2006. Successful leaders in successful schools: A case study of a government primary school principal in Victoria, Australia. M. Ed. thesis. Melbourne: The University of Melbourne.

Harris, A. and Muijs, D., 2005. *Improving schools through teacher leadership*. Maidenhead, Berkshire, UK: Open University Press.

Hoy, W. G. and Miskel, C. G., 1987. *Educational administration: Theory, research and practice*. 3rd ed. New York: Random House.

Huey, J. and Sookdeo, R., 1994. The new post-heroic leadership. *Fortune*, 129(4), pp. 42–46.

Jacobson, S. L. and Ylimaki, R., 2011a. Comparative perspectives: An overview of seven educational contexts. In R. Ylimaki and S. Jacobson, eds., *US and crossnational policies, practices and preparation: Implications for successful instructional leadership, organizational learning, and culturally responsive practices* (pp. 1–16). Dordrecht, the Netherlands: Springer.

Lakomski, G., 2005. *Managing without leadership: Towards a theory of organizational functioning*. Oxford: Elsevier.

Lambert, L., 2000. *Building capacity in schools*. Australian Principal Centre. Monograph Number 1. http://research.acer.edu.au/apc_monographs/2

Leithwood, K., 2005. Understanding successful principal leadership: Progress on a broken front. *Journal of Educational Administration*, (43)6, pp. 619– 629.

Leithwood, K. and Riehl, C., 2005. What we know about successful school leadership. In W. Firestone and C. Riehl, eds., *A new agenda: Directions for research on educational leadership* (pp. 22–47). New York: Teachers College Press.

Leithwood, K. and Day, C., 2007a. Starting with what we know. In C. Day and K. Leithwood, eds., *Successful school leadership in times of change* (pp. 1–16). Dordrecht, the Netherlands: Springer.

Leithwood, K. and Day, C. 2007b. What we learned: A broad view. In C. Day and K. Leithwood, eds., *Successful school leadership in times of change* (pp. 189–203). Dordrecht, the Netherlands: Springer.

Leithwood, K., Louis, K. S., Anderson, S. and Wahlstrom, K., 2004. *How leadership influences student learning*. New York: The Wallace Foundation.

Leithwood, K., Day, C., Sammons, P., Harris, A. and Hopkins, D., 2006. *Seven strong claims about successful school leadership*. Nottingham, UK: National College of School Leadership.

Lewin, K., 1935. *A dynamic theory of personality*. New York: McGraw-Hill.

Luthans, F., 2011. *Organizational behaviour: An evidence-based approach*. Boston, MA: McGraw-Hill Irwin.

Manz, C. C and Sims, H. P., 1991. Superleadership: Beyond the myth of heroic leadership. *Organisational Dynamics*, 19(4), pp. 18–25.

Moos, L., Johansson, O. and Day, C., eds., 2011a. *How school principals sustain success over time: International perspectives*. Dordrecht, the Netherlands: Springer-Kluwer.

Moos, L., Johansson, O. and Day, C., 2011b. New insights: How successful school leadership is sustained. In L. Moos, O. Johansson and C. Day, eds., 2011a. *How school principals sustain success over time: International perspectives* (pp. 223–230). Dordrecht, the Netherlands: Springer.

Mulford, B. and Edmunds, B., 2009. *Successful school principalship in Tasmania*. Launceston, Tasmania: Faculty of Education, University of Tasmania.

Mulford, B., and Silins, H., 2011. Revised models and conceptualisation of successful school principalship for improved student outcomes. *International Journal of Educational Management*, 25(1), pp. 61–82.

Murphy, J. T., 1988. The unheroic side of leadership: Notes from the swamp. *Phi Delta Kappan*, 69(9), pp. 654–659.

Newmann, F. M., King, M. B. and Carmichael, D. L., 2007. *Authentic instruction and assessment: Common standards for rigor and relevance in teaching academic subjects*. Des Moines, IA: Iowa Department of Education.

Notman, R. and Henry, D. A., 2011. Building and sustaining successful school leadership in New Zealand. *Leadership and Policy in Schools*, 10(4), pp 375–394.

Owens, R. G. and Valesky, T. C., 2011. *Organizational behaviour in education: Leadership and school reform.* Boston, MA: Pearson.

Robbins, S. P. and Judge, T. A., 2011. *Organizational behaviour.* New Jersey: Prentice Hall.

Sammons, P., 1999. *School effectiveness: Coming of age in the twenty-first century.* Lisse: Swets and Zeitlinger.

Sergiovanni, T. J., 1991. *The principalship: Reflective practice perspective.* 3rd ed. Boston: Allyn and Bacon.

Stogdill, R. M., 1974. *Handbook of leadership: A survey of theory and research.* New York: Free Press.

The Wallace Foundation, 2013. *The school principal as leader: Guiding schools to better teaching and learning.* New York: Wallace Foundation.

Tucker, P., 2001 Helping struggling teachers. *Educational Leadership*, 58(5), pp. 52–55.

Western, S., 2012. An overview of leadership discourses. In M. Preedy, N. Bennett and C. Wise, *Educational leadership: Context, strategy and collaboration* (Part I, pp. 11–24). London: SAGE.

Whalstrom, K. L., Louise, K. S., Leithwood, K. and Anderson, S. E., 2010. *Learning from leadership project: Investigating the links to improved student learning. Executive summary of research findings.* New York: Wallace Foundation.

Ylimaki, R. and Jacobson, S., eds., 2011a. *US and cross-national policies, practices and preparation: Implications for successful instructional leadership, organizational learning, and culturally responsive practices.* Dordrecht, the Netherlands: Springer-Kluwer.

Ylimaki, R. M. and Jacobson, S. L., 2011b. Comparative perspective on organisational learning, instructional leadership, and culturally responsive practices: Conclusions and future directions. In R. Ylimaki and S. Jacobson, eds., 2011a. *US and cross-national policies, practices and preparation: Implications for successful instructional leadership, organizational learning, and culturally responsive practices* (pp. 179–190). Dordrecht, the Netherlands: Springer-Kluwer.

12 The future of leadership

New directions for leading and learning

*Gabriele Lakomski, Colin W. Evers
and Scott Eacott*

Introduction

The chapters in this book raise a great number of critical issues about leader-centrism that scholars of leadership need to address. It is important to recall that the primary motivation for *Questioning Leadership* was to investigate, if not restore, the balance in explanation that since the 1980s has favoured leader-centrism as the dominant, *a priori*, account for organisational functioning at the expense of organisational–institutional factors that have both provided the context for leadership and exercised their own constraints on organisational performance (e.g. Perrow, 1986 [1993]). Different answers and solutions have been offered in the chapters of this book on how to address, or redress, leader-centrism from a variety of theoretical and philosophical perspectives.

The three sections of this final chapter discuss some key issues we think will contribute to knowledge of how to create effective learning in schools, individually and collectively, on the assumption that student learning is the core business of schools and that it is the role of principals to make that happen. First, Lakomski proposes that a new direction in leadership studies is called for that would recalibrate the explanatory balance, in that cognition as a dynamical system (see Chapter 1) locates leadership as part of the 'cognitive ecology' (see Hutchins, 2010) of organisational functioning. In the context of this broader conception of cognition, it is important to emphasise that cognition is fundamentally *social* and integral to human learning in general and to classroom learning in particular. How knowledge of social cognition might improve classroom learning is briefly discussed at the end of this part of the chapter.

In the second part, Evers looks at a number of constraints that shape what might be required to meet the onus of proof in demonstrating the importance of leadership in explaining and advancing an organisation's performance. Taking note of Hutchins' (2014) distinction between the extended mind thesis and distributed cognition as being primarily about the centredness of the cognitive unit, Evers argues for a continuum of centredness from none to strong. This both explains the possibility of shifting levels of influence between the three elements comprising Lakomski's account of social cognitive neuroscience – the social, cognitive and neural – and shows that there is no one answer concerning where leadership might be located and whether it is present at all. Determining whether or not leadership obtains depends on the degree of centredness a cognitive unit requires to accomplish tasks and solve problems, something that will vary from issue to issue.

In the final section, Eacott challenges the educational leadership research community to engage with one another actively and to move beyond the parallel monologues that fill journals, books, theses and conferences. Such a move connects to the social epistemological arguments of the preceding sections of this book, albeit from a different perspective, in that knowledge production is seen as a relational activity. Central to Eacott's argument is that any contribution to knowledge must be able to demonstrate how it relates to the arguments of others if it is to advance the growth of knowledge.

Leadership as part of the cognitive ecology of organisational functioning

Gabriele Lakomski

Cognition as a dynamic system

In leader-centric views, so we argued in Chapter 1 (also Evers and Lakomski, 2015), the individual principal is mistakenly imbued with cognitive autonomy (if not hegemony) and accorded a conception of agency, the 'self-as-controller', based on traditional understandings of 'self'. 'Context', in the form of organisational, institutional or environmental features, is not considered to exert control or constraint over principal autonomy and 'degrees of freedom' for action. We raised a number of objections against this view and suggested a more nuanced way to recast the interrelationship between individual and context/world. Understanding the nature of human cognition as 'social' (e.g. Gillett, 2009), that is, as constituting a dynamic system that includes non-biological resources as well, offers a coherent and unifying explanatory framework of organisational functioning *as a cognitive ecology*. School leaders and principals are natural parts of this larger cognitive web (Lakomski, 2005). Adopting this approach brings with it several advantages. First, it is based on real knowledge of human cognitive functioning and capacity (leaders are not omniscient and knowledge does not flow downhill). Second, it includes as potential causal factors non-neural components such as artefacts, the built and natural environments and organisational and institutional factors. Third, and most importantly, it sanctions a radical re-direction of educational leadership research – away from a myopic focus on 'what leaders do', as represented, for example, in the school effectiveness and student learning literature – to ask, what are the conditions that are most advantageous for the design of learning environments?

This question supports the development of a progressive research programme worth investing in as it has the capacity to deliver real, empirically defended results that will, in effect, help improve lifelong learning (Evers, 2012). For the moment, we can only discuss briefly what lies at the core of all human learning: social cognition. The specific contribution that non-biological components make in the cognitive ecology, as indicated in Chapter 1, is a complex and controversial question that needs more time and space than is available here.

Social cognition

Social cognition is the research focus of *social cognitive neuroscience* (SCN) (Adolphs, 1999, 2009; Ochsner, 2007; Ochsner and Lieberman, 2001; Lieberman, 2007, 2010). SCN is less a departure from cognitive and affective neuroscience as an explicit recognition of the social level of human (inter-)action, which appears to make it particularly useful for education. Social cognition is largely compatible with theories of cognition, variously described, or expressed as *the extended mind* (a comprehensive overview can be found in Anderson, 2003; Clark, 2008, 2010). Specifically, social cognitive neuroscience wants to under-stand the interactions between three levels of analysis – the social, cognitive and neural – not in the sense of just adding neuroscientific data to social psychology but by trying to understand 'how contexts impact the way on which socioemo-tional contents are construed, thereby providing invaluable data about the func-tions associated with specific brain systems.' (Ochsner, 2007, p. 59). Interaction between these three levels, according to Adolphs (2006, p. 27), 'involves loops of processing that are extra-neural. It involves the bodies, and the social environ-ment, in which brains are embedded', as well as a third feature: 'mechanisms for exploring the social environment and for probing it interactively'. What is par-ticularly important is that such processing is to some degree specialised, in that the processing of faces and empathising with others is domain specific.

Importantly, the ability to empathise with another means that emotion is closely related to social cognition, as both share processing strategies and are sup-ported by shared neural substrates. As Adolphs (1999, p. 477) concludes, 'The common ingredient may be what we commonly call 'feeling': the representation of emotional body states, either in regard to one's own emotional reaction or in regard to the empathy for, or simulation of, another person's internal state' (Damasio, 1999). Social cognition, then, is *feeling* as described above. If the neural substrates supporting both emotion and social cognition are healthy, we are able to judge situations in the world as either advantageous or not, with a natural preference for choosing the good over the bad. Where neural pathways are impaired, as shown in autism research (e.g. Baron-Cohen et al., 2013) and in studies of patients with brain lesions (Bechara, 2004; Damasio et al., 1991), *feeling*, or the 'emotional rudder' (Immordino-Yang and Damasio, 2011) that normally guides decision-making, is seriously compromised and leads to bad choices because of an inability to learn from past experience.

We feel, therefore we learn[1]

One interesting way to highlight the importance of social cognition in (school) learning is to consider research on educational attainment. Lieberman (2012) makes the point that in over 75 years of research, there has been consistent evidence that children retain only a small fraction of classroom learning 'even a year after learning' – after having undergone about 20,000 hours of classroom teaching by the age of 18 (in North American contexts). This outstrips the amount of time children spend on any other activity over the course of their development. This result hardly represents 'value for money'. So can knowledge of social cognition both help understand and possibly ameliorate this outcome?

Our brain contains a relatively large-scale network, the *mentalizing network*, (Lieberman, 2012; Baron-Cohen, 1994; Baron-Cohen et al., 2013), which allows us to track our own feelings, motives and thoughts and those of others that might differ from our own. An interesting feature of this network is that it keeps in active 'wandering' mode even when we are asked to execute a specific mental task; this network is known as the *default mode network* (Buckner et al., 2008). It keeps operating in the background by scanning the environment in order to increase our social cognitive grasp and how to deal with it – which is precisely the function for which evolution has been designing it.

In classroom learning, analytical reasoning, attention and memory are the aspects of cognition most emphasised, and these rely on the *working memory network*. The problem, as Lieberman (2012) explains, is that the social brain is biased towards 'free-wheeling' (my term) and that this state of activation competes with the working memory network. Such neurocognitive competition, says Lieberman (2012, p. 5), is unfortunately treated 'as a zero-sum battle between actual learning and social distractions like note passing or texting during class'. But there is evidence that using the social brain's natural tendencies can improve (classroom) learning and retention, especially in non-social subjects that do not naturally draw on the mentalising network, such as science, technology, engineering and mathematics (STEM) subjects, when a non-social task is learned for the benefit of teaching someone else (e.g. Bargh and Schul's 1980 *learning-for-teaching* study). Lieberman (2012) also suggests that *peer tutoring* might be another fruitful strategy in that it encourages student interaction, which, when suitably guided, is likely to improve educational attainment for both parties, especially when the roles of tutor and tutee are exchanged, as there is evidence that tutors often benefit more (Rohrbeck et al., 2003). There is preliminary neuroscientific/neuroimaging evidence that social motivation alone may indeed engage the mentalising system (rather than the traditional memory regions) during encoding of non-social information. (Lieberman, 2012, p. 7).

The long and short of this brief excursion into social cognition and (classroom) learning is that closer attention to how the social brain learns provides the best possible foundation for improving school learning and retention beyond the classroom. The social, affective and cognitive neurosciences open up many exciting avenues for future research that will enhance our knowledge of learning (and teaching) by getting a better grasp on such central topics as memory, attention, motivation and importantly, the complex area of social interaction so fundamental to understanding what happens between students and between students and teachers. Although there is as yet no formal *social* neuroscience of education, there is increasing and rapidly growing recognition of the importance of the neurosciences for education (e.g. Blakemore and Frith, 2005; Byrnes, 2001; Sylwester, 2000) and educational administration and leadership studies (Evers and Lakomski, 1996, 2000; Lakomski, 2005).

From the perspective of social cognition, school effectiveness and student learning, for example, would be determined 'from the ground up', be studied naturalistically in the context in which learning happens, where a school's socio-economic status, composition of student body, gender, languages spoken, qualifications and experience of teachers and principal and the built and natural environments may all be part of the causal picture that makes up the cogni-tive ecology of organisational functioning. School principals, as always, have an important role to play, and they are part of this larger picture.

The leadership–no leadership continuum

Colin W. Evers

In my contribution to this discussion, I want to add to and develop an aspect of one of Lakomski's key points. The main focus of her argument is to high-light the importance of a particular approach to theorising social cognition, notably through the lens of social cognitive neuroscience (SCN). As she notes, this involves understanding 'the interactions between three levels of analysis, the social, cognitive, and neural'. At first glance, there appears to be a significant tension among these levels. Hutchins (2014, pp. 35–38) formulates the issue in terms of whether a cognitive system has a centre or not (although this can come in grades). If the centre is the individual brain, then the interaction between the social and the mind as brain will need to be theorised in terms of the skin functioning as a boundary between inside and outside. It will deal with how the inside is shaped by the outside and vice versa. For a system with a centre in this case, the system can still be described with the language of leadership construed individualistically. But if a cognitive system has no centre, that is, if cognition is thoroughly distributed, matters are different.

Resnick (1997, pp. 3–19) takes aim at what he calls the 'centralized mindset' (p. 4) and offers examples of decentralised systems, some of which are obviously cognitive. The functioning of markets is one of his examples. No-one is telling pro-ducers how much to produce, what products they should produce or how much to charge. Nor is anyone telling buyers what to buy, how much or, in the case of bargaining, how much to pay. Price setting, production and consumption are cognition-laden decisions that are made within a cognitive system that arguably has no centre. No one is in charge of these decisions. A cognitive system that has no centre fails to comport with the more individualistic discourses of leadership.

This formulation of the tension between the three levels of analysis characteris-ing SCN is in part an artefact of Hutchins's way of drawing a distinction between the extended mind thesis as centre-oriented and distributed cognition that can deal with systems that have no centre. In addition to the centredness of a cogni-tive system, another useful metric that Hutchins draws attention to is its spatial scale. Thus a brain is not centred in the sense that it contains some homunculus constituting the 'I' of a person. No such homunculus exists, the 'I' being an emergent feature of aggregate neural activity. But it is spatially confined. Given the above accounts of centre and space, it is worth elaborating a bit more how they are used in the work that Lakomski and I do and what aspects we consider to be most important.

The main reason for not drawing a sharp distinction between the extended mind and distributed cognition is because educational organisations such as schools contain cognitive systems that come in grades of both centredness and size. With regard to size, the scale can run from individual brains all the way up to school communities that articulate with wider communities well beyond the boundary of a school community. With regard to the presence of a centre, classrooms are best characterised as having a centre in the person of a teacher and, in some of their administrative functions, school principals are a centre. But some school cognitive systems are relatively de-centred. Informal groups of parents, especially in primary or elementary schools, can be like this, as can faculty staff rooms. And the practice of aiming for de-centred school self-evaluation systems has merit where there may be conflict-of-interest issues for the school's leadership or where there is a desire to minimise the possibility of confirmation bias. This can also be extended to models of organisational learning when applied to schools. In addition, members of the school community may participate in multiple systems varying in both size and degree of centredness.

There are two points I want to emphasise here in thinking about leadership in cognitive systems. The first concerns what is known as the 'royal family' result, a result derived from computer simulations of cognitive processes in social networks (Hutchins, 1995, pp. 250–262; Zollman, 2007, p. 583). Strong leadership, in the sense that an individual leader has a strong influence over what other members of the system think, while it makes for rapid decision-making, also makes confirmation bias more likely. Errors, when they occur, are hard to correct. Weak leadership, in the sense that members of the system have more autonomy over what they think, engenders cognitive systems that can more readily resist confirmation bias but at the expense of slowing decision-making. Degree of centredness can thus affect a cognitive system's learning.

The second point is conceptual. In talk of the extended mind, it is customary to see a person and a cognition-supporting artefact, such as a calculating device, as part of a whole cognitive unit. That is, we don't say that the person is calculating in the context of a calculating device. However, this parsimony of usage fails to carry over when we shift from artefacts to other people. A leader-centric mind-set tends to posit an individual as leading in such-and-such a context: school leadership, departmental leadership, military leadership and the like. But task achievement in organisational contexts is mostly distributed and can sometimes be described in the explicitly epistemic terms of a social epistemology. Here is an example.

Suppose a school has an identified problem, say low student achievement scores, low staff morale or difficulty in reaching enrolment targets. We see the problem defined as a set of constraints plus the demand that something be done

(Evers, 2015). Let us further suppose that, given the limits of social science and the complexity of school environments, any theory that is proposed for implementation to solve the problem will be a tentative theory, one that may turn out to be unhelpful. During the process of implementation, more often than not, weaknesses in the theory, or errors, are discovered. In trying to boost enrolments, a proposed publicity campaign may turn out to be ineffective because the school is held in poor regard by the local community, thus implying another problem that needs to be solved in addressing the enrolment issue.

The social epistemology here can be regarded as having the same structure as that proposed by Popper (1979) in accounting for the growth of scientific knowledge (see Evers, 2012). Popper's schema captures the various components and the order in which knowledge building proceeds as follows:

$$P_1 => T_1 => EE_1 => P_2$$

P_1 is the problem to be solved, T_1 is the first tentative theory to be tried, EE_1 is the process of error elimination that comes from the implementation of the theory and P_2 is some new problem that emerges (although it could be just the original problem again). Calling Popper's schema a Popper Cycle, it is quite common for the solution of a particular problem to emerge only after a series of Popper Cycles have been undertaken. This social epistemology thus takes the form of a trajectory through time.

Viewed from the perspective of leader-centrism, this example of cognition can be described as a leader attempting to solve a problem in the context of their school and (outside) environment. The trouble with this characterisation is that it lumps together a whole lot of epistemic processes and their constituents into a single background entity called 'context'. When we look carefully at each of the elements in Popper's schema, it is possible to identify many constituents that comprise them. Thus, in organisational life, a problem owned by just one individual is less likely to elicit change than one owned across the organisation. Similarly, effective theories need to be formulated with an eye to how they might be implemented, and implementation in organisational life is almost always a collective matter, one that requires a range of participants. The processing of feedback that provides evidence that the problem is being solved or not can also be a collective matter. What this means, therefore, is that the unit of cognition is more likely to be spatially extended and, given the possibility of problem solving requiring a trajectory of Popper Cycles, it is more likely to be temporally extended. This is the reason why leadership, where it is practiced, is only part of the ontology of a cognitive system and why it is better to conceive these systems in the same inclusive way that applies to the person plus calculator cognitive system.

With numerous actors involved in this exercise of distributed cognition, does it nevertheless have a centre? There is no one answer to this question, for it will depend on the nature of the problem and the ontology and dynamic configuration of the unit of cognition required by the trajectory to solve it. The three levels of analysis posited for social cognitive neuroscience will also be variously engaged.

The upshot of this discussion is that if the conditions for leadership require a cognitive system to possess some identifiable centre, and if this changes from problem to problem, then for a wide class of plausible social epistemologies, an onus of proof will exist in maintaining the explanatory merits of leadership in accounting for organisational performance.

In Chapter 1, it was argued that leader-centrism is biased towards agency-oriented accounts of organisational performance at the expense of adequately accounting for structural constraints. I conclude by noting a difficulty in providing good empirical research evidence for meeting the onus of proof requirement. Roughly speaking, quantitative research designs that seek to give a result on, say, the influence of principal leadership on student learning outcomes must make some assumptions about what descriptors of leader action can function as variables to be investigated. But this selection process will, in turn, embody assumptions about the scope of leader agency. The widely cited meta-analysis by Robinson et al. (2008) that seeks to measure the effect sizes of transformational versus instructional leadership on students' academic performance posits categories of leader actions with almost no reference to structural factors. Even those factors that looked structural, such as resource acquisition, were presented as the result of agency related principal actions (p. 661) with the studies in the meta-analysis mainly taking the form of using teacher views of principal leadership and then relating these to student learning outcomes. A closer examination of the assumptions about the scope of leader agency in these kinds of research designs and what it means for justifying the importance of leadership is a challenge for some of our future work.

Beyond parallel monologues

Scott Eacott

Continuing the focus on social epistemology, although from a sociological rather than cognitive science perspective, I argue for purposeful dialogue and debate in the educational leadership scholarly community. Critical dialogue is something that we have aspired to embody in this book as an overall project, including the contributions by the commentators.

For the student of educational leadership or those new to the area, the volume of research generated means that one is spoilt for choice. Millions of words are generated annually, yet as far back as the 1960s, Taylor (1969) questioned the scholarly value of much that was written. With the expansion of information technologies that can be said to constitute a globally distributed cognitive system, one can only guess what Taylor would say today. This production of 'new' knowledge obscures a major issue, one less concerned with the volume of work and more with the organisation of scholarly communities and activities. Despite all of the conceptual attention to shared visions, collective responsibility and group/organisational performance, educational leadership is a fragmented and piecemeal domain of inquiry. Although I am against the pursuit of a single over-arching meta-narrative of what is educational leadership, or declaring how research should be conducted forevermore, the fragmentation of scholarship or absence of meaningful dialogue and debate across research communities is a major impediment to advancing knowledge. For the most part, educational leadership research is little more than a set of parallel monologues.

The question that drives my contribution in this chapter is 'Where are new theories of educational leadership coming from?' My use of the term *new* here requires some, albeit brief, attention. I mobilise the label not in the sense of appropriation or novelty, as importing, overlaying or mapping a terrain leaves the received terms remain intact. I am less interested in the logic of validation (e.g. the current trend of meta-analyses) and more in the logic of discovery – mindful that such artificial partitioning is not always helpful (Bourdieu et al., 1991). As would be expected in a book questioning the explanatory value of 'leadership', the grounds on which knowledge claims are based is of particular interest. The epistemological preliminaries of research, how we come to know something and the legitimacy of knowledge claims require explicit attention and engagement with alternatives – and this is a point shared by all three of us in this chapter. To contribute, one must be able to demonstrate a distinction between one's own ideas and those of others. This can only be achieved by engaging with differing arguments and developing claims that can be defended in the face of critique. Parallel monologues constrain the advancement of knowledge courtesy of their self-sustaining rhetoric and selective – if any – engagement with different approaches.

While there exist some forms of commentary (e.g. Oplatka, 2010) or classification work (e.g. Gunter, 2016) on the field at large, educational leadership researchers seldom seriously engage with scholarship emanating from scholarly traditions different from their own. The most notable exceptions are Greenfield (e.g. Greenfield and Ribbins, 1993) and Evers and Lakomski (1991, 1996, 2000), who explicitly engage with different approaches to justify how their programmatic approach to scholarship offers a productive means to theorise educational administration. Greenfield drew particular attention for his questioning of the central logic of the *theory movement* and the validity of its knowledge claims. However the complexity of his scholarly argument is often reduced to constructing a binary between objectivist and subjectivist knowledge production. Evers and Lakomski adopted a systematic approach to illuminating what they saw as limitations in the perspectives of leading thinkers at the time before offering their own version of a more appropriate means of researching educational administration – *natural coherentism*. Unlike most 'new' perspectives, following the first book, Evers and Lakomski invited those they critiqued to comment/reply in a series of special issues, leading to a second book. The final contribution to the trilogy represents a refined version of their approach that is built upon the dialogue and debate with alternatives. Whether you align with the perspective of Evers and Lakomski is less important than what their approach to scholarship demonstrates. First and foremost, it is programmatic as opposed to project based. Significantly, this research programme is built upon systematic engagement with the epistemological/methodological preliminaries of alternate approaches. That is, Evers and Lakomski sought to understand contemporary ways of knowing and, through the analysis of their strengths and limitations, proposed an alternative – and in their view better – way of approaching work. Unlike the parallel monologues that plague educational leadership research, this is an example of seriously engaging with alternatives for the purpose of advancing knowledge.

Despite these examples of engaging with the other, at scale, educational leadership research continues to take place in parallel discourse communities. There is a well-recognised lack of engagement across differing traditions and, at best, a benign neglect of those with whom we disagree (Donmoyer, 2001; Thrupp and Willmott, 2003). This becomes problematic when end-users – including graduate students – are only exposed to a particular literature (Thrupp, 2005) and/or research training remains within the confines of a single tradition.

It would be naïve to assume that as a scholarly community grows in size and scale that different discourse communities do not emerge. These communities develop their own networks, journals, conferences and, arguably, citation patterns. The emergence of such communities is not problematic and is arguably evident in all forms of the social sciences. What is problematic for the quality of research, and thus the advancement of scholarship, is the absence of dialogue and debate across different traditions. A once fertile scholarly field of research and inquiry (Smyth, 2008) has broken down to a series of self-sustaining communities advancing their own trajectories irrespective of thought and analysis developed elsewhere. This is not about constructing imperialistic boundaries around educational leadership as a domain of inquiry – although that, too, is arguably worthy of attention – but a genuine lack of engagement with other ways of knowing educational leadership.

Such a lack of engagement denotes a break from the logic of scholarship. Argument and refutation are the basis on which scholarly activity is based. The book, book chapter, article, even the lecture can constitute an argument. This argument is built upon a set of claims grounded in previous work (by an author and others) and is defensible in the face of critique. This is more than locating in the field – a role often limited to the literature review – as it is only possible to have a position in the presence of alternatives. In other words, without the many, the one would not be possible. Having a defensible position is a relational activity. It can only be understood in relation to others. The markers of an argument are spatio-temporal. Ideas have a history, or more specifically histories; the moment of genesis is the coming together in a particular space. Having these ideas locates one within a field. Positions are dependent on the abstract systems of distance – distinctions – between ideas, and these ideas travel beyond geographic boundaries. Unlike the particular claims of the empirical studies, ideas are a global enterprise and therefore to advance them requires attention to a breadth of literatures and perspectives.

Beyond any strict content work within research, the social scientist engages in the craft of social analysis. Scholarship is not simple reporting but arguing. To this end, scholarship is pedagogical. However, educational leadership journals are somewhat notable for the absence of commentaries, responses to papers and genuine dialogue and debates. Even special issues frequently lack a critical response, instead opting for the concluding or summative piece by a sympathetic reader. Debates such as those between Gronn (1982, 1984, 1987) and Thomas (1986; Thomas et al., 1981) over the value of observational studies, primarily through the pages of *Educational Administration Quarterly*, rarely take place any more, at least publicly. Possibly this is done during the peer review process – another process worthy of attention in educational leadership – but if so, it remains behind closed doors. The pedagogical value of refining and extending arguments is lost. The work of scholarship becomes a rare undertaking in the context of rapid knowledge production.

Moving beyond parallel monologues and explicitly engaging with alternative approaches is about asking questions about where knowledge of educational leadership's frontiers lie, building on its successes and pushing those frontiers further. This is difficult work. It is risky work. After all, editors and reviewers are to some extent the custodians of a field's traditions, challenging prevailing views and trends is difficult (Natriello, 1996) and theoreticians often have few peers (Tsang, 2013). To overcome potential scepticism about new claims and/ or substantial departures from the orthodoxy, arguments need to be grounded in the logic of academic work – argument and refutation. If we embrace the notion that scholarship is pedagogical, then the publication of an argument is not the end of it. Publication serves, as Berger (1966) argues, as an invitation – an invitation to think with, through and, where necessary, against in the spirit of the scholarly enterprise. Through the composing of a systematic argument, others can engage with your knowledge claims to support, extend or challenge them. This is only possible through engagement. By engaging with counter claims, refinements lead to greater clarity. With greater clarity come advances in knowledge. If educational leadership aspires to advance knowledge and not simply produce more, then it is imperative to engage with the other and move beyond parallel monologues.

Note

1   This heading is part of the title of an article by M. H. Immordino-Yang and A. Damasio; see references.

References

Adolphs, R., 1999. Social cognition and the human brain. *Trends in Cognitive Sciences*, 3(12), December 1999, pp. 469–479.

Adolphs, R., 2006. How do we know the minds of others? Domain-specificity, simulation, and enactive social cognition. *Brain Research*, pp. 25–35.

Adolphs, R., 2009. The social brain: Neural basis of social knowledge. *Annual Review of Psychology*, 60, pp. 693–716.

Anderson, M. L., 2003. Embodied cognition: A field guide. *Artificial Intelligence*, 1491, pp. 91–103.

Bargh, J. A. and Schul, Y., 1980. On the cognitive benefits of teaching. *Journal of Educational Psychology*, 72, pp. 593–604.

Baron-Cohen, S., 1994. The mindreading system: New directions for research. *Current Psychology of Cognition*, 13, pp. 724–750.

Baron-Cohen, S., Tager-Flusberg, H. and Cohen, J. D., eds., 2013. *Understanding other minds: Perspectives from developmental cognitive neuroscience.* 2nd ed. New York: Oxford University Press.

Bechara, A., 2004. The role of emotion in decision-making: Evidence from neurological patients with orbitofrontal damage. *Brain and Cognition*, 55, pp. 30–40.

Berger, P., 1966. *Invitation to sociology: A humanistic perspective.* Harmondsworth: Pelican.

Blakemore, S.-J. and Frith, U., 2005. *The learning brain.* Oxford: Blackwell.

Bourdieu, P., Chamboredon, J.-C., and Passeron, J.-C., 1991. *The craft of sociology: Epistemological preliminaries.* R. Nice, Trans. New York: Walter de Gruyter.

Buckner, R. L., Andrews-Hanna, J. R. and Schacter, D. L., 2008. The brain's default network: Anatomy, function, and relevance to disease. *Annals of the New York Academy of Sciences*, 1124, pp. 1–38.

Byrnes, J. P., 2001. *Minds, brains and learning.* New York: The Guildford Press.

Clark, A., 2008. *Supersizing the mind.* New York: Oxford University Press.

Clark, A., 2010. Memento's revenge: The extended mind, extended. In: R. Menary, ed., *The extended mind,* pp. 43–66. Cambridge, MA: MIT Press.

Damasio A. R., 1999. *The feeling of what happens.* New York: Harcourt.

Damasio, A. R., Tranel, D. and Damasio, H., 1991. Somatic markers and the guidance of behavior: Theory and preliminary testing. In H. S. Levin, H. M. Eisenberg and A. I. Benton, eds., *Frontal lobe function and dysfunction*, New York: Oxford University Press.

Donmoyer, R., 2001. Evers and Lakomski's search for leadership's holy grail (and the intriguing ideas they encountered along the way). *Journal of Educational Administration*, 39(6), pp. 554–572.

Evers, C. W., 2012. Organizational contexts for lifelong learning: Individual and collective learning configurations. In D. N. Aspin, J. D. Chapman, K. R. Evans and R. Bagnall, eds., *Second international handbook of lifelong learning.* Dordrecht: Springer, pp. 61–76.

Evers, C. W., 2015. Decision making as problem solving trajectories. In S. Chitpin and C. W. Evers, eds., *Decision making in educational leadership.* New York: Routledge, pp. 57–71.

Evers, C. W. and Lakomski, G. 1991. *Knowing educational administration.* Oxford: Elsevier.

Evers, C. W. and Lakomski, G., 1996. *Exploring educational administration: Coherentist applications and critical debates.* Oxford: Pergamon/Elsevier.

Evers, C. W. and Lakomski, G., 2000. *Doing educational administration: Coherentist naturalism into administrative practice.* Oxford: Pergamon/Elsevier.

Evers, C. W. and Lakomski, G., 2015. Naturalism and educational administration: New directions. In S. Eacott and C. W. Evers, eds., *Educational Philosophy and Theory,* special issue on *New frontiers in educational leadership, management and administration theory*, 47(4), pp. 402–419.

Gillett, G. R., 2009. The subjective brain, identity, and neuroethics. *The American Journal of Bioethics*, 9(9), pp. 5–13.

Greenfield, T. B. and Ribbins, P., eds., 1993. *Greenfield on educational administration: Towards a humane science.* London: Routledge.

Gronn, P., 1982. Neo-Taylorism in educational administration? *Educational Administration Quarterly*, 18(4), pp. 17–35.

Gronn, P., 1984. On studying administrators at work. *Educational Administration Quarterly*, 20(1), pp. 115–129.

Gronn, P., 1987. Obituary for structured observation. *Educational Administration Quarterly*, 23(2), pp. 78–81.

Gunter, H., 2016. *An intellectual history of school leadership practice and research.* London: Bloomsbury Academic.

Hutchins, E., 1995. *Cognition in the wild.* Cambridge, MA: MIT Press.

Hutchins, E., 2010. Cognitive ecology. *Topics in Cognitive Science*, 2, pp. 705–715.

Hutchins, E., 2014. The cultural ecosystem of human cognition. *Philosophical Psychology*, 27(1), pp. 34–49.

Immordino-Yang, M. H. and Damasio, A., 2011. We feel, therefore we learn: The relevance of affective and social neuroscience to education. *LEARNing Landscapes*, 5(1), pp. 115–131.

Lakomski, G., 2005. *Managing without leadership.* London: Elsevier.

Lieberman, M. D., 2007. Social cognitive neuroscience: A review of core processes. *Annual Review of Psychology*, 58, pp. 259–289.

Lieberman, M. D., 2010. Social cognitive neuroscience. In S. T. Fiske, D. T. Gilbert and G. Lindzey, eds. *Handbook of social psychology.* 5th ed., pp. 143–193. New York: McGraw-Hill.

Lieberman, M. D., 2012. Education and the social brain. *Trends in Neuroscience and Education*, 1, pp. 3–9.

Natriello, G., 1996. For the record – lessons for young scholars seeking to publish. *Teachers College Record*, 97(4), pp. 509–517.

Ochsner, K. N., 2007. Social cognitive neuroscience: Historical development, core principles, and future promise. In A. Kruglanski and E. T. Higgins, eds., *Social psychology: A handbook of basic principles.* 2nd ed., pp. 39–66. New York: Guilford.

Ochsner, K. N. and Lieberman, M. D., 2001. The emergence of social cognitive neuroscience. *American Psychologist*, 56, pp. 717–734.

Oplatka, I., 2010. *The legacy of educational administration: A historical analysis of an academic field.* Berlin: Peter Lang.

Perrow, C., 1986. *Complex organizations: A critical essay.* New York: McGraw-Hill. Reprinted 1993.

Popper, K. R., 1979. *Objective knowledge.* Oxford: Oxford University Press.

Resnick, M., 1997. *Turtles, termites and traffic jams: Explorations in massively parallel microworlds.* Cambridge, MA: MIT Press.

Robinson, V. M. J., Lloyd, C. A. and Rowe, K. J., 2008. The impact of leadership on student outcomes: An analysis of the differential effects of leadership types. *Educational Administration Quarterly*, 44(5), pp. 635–674.

Rohrbeck, C. A, Ginsburg-Block, M. D., Fantuzzo, J. W. and Miller, T. R., 2003. Peer-assisted learning interventions with elementary school students: A meta-analytic review. *Journal of Educational Psychology*, 95, pp. 240–257.

Smyth, J., 2008. Australia's great disengagement with public education and social justice in educational leadership. *Journal of Educational Administration and History*, 40(3), pp. 221–233.

Sylwester, R., 2000. *A biological brain in a cultural classroom.* Thousand Oaks CA: Corwin Press.

Taylor, W., 1969. Issues and problems in training the school administrator. In G. Baron and W. Taylor, eds., *Educational administration and the social sciences*, pp. 97–123. London: The Athlone Press of the University of London.

Thomas, A. R., 1986. Seeing isn't believing? Neither is hearing! In defense of observational studies. *Educational Administration Quarterly*, 22(1), pp. 29–48.

Thomas, A. R., Willis, Q. and Phillipps, D., 1981. Observational studies of Australian school administrators: Methodological issues. *Australian Journal of Education*, 25(1), pp. 55–72.

Thrupp, M., 2005. The National College for School Leadership: A critique. *Management in Education*, 19(2), pp. 13–19.

Thrupp, M., and Willmott, R., 2003. *Educational management in managerialist times: Beyond the textual apologists*. Buckingham: Open University Press.

Tsang, E. W. K., 2013. Is this referee really my peer? A challenge to the peer-review process. *Journal of Management Inquiry*, 22(2), pp. 166–171.

Zollman, K., 2007. The communication structure of epistemic communities, *Philosophy of Science*, 74, pp. 574–587.

Commentary
Silos, bunkers and their voices

Peter Gronn

Introduction

During periods of disillusionment when I bemoan (what I perceive as) a lack of progress in knowledge gains in the academic domain of leadership, I wonder whether (if I had my time over again) scholarly life might not have been more straightforward had I been a physicist. The reason is that in the domain of physics (I imagine) one would be dealing with the inanimate phenomena of matter that are governed by laws and about which there is an agreed-upon language and commonly shared definitions of problems to the resolution of which (through experimentation) one's colleagues devote their energies. There might also be, of course, the added attraction of nice big toys to play with like a synchrotron or the Large Hadron Collider. And, what is more, unlike humans and their fickle behaviour, matter doesn't answer one back. It was while musing along these lines recently, however, that I stumbled on Hilary Putnam's (2004, pp. 25–26) brief discussion of a legacy of philosophical thinking devoted to trying to render language meaningful according to a model of the language of physics. It was after absorbing Putnam's demolition of this endeavour that my courage failed me and the physics thought bubble burst.

Having just publicly paraded my (rather silly) fantasy and probably also having betrayed my gross ignorance of the work of physicists, what has this lament to do with leadership? Little point would be served by rehearsing the reasons why leadership can never hope to approximate (what I perceive to be, probably naively) the certainties of a field such as physics, but the present choice of chapters causes me to wonder whether there might ever be an occasion when there is agreement about leadership fundamentals (such as those associated with epistemology and ontology). Those members of my generation who were weaned as postgraduate students (in the 1970s) on the idea of paradigms and paradigm wars and witnessed the collapse of (and, indeed, fired numerous salvos at) one of the few attempts in this field – the self-styled, US-originated, behavioural science–inspired Theory Movement – to try to order a domain of knowledge have learned to live with the existence of diverse voices and an overall lack of cumulative knowledge advancement. But none of that splintering into silos and bunkers helps me to answer satisfactorily the following questions, each of which I am prompted to ask as a result of points made in the four chapters. As (mostly) tenured scholars funded out of the public purse, do we not have some responsibilities to the hands that feed us? To what extent are we under some obligation to try to solve the leadership-related problems that beset policy-makers and practitioners, therefore, as distinct from treating policies and practices as targets – field sport-like – either for critique or for dismissal as vehicles for hegemonic discourse (i.e. biting the hand)? And should we view the institution-based academic autonomy made possible by public purse funding as offering us a licence to do our own thing? Finally, is there any sense in which as academics we ought to be trying to facilitate student betterment and the improvement of their learning, however that might be measured – after all, were it not for the presence of students at all levels of education systems, there would be no systems as such. These questions (and others like them) have bothered me from time to time over the past three or four decades and they still do and, to be honest, having read these four chapters, I'm no nearer having answers to them. Part of the reason is that the chapters' authorial voices are quite discordant. I discuss below a selection of the key claims made in each chapter. While this discussion adheres to the chapter sequence, I also cross-reference points of inter-connection.

Framing, defining and positioning leadership

Howard Youngs is perfectly correct to point to the lack of agreement about definitions of leadership – part of my earlier lament about ontology – although Rost (1993) made a valiant effort some two decades ago to try to bring order to the confusion. Youngs is also right to point to the recent upsurge of interest in distributed or shared understandings of leadership – Richard Bolden's (2011) data has provided the definitive evidence of a graphed north-bound trend line on its uptake. One point on which I differ from Youngs, however, is in regard to his claim that part of distributed leadership's popularity may be due to its democratic flavour. I think this is illusory, and Philip Woods and I (Woods and Gronn, 2009) raised concerns about this presumed democratic attribute some years ago. My own view, for what it is worth, is that the popularity of distributed leadership is attributable to two main factors. First, the idea of distributed leadership represents an understandable reaction to a post-1970s resurgence of heroic individualism that attained nigh on hegemonic dominance in the field. Second, as a corollary of this first point, perhaps, distributed leadership has also become a catch-cry in a parallel way that 'participation' did – a word on which Youngs relies, interestingly, in his fifth empirical instance of leadership practice – consequent on the social and cultural turmoil unleashed in the 1960s in the West (Pateman, 1970). The commonality of the appeal in both cases is numerical: with participation, the core idea was that those persons likely to be affected by the impact of decisions ought to take part in the making of them; with distributed leadership, the notion is that the more people who share in the burden of decision-making the merrier. (Intriguingly, Riveros, Newton and Burgess – hereafter Riveros et al.—refer to both terms as well.) A less populist, and more sophisticated, vehicle of justification for distribution proponents would be to connect with Lakomski's, Evers' and Eacott's argument about social cognition. Youngs' point made in passing about work intensification could have provided a link here, except that the theoretical knitting to which he chose to stick was official discourse. Whether distributed leadership will exit the academic lexicon just as quickly as participation did following its brief day in the sun, however, is a matter for speculation.

Whereas Youngs wants to 'reposition' distributed leadership (for the most part) discursively, for the past few years I personally have been back-pedalling from it as fast as I can, so much so that now my preference (for the reasons of ontology outlined in Gronn, 2011 and 2015) is to abandon it altogether. As for some of the other ideas in Youngs' conceptual quiver, I cannot really see a lot of virtue in applying Bourdieu's ideas of fields and capital here, if I am being honest. Where in his case study school B, for example, Youngs writes of the deans as lacking symbolic capital, a word like *reputation* might just as well have sufficed. On the other hand, his idea that school leaders are being positioned as agents of educational reform can be readily endorsed, of course, except that once again we don't need Bourdieu to point this out to us (because this fact is self-evident to anyone working in the field anyway). Having said that, for the life of me I cannot see how the dualism between formal and informal leadership (let alone its significance) to which he points has any meaningful merit in practice. To be equally frank, I am also wary of the emphasis on New Public Management (NPM). Certainly, this idea had currency for a good while in leadership and administration circles, and, even though it has not entirely disappeared from scholarly purview, writers working in sub-domains of leadership other than education have tended to cast it adrift. Also, I am not clear about the purposes served by the elucidation of Gunter's four-fold mapping of usages of distributed leadership. To be sure, there is some point in knowing that the term lends itself (like numerous other concepts in this field) to differing interpretations, but is that really a useful endpoint of (and for) knowledge?

When Youngs turns to his empirical data, he makes some interesting points. He is dead right in my experience that practitioners tend to shy away from using, and thinking in terms of, 'follower(s)'. The significance of this observation should be obvious for a field in which scholars (mostly outside of the educational leadership sub-domain, it has to be said) still cannot help talking in terms of leaders and leadership without the categories of followers and followership. This is where Youngs' adoption of Goffman's idea of deference – directed towards those possessing high status capital, for Bourdieusians – is helpful, because deference carries with it implicit notions of what psychologists refer to as learned helplessness. In this sense, followers are those people who are done to – a status that amounts to agent passivity with a vengeance. But learned helplessness (my term, not Youngs') should not mislead readers into thinking that the preparedness of his case study A school deans to step up or to have matters left to them for decision ('participation', anyone?), to paraphrase his terminology, is necessarily evidence of learned helplessness. This is because, at its most benign, the leaving of decisions by deferrers to someone else might constitute straightforward evidence on their part of taking the easy option of convenience or, to express it in slightly vulgar terms, evidence of the sheer rat cunning of the deferring people who, in the hands of someone less sensitive than Youngs, might find themselves residual-ised as members of that wretched follower category. (Riveros et al. are also alert to the problems for agency created by reliance on the idea of followers.)

There is another point in the dynamics of the relationship between the leading groups in schools A and B that may have been underscored by Youngs, if not missed altogether. This point occurred to me when I read the words 'taking responsible risks'. Part of what is entailed in the incumbency of higher positions (in formal hierarchical terms) is exactly that: risk-taking. That is, such positioned people are accountable for and are remunerated for managing and taking risks, and it is this latter understanding that that's what the higher-ups are there for (if I may express it in the vernacular) that can fuel the idea of being willing to leave decisions to 'them'. Deference or no deference, such a response by a deferrer is a knowing form of a cold, hard calculation of self-interest. Finally, what I thought was missing in Youngs' discussion, particularly at the end of it, was any revisit-ing of the framework that he tried (with modest success) to meld together at the outset.

Re-positioning and professionalising leadership

Riveros et al. provide readers not only with more leadership re-positioning but also with more additional discursive re-positioning at that. This chapter manifests an antipathy (one that is not uncommon in the field) to instrumental views of leadership and what leaders conceived in these terms might or might not be said to accomplish. To that extent, the authors' discussion hearkens back to my earlier observation about what, from the perspective of those responsible for the running of an education system, might count as a reasonable expectation of scholars who feed off its policy outputs and whether this ought to add up to something more than ivory tower stick-poking. Part of the focus of Riveros et al. is on leadership standards and, given the current attention being accorded standards, this is a very apposite choice. There can be no doubt, as the authors suggest, that there is a potentially sinister side to standards-writing and the assessment of leader perfor-mance in accordance with standards – indeed, I said as much myself some years ago when I articulated a concern about the potential dangers of what I detected as designer-style leadership (Gronn, 2002), except that I have since learned that it doesn't have to be this way. In my view, the authors' concern with standards being centrally mandated and operating in apparent ignorance of local (or site) contexts may slightly miss or muddle up the real point. In their eagerness to dis-parage standards, the authors take the notion of central mandate to mean system-level or employer mandate. But suppose that the teaching profession itself were to (centrally) mandate standards for its members that were evidence-informed and teacher-authored, against which teacher performance was assessed by their fellow teachers, as part of an advanced certification system, would the same criticism then apply? I think not. In light of the fact that other professions (e.g. medicine) determine standards of accomplished practice for and on behalf of their members and then discipline the work of their own members in relation to such standards, there is no reason in principle (other than pig-headed government and employer refusal to countenance the possibility) why the teaching profession ought not to be doing likewise. This is not the place for me to pursue the argument – perhaps the US National Board for Professional Teaching Standards (NPBTS) offers a prototype (see Darling-Hammond, 2008; Hattie, 2008) – other than to say that there is an alternative view of leadership standards apart from the authors' invocation of commentary (early in their chapter) to the effect that a resort to standards simply compounds the ubiquity of a neo-liberal, market-driven approach to education reform.

Riveros et al. then claim that principal standards reinforce the idea of leaders as experts. This is correct – except that such a claim is a statement of the obvious – and yet I am not sure why the resort to such principal standards and competencies (or, as I would prefer, *capabilities*) is necessarily a problem, as the authors assert that it is, given that claims to professional status by occupational groups rest in large measure on the very idea of possessing a distinctive knowledge or expertise base. There is, however, an added difficulty. This arises, as is rightly pointed out by Riveros et al., whenever employers try to rely on leadership standards for their own appraisal and evaluation purposes. In the employers' defence, however, such a reliance is surely understandable; can anyone seriously question the right of those employing authorities not to have a direct interest in the work of leadership and teaching, given that teachers and principals in publicly funded school systems are, after all, civil, or public, servants or employees? To that extent, educationists are inescapably answerable for what they do (and do not do) in respect of official policy. It is useful in discussions of standards, therefore, to keep in mind two separate strands. On the one hand, there are these latter legitimate industrial or performance management requirements that are intended to that ensure teachers and principals fulfil their employment contractual obligations. On the other, there is the profession's expertise-based claim to determine its own evidence-informed standards (as canvassed in the previous paragraph) as part of a profession-based certification system (Ingvarson, 2013, p. 8). Unfortunately, this distinction has passed the authors by. Their concerns about current principals' standards also infuse their discussion of leadership standards for teachers, except that their emphasis here tends to be on what they regard as the denial of the agency of those teachers not officially legitimised (discursively) as leaders. The question that such allegations of discursive positioning always leave begging, of course, is whether or not the pattern of daily leadership practice in schools conforms to or occurs in its own unique configuration, regardless of whatever might be the dictates of official discourse.

What about leadership's causal powers, the next focus of Riveros et al. (and which is also an issue of direct relevance to Drysdale's and Gurr's chapter)? Their discussion of this point is somewhat equivocal: at the same time as they are critical of the attribution of causal agency to principals as leaders, Riveros et al. acknowledge the good sense (their words) of officialdom in seeking entry points for principal-led change and system re-design. (This section of the chapter does not seem to go anywhere and ends with an oblique characterisation of leadership's power as a mere doxa.) I can't help thinking that, in respect of leadership, officialdom generally finds itself in a bit of a bind. While being responsible for school systems and their effectiveness, public officials rely heavily on academic (and management consultant) language to tell them what they ought to be thinking. Every so often, this dependence results in wasted energy. Riveros et al. highlight one classic instance (and they are right to do so): the distinction between leadership and management. Few matters have generated so many pointless disputes among leadership scholars about whether there is such a distinction or not and what the implications might be if there is. Culpability here probably stems back as far as Zaleznik's (1977) landmark discussion of this topic, following which, while extensive evidence existed that executive down-sizing was beginning to take place on a substantial scale in the 1980s, scholars became embroiled in debates about whether organisations were over-managed and under-led or the reverse, and what the consequences in each instance might have been. These disputes have now largely fizzled out, thankfully, and maybe this will be the fate of the leadership framework adopted by the Canadian province of Alberta, as discussed by the authors.

Internationalising and centring leadership

Whereas Riveros et al. call into question the entire justification for and apparatus of principal-led school transformation, Drysdale's and Gurr's intention is to indicate not only that this approach works but also to show how principal leadership can be inclusive of others in schools. (Is this a version of distributed leadership masquerading as non-distributed leadership, I ask myself? These authors come close to admitting as much in their conclusion.) By any measure, the International Successful School Principalship Project (ISSPP) that they describe is a big project, as their boosterish claims on its behalf indicate. With their statement that the output yield of the ISSPP stands at more than 100 publications, one is entitled to ask whether (and how) the totality of this project's findings might have resulted in a re-structuring of the evidence base. On this point, unfortunately, the authors are somewhat opaque. As with the two previous chapters, there is evidence of positioning going on in this one as well. On the one hand, like Youngs, these authors situate their work in relation to Gunter's four-fold typology of leadership studies, although the real angels that Drysdale and Gurr want to be on the side of (understandably) are studies of principal effects. If this represents the terrain of purity, then there is also a domain of danger for the ISSPP, because on the other hand they want to distance their project from a school effectiveness focus in favour of a spotlight on school success, mainly on the grounds that they regard the latter as a broader concept that is concerned with outcomes. (Fair enough, although I cannot help thinking that this might be an instance of academic hair-splitting.)

Readers are then provided with a synthesis of findings about the ISSPP principal leaders. These people are shown, first, to not be powerless in the face of contextual constraints on their work. Context tends to be a much used word in the study of leadership – and in their earlier discussion, Riveros et al. saw the variability of school contexts as posing problems for mandated standards. Sadly, however, context is often either ill-defined or not defined at all. But to Drysdale's and Gurr's credit, they do take the trouble – unlike some other chapter authors (although not Lakomski and Evers) – to spell out what they mean by it. That said, there then comes some uncertainty, because the qualities that ISSPP principals have been shown to manifest (in respect of their battles with contextual factors) may not necessarily be evidence of leadership as such (readers are told), and the authors revert to (long since abandoned) trait theory to emphasise their point. With this reversion, the chapter discussion begins to take on a back-to-the-future character, which at first blush the authors seem to reinforce with their endorsement of heroic-style leadership. But that is only part of the story, because with their collaborative approaches and willingness to empower colleagues, the ISSPP principals are shown to be simultaneously post-heroic. Drysdale and Gurr then touch on the point about leadership definition that was raised initially by Youngs. Here, unlike other scholars who may be inclined to leave their readers adrift in a swamp of competing adjectival definitions of leadership, Drysdale and Gurr are quite prepared to nail their colours to the mast, with a conceptual map (derived from the ISSPP findings) to help drive forward future research. Following another brief back-to-the-future lurch (in the guise of mentions of references emanating from the aforementioned era of the Theory Movement), Drysdale and Gurr re-work social systems theory to arrive at a principal-impact model. Implicit (and at times explicit) in their entire approach here is a laudable attempt by them to take seriously the question that I posed at the outset of this commentary about whether or not leadership researchers have an obligation to try to make a contribution to the enhancement of student learning outcomes. In their search for workable interventions, Drysdale and Gurr are steadfastly unequivocal on this point.

Cognitivising, de-centring and knowing leadership

On one interpretation of leader-centricity (a core anchoring theme of this book), then, Drysdale's and Gurr's chapter is clearly (and unapologetically) an instance of such centrism, except that how could any author whose focus, at least to some extent, is on leadership and the people who embody it – singly, in pairs or in multi-member units – *not* be fingered for being leader-centric? On this reckoning, even distributed leadership proponents stand accused of leader-centricity, in which case, unless a narrow definitional approach is taken to such centrism viz. individuals as leaders, then this is a dock in which all of us, the present author included, stand together accused and guilty as charged. Lakomski and Evers try to tackle this theme through an understanding of cognition, in particular the idea of a cognitive ecology. I am reminded here that in the same breath that he was commending caution in respect of physics, Putnam (2004, p. 26) also hit out at those philosophers who were inclined to dismiss ordinary language psychology usage as 'folk' and who insisted on psychological descriptions being reduced to brain, or neurological, states.

Like Drysdale and Gurr, Lakomski introduces the idea of a system, albeit with a quite different meaning and emphasis, on this occasion with a focus on social cognition and the environments (contexts?) in which leadership and learning occur. For the uninitiated reader, the topography of this knowledge domain can be tricky to traverse. It is the decision-making of feeling and thinking beings with bodies and brains that is of concern here for Lakomski. The research that she reviews shows that brains (and we are talking here about social brains), thanks to evolutionary pressures, learn. Certainly. But when taking this idea on board, we ought to be mindful of the fact that a brain is not the equivalent of an individualised person. As humans, we inhabit worlds made up of persons, each with a social brain. In principle, the naturalistic (or bottom-up) research agenda proposed by Lakomski ought to be able to shed light on how the two phenomena (persons and social brains) come together to facilitate or impede both leadership and learning. Somewhat enticingly, perhaps, Lakomski leaves her readers dangling with the very last sentence of her section, in which she concedes that school principals play a role in these naturalistic environments of social cognition, except that the specifics of their role are left unelaborated.

Once more, with the idea of a system in mind, in his section Evers confronts the question of whether there is a centre (or brain?), and whether indeed the notion of centre makes any sense in a social cognition framework. Here, Evers draws on examples of decentralised systems that lack centres, and for him markets offer a quintessential illustration (just as they did, incidentally, for Hayek [1945] – for a discussion of which see Gronn, 2008). The contentious element here for me, in respect of brains, however, is that the notion of 'I' (which in lay terms is a person's sense of selfhood and their own neurological centre, so to speak) is made coterminous with emergent aggregated neural activity. Ouch! This, surely, is physicalist reductionism par excellence. In light of this presumed equivalence, therefore, one is bound to ask: Where do minds fit in relation to social brains? And is the assertion about aggregated neural activity tantamount to claiming that any notion of individualised consciousness (i.e. one's awareness that this 'I' is or might just be me) is a fiction? Evers still permits individualised leadership to squeak into this analysis, although his answer to the question of whether or not extended cognitive systems have (or require) centres is that that depends – with problem definition and the ontology of cognitive units being posited as possible key determinants. As with Lakomski, there is something of a promissory note here for the reader concerning the scope for leaders' agency, with Evers' concluding comment being that this remains a challenge for future work.

Finally, in his appeal for critical dialogue in the leadership field, Eacott echoes my characterisation of it as siloed and bunkered. Such fragmentation he regards as impeding knowledge advancement. Instead of parallel monologues, he wants new knowledge (but then, don't we all?) As I did at the outset of this commentary, Eacott recognises the difficulties posed for end users (his term) by the cacophony of voices in leadership. Equally, however, he dismisses any notion of scholars signing on to an over-arching grand narrative. If Eacott is right, that we – that is, all of us with scholarly claim to tenure in this field – by and large occupy comfort zones that have provided us with intellectual anchorage along with the wherewithal to fashion careers for our own advancement, then for me that is the legacy of the post-paradigmatic warfare settlement. The 1970s and 1980s chickens have come home to roost. Maybe Eacott is also right about the need for critical debates across and between the various bubbles and comfort zones that he has in mind. And yet another, perhaps for him less appealing and idealistic, alternative might be to adopt a more hard-nosed view of where we all are. Why not just accept the fact that fragmentation has been and is likely to go on being the order of the day, that (with apologies to W. B. Yeats) not only is the leadership centre never going to hold, but that there is not and cannot ever be such a centre anyway? After all, if part of what this book has set out to question is the very idea of leader-centrism, then presumably any notion of knowledge-centrism (if I may put it that way) is likewise up for grabs. Fission trumps fusion. The other point here is that at the end of the day, leadership (like any other knowledge domain) can only ever be sustainable while there is a public need and demand for it. Drysdale and Gurr quote Ken Leithwood and Chris Day as remarking on the 2000s as having been leadership's golden age. Well, these years might have been, and yet because all good things come to an end sooner or later, perhaps we leadership scholars have to reconcile ourselves to the fact that, for this field anyway, twilight time might be beckoning.

References

Bolden, R., 2011. Distributed leadership in organizations: A review of theory and research. *International Journal of Management Reviews*, 13(3), pp. 251–269.

Darling-Hammond, L., 2008. Reshaping teaching policy, preparation, and practice: Influences of the national board for professional teaching standards. In L. Ingvarson and J. Hattie, eds., *Assessing teachers for professional certification: The first decade of the National Board for Professional Teaching Standards*. Oxford: Elsevier JAI, pp. 25–53.

Gronn, P., 2002. Designer-leadership: The emerging global adoption of preparation standards, *Journal of School Leadership* 12(5), pp. 552–578.

Gronn, P., 2008. Hayek, learning and leadership. In E. A. Samier and A. G. Stanley, eds., *Political approaches to educational administration and leadership*. London: Routledge, pp. 73–88.

Gronn, P., 2011. Hybrid configurations of leadership. In A. Bryman, D. Collinson, K. Grint, B. Jackson and M. Uhl-Bien, eds., *Sage handbook of leadership*. London: Sage, pp. 435–452.

Gronn, P., 2015. The view from inside leadership configurations. *Human Relations*, 68(4), pp. 545–560.

Hattie, J., 2008. Validating the specification of standards for teaching: Applications to the National Board for Professional Teaching Standards assessments. In L. Ingvarson and J. Hattie, eds., *Assessing teachers for professional certification: The first decade of the National Board for Professional Teaching Standards*. Oxford: Elsevier JAI, pp. 93–111.

Hayek, F. A., 1945. The use of knowledge in society. *American Economic Review*, 13(4), pp. 33–54.

Ingvarson, L., 2013. Professional certification: Promoting and recognising successful teaching practices. Paper presented to the 'Sustaining teachers' professional growth Cambridge seminar, Moller Centre, Churchill College, Cambridge (February 18–19).

Pateman, C., 1970. *Participation and democratic theory.* Cambridge: Cambridge University Press.

Putnam. H., 2004. *The collapse of the fact/value dichotomy and other essays.* Cambridge, MA: Harvard University Press.

Rost, J. C., 1993. Leadership for the twenty-first century. Westport: Praeger.

Woods, P. A. and Gronn, P., 2009. Nurturing democracy: The contribution of distributed leadership to a democratic organisational landscape. *Educational Management, Administration and Leadership,* 37(4), pp. 430–541.

Zaleznik, A., 1977. Managers and leaders: Are they different? *Harvard Business Review,* 55(3), pp. 67–78.

About the contributors

Jeffrey S. Brooks is Professor of Educational Leadership in the Faculty of Education at Monash University. He is a J. William Fulbright Senior Scholar alumnus who has conducted studies in the USA and the Philippines. His research focuses broadly on educational leadership, and he examines the way leaders influence (and are influenced by) dynamics such as racism, globalisation, distributed leadership, social justice and school reform. Jeff is the author of *The Dark Side of School Reform: Teaching in the Space between Reality and Utopia* and *Black School, White School: Racism and Educational (Mis)leadership*, as well as the editor of an additional 11 volumes and the author or co-author over 50 peer-reviewed journal articles and book chapters. Dr. Brooks is former editor of the *Journal of School Leadership* and series editor for the *Educational Leadership for Social Justice* book series. He has served in several leadership positions in the American Educational Research Association.

David Burgess is Head of and Associate Professor in the Department of Educational Administration at the University of Saskatchewan. His research interests include philosophy of organisation, organisation theory and organisational modelling; educational law; and methods in legal instruction and research. Burgess holds university teaching concentrations in history of organisational theory, philosophy of organisation and educational and administrative law. He has served as co-editor of *the Journal of Educational Administration and Foundations* (JEAF) and, prior to academia, worked with the United Nations Non-Governmental Liaison Service (UN/NGLS) in Geneva. Burgess is author, co-author and co-editor of four books and over a dozen scholarly chapters and papers.

Tony Bush is Professor of Educational Leadership at the University of Nottingham (UK and Malaysia) and Visiting Professor of Education at the University of the Witwatersrand, Johannesburg. He is a vice-president and council member of the British Educational Leadership, Management and Administration Society (BELMAS) and was given the society's Distinguished Service Award in 2008. He has edited the leading international journal *Educational Management, Administration and Leadership* (EMAL) since 2002. Tony has published extensively on many aspects of school leadership and management, including his influential *Theories of Educational Leadership and Management*, which is now in its fourth edition. He has directed many research projects for the former National College for School Leadership and for many other clients in the UK and internationally. Tony has been a consultant, external examiner, invited keynote speaker or research director in more than 20 countries on all six continents. He is also a fellow of the Commonwealth Council for Educational Administration and Management (FCCEAM).

Robert Donmoyer is currently Professor of Leadership Studies at the University of San Diego. Previously, he served for 20 years as Professor and the Director of the School of Educational Policy and Leadership at Ohio State University. Dr. Donmoyer has published extensively on research methodology, research utilization in policymaking and practice and the leadership and management of schools. His work has appeared in books and academic journals focused on school administration/leadership and research methods. Recently, journals in the non-profit and philanthropic studies field also have published his work. Dr. Donmoyer has served as the editor of a number of scholarly journals, including the American Educational Research Association journal *Educational Researcher*. He currently serves as a board member and treasurer for the non-profit Academic Centers Council. Several years ago, he took a leave of absence from his university position to serve as acting principal of a middle school.

Lawrie Drysdale is Associate Professor in the Melbourne Graduate School of Education, the University of Melbourne. Lawrie teaches in leadership, human resource management, marketing, school effectiveness and improvement and learning communities. His research interests are in marketing in education and successful school leadership. Currently, he is a member of the International Successful School Principalship Project (ISSPP) and the International School Leadership Development Network (ILSDN). Both organisations include teams of international researchers who are investigating successful school leadership in a range of contexts in over 18 countries. Lawrie is co-editor of *International Studies in Educational Administration (ISEA)*, the journal for the Commonwealth Council for Educational Administration and Management (CCEAM). His publications include 16 scholarly book chapters, 26 refereed journal articles and over 50 presentations at international conferences. He is currently a board member of the Australian Council for Educational Leadership (ACEL) and Overnewton Anglican Grammar School, Melbourne.

Scott Eacott is Director of the Office of Educational Leadership in the School of Education, the University of New South Wales; and Adjunct Professor of Educational Leadership in the Department of Educational Administration at the University of Saskatchewan. His scholarship sits at the intersections of organisational theory, sociology and educational administration and leadership. Scott is widely published, with his research interests and contributions falling into three main areas: i) relational approaches for studying educational organisations, ii) leadership preparation and development and iii) Bourdieusian theorising in educational leadership. He is currently working on a follow-up project to *Educational Leadership Relationally* (2015, Sense), where he further articulates his relational approach and engages with critiques of it. Scott is on the editorial board of a number of leading educational leadership journals, including *Journal of Educational Administration and History* and *International Journal of Educational Management.* He is a Fellow of the Australian Council for Educational Leaders.

Lisa Catherine Ehrich is Associate Professor in the School of Cultural and Professional Learning in the Faculty of Education at Queensland University of Technology. Her research interests include educational leadership, mentoring for professionals and phenomenology as a methodology. She has published three co-edited books, three co-authored books and over 100 journal articles and book chapters. Her most recently published book (with Fenwick English) is titled *Leading Beautifully: Educational Leadership as Connoisseurship.* In 2014, in recognition of her contribution to educational leadership, she was awarded an Australian Council for Educational Leaders (ACEL) Fellowship and was made a Fellow of its Queensland Branch. She is a member of two editorial boards: *The International Journal of Educational Management* and *Leading & Managing.*

Fenwick W. English is the R. Wendell Eaves Senior Distinguished Professor of Educational Leadership in the School of Education at the University of North Carolina at Chapel Hill. His record of publications includes more than 40 books and over 100 referred journal articles. In addition he has served as General Editor of the *2015 SAGE Guide to Educational Leadership and Management;* the *2005 SAGE Handbook of Educational Leadership;* the *2006 SAGE Encyclopedia of Educational Leadership and Administration* (2 volumes); and the *2009 SAGE Major Works Series in Educational Leadership and Administration* (4 volumes). He is also the co-author with Lisa Ehrich of the 2016 book *Leading Beautifully: Educational Leadership as Connoisseurship* released by Routledge. He served as President of UCEA 2006–07 and later President of NCPEA 2011–12. He received the NCPEA 'Living Legend' award for his lifetime contributions to the field in 2013.

Colin W. Evers is Professor of Educational Leadership in the School of Education at the University of New South Wales. He has a disciplinary background in mathematics and philosophy and research, and his teaching interests lie in the areas of educational administration and leadership, philosophy of education and research methodology. He is co-author and co-editor of 11 books and over 100 scholarly papers. He has recently published with co-authors/editors *Teacher Leadership: New Conceptions for Autonomous Student Learning in the Age of the Internet* (Routledge, Oxford, 2014), *Decision Making in Educational Leadership* (Routledge, New York, 2015) and *Realist Inquiry in Social Science* (SAGE, London, 2016). His current research projects concern decision-making in educational administration, developing a model for theorizing the nature and scope of the distribution of leadership in organisational contexts, exploring links between emotion and leadership and systematically developing a view of educational leadership as critical learning.

Brad Gobby is Lecturer in the School of Education at Curtin University. His research interests are in the areas of education policy and governance. His current research uses post-structuralist notions of governmentality, power, subjectivity and materiality to examine contemporary programmes and modalities of government. He is an executive member of the Western Australian Institute for Educational Research.

Christina Gowlett is currently Lecturer in the School of Education at the University of Queensland. Prior to this, Christina was a McKenzie Postdoctoral Research Fellow at the University of Melbourne. One of her main research interests is the use of queer theory (especially the use of Judith Butler) in new empirical research spaces within education. Christina has recently co-edited a book regarding this topic with Associate Professor Mary Lou Rasmussen entitled *The Cultural Politics of Queer Theory in Education Research*, which is published by Routledge.

Peter Gronn is Professor Emeritus at the University of Cambridge and Monash University. His research interests include leadership configurations, historical and evolutionary perspectives on leadership, recruitment and selection of leaders, leader succession and biographical studies of leaders. He has recently completed a biography of Sir James Darling, headmaster of Geelong Grammar School (1930–1961) and chairman of the ABC (1961–1967). With James Biddulph, Peter is currently editing a book on the newly opened University of Cambridge Primary School (to be published by Cambridge University Press), of which he was deputy chair of the trustees. He has been a member of a number of leading journal editorial boards, including *Administrative Science Quarterly, Leadership, Leadership Quarterly, Leadership & Organization Development Journal* and *Educational Administration Quarterly*. Peter has held a number of senior university appointments and was head of the Faculty of Education, University of Cambridge (2011–2014). He is a Fellow of the Academy of Social Science.

David Gurr is Associate Professor in Educational Leadership at the Graduate School of Education of the University of Melbourne. He has a 36-year background in secondary teaching, educational psychology, school supervision and research in educational leadership. He is a founding member of the ISSPP and the ILSDN. He has authored more than 100 publications and more than 100 international conference presentations. David has served as the Vice President of the Australian Council for Educational Leaders and was awarded its National Presidential Citation in 2004, the Hedley Beare Educator of the Year in 2012, and the Council's Gold Medal in 2014, which is the most prestigious award presented annually by the Council to an educator whose contribution to the study and practice of educational administration and leadership is assessed as most outstanding, nationally. David was the editor of *Leading and Managing* and is co-editor of *International Studies in Educational Administration*. He is associated with universities in Hong Kong (Asia Pacific Centre for Leadership and Change, HKIED), Canada (Western University) and Scotland (Robert Owen Centre for Educational Change at the University of Glasgow).

Gabriele Lakomski is Professor Emeritus in the Melbourne Centre for the Study of Higher Education at the University of Melbourne. Her research interests are in the areas of leadership, organisational learning and culture, education and training in the higher education sector. Her current research focuses on neuroscience and the emotions, the relation between cognition and emotion and what this means for rational decision-making in organisational contexts. Gabriele was editor of the *Australian Journal of Education*, section editor of the *Second International Encyclopedia of Education*, senior editor of *Organization Studies* and section editor of the Springer *Encyclopedia of Educational Philosophy and Theory* (Educational Leadership). She is a member of a number of editorial boards, such as the *Journal of Educational Administration* and *Management Learning*. She is author, co-author and co-editor of six books and over 80 scholarly papers. She is Deputy Chair of the board of St. Michael's Grammar School, Melbourne.

Paul Newton is Associate Professor and Graduate Chair in the Department of Educational Administration, University of Saskatchewan. Prior to coming to the University of Saskatchewan, he was Associate Professor in the Department of Educational Policy Studies at the University of Alberta and a principal in the North East School Division. He serves as co-editor of the *Journal of Educational Administration and Foundations*. Newton is the editor of two books on educational leadership and has authored more than 25 research articles and book chapters on school improvement, educational leadership and theories of educational administration.

Richard Niesche is Senior Lecturer in the School of Education at the University of New South Wales, Sydney, Australia. He has worked as a teacher in Queensland and New South Wales at both primary and secondary levels. His research interests include educational leadership, headteachers' work and social justice. His particular research focus is to use a range of critical perspectives in educational leadership to examine the work of headteachers in disadvantaged schools and how they can work towards achieving more socially just outcomes. He has published his research in a range of peer-reviewed journals and is the author of a number of books, including *Foucault and Educational Leadership: Disciplining the Principal* (Routledge, 2011) and *Deconstructing Educational Leadership: Derrida and Lyotard* (Routledge, 2013). His most recent publication is *Leadership, Ethics and Schooling for Social Justice*, co-authored with Dr. Amanda Keddie of the University of Queensland (Routledge, 2015).

Augusto Riveros is Assistant Professor in the Faculty of Education at Western University in Ontario, Canada. His research interests include leadership theory and the intersections between philosophy, educational administration and policy analysis. His work has been published in the *Journal of Educational Administration*; the *Canadian Journal of Education*; *Educational Philosophy and Theory*; *Discourse: Studies in the Cultural Politics of Education*; and *Studies in Philosophy and Education*, among other journals and edited books.

Bev Rogers is Lecturer in Leadership and Management (L&M) within the Masters of Education programme at Flinders University. Bev was previously a secondary principal in both country and disadvantaged areas of Adelaide and

Director of Teaching and Learning within the Department of Education and Child Development prior to joining Flinders University in 2014. Her research interest is in rethinking and challenging current dominant and culturally limited Western models of educational leadership. Her current research focuses on leading practices and the connection with working with teachers to theorise and critically examine what they do. She is also exploring culturally sensitive leadership interactions in diverse contexts. As an early career researcher, Bev is topic coordinator for three topics within the Masters of Education (L&M) and author of eight peer-reviewed papers.

Howard Youngs is Senior Lecturer in Educational Leadership in the School of Education at Auckland University of Technology. His research interests are in the areas of leadership, leader development, group processes, organisational development and education. His current research focuses on distributed forms of leadership and associated collaborative processes within and across networks of schools and how these are associated with professional learning. Howard is a member of the editorial boards of the *Journal of Educational Administration and History* and the *Journal of Educational Leadership Policy and Practice*.

Index